THE WORST WE CAN FIND

THE WORST WE CAN FIND

MST3K, *RiffTrax*, and the History of Heckling at the Movies

DALE SHERMAN

APPLAUSE
THEATRE & CINEMA BOOKS

Essex, Connecticut

APPLAUSE
THEATRE & CINEMA BOOKS

An imprint of Globe Pequot, the trade division of
The Rowman & Littlefield Publishing Group, Inc.
4501 Forbes Blvd., Ste. 200
Lanham, MD 20706
www.rowman.com

Distributed by NATIONAL BOOK NETWORK

Library of Congress Cataloging-in-Publication Data Available
ISBN 978-1-4930-6391-8 (pbk.: alk. paper)
ISBN 978-1-4930-6392-5 (electronic)

∞™ The paper used in this publication meets the minimum requirements of American
National Standard for Information Sciences—Permanence of Paper for Printed Library
Materials, ANSI/NISO Z39.48-1992.

To Claudene, Joel, John, and Haley, who understand.
And to Joe Don Baker, who tolerates it.

Special thanks to Ken Plume for allowing me to use excerpts from his many excellent interviews with members of the *MST3K* crew. You can find those and more over at http://asitecalledfred.com.

Additional thanks to Joshua Murphy and the JM Archives for his clear and thorough interviews with Jim Mallon (https://www.youtube.com/watch?v=SWMDzjhSgGc&t=1728s) and Wade Williams (https://www.youtube.com/watch?v=0wQVUfvoDfQ&t=2257s).

Contents

Introduction

I was digging around on the internet and ran across a newspaper ad from October 1984 for Wright State University, in Dayton, Ohio, and its film series, which was held in one of the lecture rooms on campus every weekend. The ad was for the Tom Hanks movie *Splash*, showing October 12 through 14, with admission at $1.50 per person.

That movie doesn't tie into my story here, however.

Like many college campuses at the time, Wright State ran recent second-run movies, classics, and cult films to raise money. I had been going to movies there on a regular basis since I was a sophomore in high school and even worked as an usher (as much as one can be an usher in a lecture hall) when I attended college there. Each Friday or Saturday night was typically a greasy burger over at a pub called the Rat on the other side of campus and then wandering the catacombs system under the school to get to Oelman Hall in time for the movies there. I once sat through *Blade Runner* four times in one weekend as an usher, got into a heated argument over the sociological implications of Uncle Scrooge with another usher (he found Scrooge McDuck to reflect a capitalist plot to seduce children to the power of money; I found the usher to be a pompous idiot), and once skipped high school in order to see Graham Chapman introduce *Monty Python's Life of Brian* to a standing-room-only hall (he came in, surveyed the room, announced, "These are some home movies we shot in Tunisia a few years ago," watched as the movie began, lit his pipe, nonchalantly stated, "Yes, this is the one," and then vanished, never to be seen again).

But this doesn't tie much into my story either.

I was past my usher days in 1984 but still going to an occasional movie at Wright State, and on the aforementioned night in October, they were showing Russ Meyer's *Beyond the Valley of the Dolls* (1970) as a midnight movie after *Splash*. I convinced a couple of friends to go with me to see the movie, and we arrived at the lecture hall with the room for *BVD* about half full. Not a ghost town, but hardly a full house. And, no, although you would think it would be the case, *Beyond the Valley of the Dolls* is not the point of this story either.

Before the film began, one of the individuals working the show came down the steps of the hall and announced that they had gotten an hour's worth of movie trailers—the three- to five-minute-long ads that appear in theaters before the main feature to promote other upcoming movies—for films they were planning to show that winter and spring. He asked if everyone wanted to see them and, since we were a smallish crowd with nothing else to do, we cheered them on.

How could I not? I love movie trailers. I can watch them for hours at a time. Yet the best of these advertisements are for movies you love or that have certain exciting and even bizarre scenes in them that transform a two- or three-minute-long trailer into a wild short film that sometimes makes for a much better movie than what the trailer is advertising. You'll be watching what looks to be a drama that suddenly shows a demon from hell, an action stunt that is the sole selling point of the movie, or a plot twist that is completely out of left field (or, better yet, a plot twist invented for the trailer that does not exist in the movie itself, thanks to clever editing). Such moments in movie trailers can make even a bad movie look good and certainly can be entertaining to watch. Besides, if one trailer is a bit dull, there will be another coming up within a couple of minutes, so a showcase of movie trailers is always a great time waster.

The problem that night was the people in charge had obviously picked movies geared toward a crowd who thought stuff like *Splash* was the pinnacle of entertainment. That is not to say *Splash* is bad, but it has a family-friendly quaintness that doesn't really lend itself to a movie trailer that is going to be "crazy." Thus, after about forty minutes of ads for movies like *Six Pack*, *Carbon Copy*, and *The Big Chill*, the luster of watching a whole hour of these things was starting to wear down on everyone. Occasionally you'd get an ad for *Scarface* or *Krull* to spice things up, but for every *Cujo*, there were three *Terms of Endearment*.

One of the last trailers was for a 1982 movie called *The Seduction*. It stars Morgan Fairchild as a television personality who is being stalked by a deranged fan, played by Andrew Stevens, with the selling point (made even in the ad) of featuring a brief nude scene with Fairchild. Un-ironically, and as expected in typical 1980s fashion for such movies, a film based on the idea of a creep stalking a woman had to make sure there's a scene where the audience can ogle her as well. So even the ad had a certain distasteful quality to it.

But, again, I'm getting away from my story.

The ad goes on for quite a while, showcasing multiple scenes of an irritated Fairchild dealing with an irritating Stevens, followed by a scene of Michael Sarrazin as the woman's boyfriend instructing Fairchild's character on how to use a shotgun. And, as per the dramatic technique of Chekhov's Gun, if you introduce a shotgun in the first minute of your trailer, it must be fired in the second minute (Anton Chekhov mentioned this in a letter about *The Seduction* in 1889; he had tremendous foresight). Thus, after several brief sequences showing Fairchild as this character being repeatedly bothered by Stevens, the movie trailer cuts to her chasing Stevens down the hall of her house with said shotgun.

At that moment in the ad, the narrator states, "Morgan Fairchild—alone, frightened, trapped like an animal. NOW, she's fighting back with the only weapon she has!"

The trailer then takes a dramatic pause before the narrator says, "HERSELF!"

However, after such a long stretch of boring ads, I found myself speaking out loud:

Narrator: Morgan Fairchild—alone, frightened, trapped like an animal. NOW, she's fighting back with the only weapon she has!

Me: (in a matter-of-fact tone) A shotgun.

I didn't realize I had said it so loud, but the audience burst out laughing in response.

At the time, I wasn't a big fan of people talking back to the movie screen in theaters, so I was a bit embarrassed about doing so. I apologized, and a guy in the row in front of me turned around and said, "No, man, that was pretty good."

And thus, my first movie riff was born. Oh, and I got to see *Beyond the Valley of the Dolls* for the first time.

One more related story before I move on.

It was July 1978, and I had convinced my family to go see the Peter Frampton/Bee Gees movie *Sgt. Pepper's Lonely Hearts Club Band* on opening night. Don't judge me; just go with that knowledge.

As the packed audience watched the movie play out with a variety of actors and musicians attempting to string together several Beatles songs in some weak-tea attempt of a plot, it was clear that the film wasn't winning us over. Even Steve Martin's goofy version of "Maxwell's Silver Hammer" was met with indifference, and George Burns talking through "Fixing a Hole" (wouldn't "When I'm 64" at least have made some type of ironic sense instead?) had people grasping the seats in front of them like George C. Scott in *Hardcore*. Only Aerosmith's attempt at "Come Together" held the audience's attention, and people began cheering on the villains in the movie just because of the pain being inflicted by the "heroes."

By two-thirds into the film, the audience had turned ugly. When it came to the late scene where Frampton's character, down on his luck, moves to the rooftop of a building in order to jump, we were supposed to be on the edge of our seats in fear of what would occur.

Instead, the audience began loudly chanting, "Jump! Jump! Jump! JUMP! JUMP!"

And the atmosphere in the theater readily changed. It was like a religious experience, even if it meant turning against the very movie we had paid

George Burns, Peter Frampton, and the Bee Gees all look to be ready to jump in the 1978 film *Sgt. Pepper's Lonely Hearts Club Band*. The audience could not have been happier.
UNIVERSAL PICTURES / PHOTOFEST © UNIVERSAL PICTURES

full-ticket price to see. People were no longer in a bad mood; they left soon afterward all smiles, thanks to this one moment of unity. The common rift had saved us all.

I have plenty of similar stories, and I'm sure these are certainly not the best ones out there, but they speak to something we've all felt when watching a movie. We've all sat in a theater or watched a movie at home where we wanted to talk back to the screen . . . and we have—sometimes for our own amusement, for the amusement of our friends, or simply because we really wanted to yell at the movie for not meeting our expectations. Although I was admittedly a slow convert to talking back to the screen in a theater, some of my fondest memories in college were sitting in the living room with my older brother at 2:00 a.m. watching bad movies and television to wind down after having both worked second shift. We all have stories about watching movies in theaters and hearing someone yell something back at the screen, and the best of those have always been when someone delivers a gem of a response out of nowhere. We even do it to movies that we love if we feel comfortable enough. As many times as I have watched *The Wizard of Oz* over the years, when the Munchkins start incessantly telling Dorothy to "follow the yellow brick road," I still want her to shout back, "Yeah, I GOT IT! Follow the yellow brick road! I'm doing it! Can't you see me doing it?! I'm right here doing it. Even the DOG is doing it."

Of course, it doesn't always work. Improvising remarks to shout back at the screen (be it the theater screen or the television) sounds simple when you're relaxing with your friends at home. And the later the night, the funnier it gets, thanks to sleep deprivation and possibly various relaxers. It's different in the theater, where you have an audience that may not appreciate the interruptions, the style of the jokes, or the repetition of material. I have witnessed many times when the audience has turned on the person making off-the-cuff remarks to try to impress everyone, and even those who had gotten off a good zinger and feel confident to continue can soon find themselves under verbal threat for talking too much.

Which is why something like *Mystery Science Theater 3000*, or *MST3K* for short, is a different beast from the guy in a side row at the theater screaming at the screen until being dragged out of the theater. It reverberates within us, as we've all had those moments of talking back to the screen, but it takes what is commonly a parting shot in the literal dark and transforms it into a slew of good jokes that we'd never be able to come up with in the spur of a moment but—man—wish we could.

MST3K is also built on a heritage of entertainment, starting with the long history of professional observational deconstruction of the play format going back to the ancient Greeks and later that of Shakespeare and many thereafter. It evolved, moving into the era of vaudeville and burlesque. The early comedians of Hollywood were masters as well at breaking the "fourth wall," the mental barrier between an audience and a performance that allows us only to observe, when such artists would turn and look directly into the camera to acknowledge a moment with the audience in response to what just occurred on the stage or screen (such as the classic moment in *Blazing Saddles* where Harvey Korman's character, addressing the camera, asks what appears to be a rhetorical question, pauses, and then says, "Why am I asking *you*?").

At the same time as sound movies entered, Hollywood quickly redubbed dialogue to make earlier serious movies humorous, going back to the days of the MGM series *Goofy Movies* from the 1930s and later with the better-known television series of the early 1960s, *Fractured Flickers*. One cannot talk further about such work without mentioning the early Woody Allen production, *What's Up, Tiger Lily?* (1966), leading to later attempts such as *J-Men Forever* (1979), *What's Up, Hideous Sun Demon* (1983), *Dynaman* (1987), and the famous *Mad Movies with the L.A. Connection* series (1985–1986), among others.

own tweaks on the genre in order to make the concept its own.

The series' bouncing off the typical hosted weekly horror movie program on a local channel remains brilliant in its simplicity. Those original horror hosts were trapped into a show featuring a bad movie, but at least you always felt that the hosts could grab a cigarette break while the films were broadcast to those unfortunates at home. *MST3K* set up a story line where that host was forced to watch those very same movies, typically horror and science fiction, and thus forced to talk back to the screen to get through the tedium and "keep his sanity." With the help of two robots, Tom Servo and Crow T. Robot, the three worked their way through each movie with funny comments, like redubbing lines or commenting on the actions on the screen. Such remarks on the show became known as "riffs," which derives from a musical term that ironically means a repeated musical phrase that helps ground a song with improvisation. (In other words, the movie itself could be seen as the riff, with the jokes layered on top of it.) Nevertheless, since riffs commonly refer to selected movements in a song that stand out ("Man, that's a great riff, keep it going!"), it is easy to see how the term was reshaped to mean the lines said back at the screen by Joel, Mike, or whoever is stuck in the theater with the robots during the program. Later episodes in the first season and thereafter involved the various comedic talents of the cast and crew reviewing the films

multiple times to come up with a heavy stream of prepared jokes that could end up being seven hundred riffs or more per episode, making it a series many fans reviewed over and again to catch all the gags that they may have missed.

As mentioned, it was not the first time something like this would be done on television, but the format of the show was unique and even risky because it included the entire movie and not just a segment or a scaled-down version of the film. Surprisingly, with comedy, usually considered a genre that cannot work past the ninety-minute mark and rarely within a television program past a half hour, the two-hour-long *MST3K* worked, and in a way that became much bigger than expected. The series went from a program on a little-remembered UHF station in Minneapolis, Minnesota, to a struggling national cable channel, and it kept chugging along until it spanned eleven seasons, 197 episodes, plus a theatrical movie during a twelve-year period and over two major cable networks. Changes that helped recalibrate the humor over time include the creator and original host, Joel Hodgson as Joel Robinson, leaving the program midway through the fifth season, to be replaced by Mike J. Nelson, as well as other cast changes. The show conceptually changed from its early days as well, evolving from two mad scientists (Trace Beaulieu and J. Elvis Weinstein) subjecting a test subject, Joel, to bad movies and occasionally showing off inventions in the "invention exchange," to an intergalactic story of the Destroyer of Worlds, Mike, and the bots he loved (on the next *Geraldo*) trying to outsmart Pearl (Mary Jo Pehl) and her hench-creatures: Professor Bobo (Kevin Murphy), an ape from the future who seemed to get dumber with each new episode, and Brain-Guy, a.k.a. the Observer (Bill Corbett), a superintelligent pain-in-the-butt who carries around his brain in a pan. As will be discussed, some of those changes were forced on the show as it moved along, but even so, those occurrences became endearing to many fans of the program.

The original series would last until 1999 and then continue in reruns for years on the Sci-Fi Channel (now Syfy) plus a syndicated package of hour-long edits of the program called *The Mystery Science Theater Hour* that would periodically pop up on various channels through the mid-2010s. But even with the cancellation of the program, *MST3K* would live on through various means, its style often parodied by other shows. In the pages ahead, we will look back on various offshoots from *MST3K*, including non-*MST3K* programs such as *The Cheap Seats*, Mike Nelson's early solo work with Legend Films, leading directly to the seemingly never-ending *RiffTrax* commentaries, as well as the short-lived *The Film Crew* and *Cinematic Titanic*.

Yet the most incredible moment of the series was to be its comeback in 2017, with the show returning for two seasons on Netflix thanks to a Kickstarter campaign by Joel Hodgson and others. After the success of the Kickstarter campaign, the show was back with new writers and fresh hosts, including Jonah Ray as Jonah Heston and the mad scientists now played by Felicia Day as Kinga Forrester and Patton Oswalt as Max. The show zipped through eighteen episodes and even a series of live shows before eventually being dropped by the streaming channel. Instead of calling it quits, however, *MST3K* was revived once again with another large Kickstarter campaign that saw the program achieve its own streaming channel, the Gizmoplex, in 2022, with more episodes, new cast members, and writers added to the expanding history of the program.

The series that was built on the dreams of all of us sitting up too late at night and casting stupid jokes at the images on the screen proved itself by living well past its thirtieth anniversary. It has become a genre, with many other programs based on the general premise, and has kicked off careers for many who worked on the program. There would also be tours, conventions, books, soundtrack albums, and even comic books over the years, all directly related to the show that kept on riffing.

Ironically, the "worst that we can find" has brought out the best in those involved. In the pages ahead, we'll see how exactly that came about and what it has taken to make riffing an art form. But to really understand how we got to this point, we have to turn back to where it all came from in the first place.

1

Don't Ever Step on My Line

Meta and a History of Professional Heckling

Servo: (noticing that the moon in the movie looks very familiar) Look! It's the MST3K *logo!*

Joel: Uh, you're not supposed to know about that. . .

Servo: Oh, uh . . . (begins to whistle)

—TOM SERVO AND JOEL, WHILE WATCHING *CRASH OF THE*
MOONS (1954) ON *MST3K*, SEASON 5, EPISODE 17 (1992)

There's a gag early on in *History of the World, Part I* by Mel Brooks that shows a caveman (Sid Caesar) proudly creating the first piece of art in human history on a cave wall. The narrator describes it as the birth of the artist. A second caveman then arrives as the "afterbirth," the critic, who proceeds to give his opinion of the art by urinating on it.

Yes, it's a pretty weak joke, and it may seem a tad astray from *MST3K*, but it does establish something that has been there from the very beginning for anyone who wants to create art: not everyone is going to enjoy what you do, and they're going to want to make sure you know it. Sometimes that disagreement is minor and doesn't hurt the overall enjoyment of the piece by the rest of the audience, but other times it can lead to people being vocal, even physically confrontational. Fortunately, with the exception of the one seen in *History of the World, Part I*, critics usually exit the show to write a lavish written piece for a publication fee in order to piss all over someone's work—to the relief of art gallery owners everywhere.

A performer in front of an audience does not have that barrier from the casual critic, however. If someone in the audience doesn't like the material, there's someone a shout, and possibly a projectile-throwing distance, away who will be forced to take the abuse of not being good enough. The only barrier is the open air, which hardly works as a defense when trying to perform onstage. Naturally, the writer and any other behind-the-scenes person can feel the immediate sting of dismissal from an audience as well, but at least they can get the car started and be gone before things get ugly. An actor who is not also a good runner doesn't have that option, and it can be even more frustrating when the actor onstage or in front of the camera knows the material is not as good as it should be (or, in words common to fans of *MST3K*, "it stinks").

Which leads us to heckling. According to Merriam-Webster, "heckle" is a verb that means to harass and try to disconcert with questions, challenges, or gibes. And for you playing at home, gibes are taunting words. And for you who are still unsure, taunting means insulting. And for you drinking heavily right now because of my rattling on here, I think I have played this gag out as far as I could go.

Heckling, a common practice of verbal disruption, is typically seen these days when someone either drunk, angry, or both takes exception to something the performer has said and shouts out in disagreement. The disagreement can range from something major, such as feeling personally insulted over politics or religion, to something as trivial as mispronouncing the name of a city or the incorrect usage of a product mentioned onstage. Rarely productive, such heckling usually throws off flow and can easily destroy a joke, a set, or even an evening for the performer and the audience (but seldom for the hecklers themselves, unfortunately, who will leave the show thinking they somehow "saved" the evening for everyone with their fits). Although rarely enjoyed by anyone, heckling is not completely uncommon, with books written on the topic and even comedians who promote their work against heckling (which, unfortunately, can sometimes insinuate that they want people heckling their work, thus feeding the beast rather than killing it off). The upside for most comics facing such hecklers is the performer is sober and—having run into it before—well prepared for such interruptions, while the heckler is typically three sheets to the wind. The audience is also usually on the side of the performer as well, unless the comic reacts poorly, like how TV's Frank managed to turn an entire virtual audience against him after calling someone "pretty ugly" when trying to do stand-up via the Virtual Comedy invention he created (*Secret Agent, Super Dragon*, season 5, episode 4).

As anyone can expect, performance pieces, whether monologues, plays, musical numbers, live television shows, or even films, all have common areas where things can go wrong. Yet sometimes the best moments in the theater are when something that did go wrong can be incorporated into the show. Hecklers are rarely funny, but the response by the performer can provide payoff for an audience. In the theater, miscues or malfunctioning props can lead to improvisation by the performers that can turn possibly disastrous moments into gold and even end up being incorporated into the shows from that point forward.

Plays, movies, and television shows build upon prepared "mistakes" or outside influences that change the narrative in surprising directions. *The Carol Burnett Show* (1967–1978), for example, had two running sketches built around recurring mistakes made in live productions: "As the Stomach Turns" typically had actors answering the front door or the phone before the Foley sound is heard, while a deeper dive into the horrors of live theater was featured in a series of recurring sketches that presented two stuck-up actors,

Funt and Mundane (usually played by Burnett and Harvey Korman), dealing with various types of malfunction: an additional actor who was unprepared or physically wrong for the role, bad props and sets, or even amateur stage crews. The program was also notorious for filming sketches twice, first per script and then allowing the actors to improvise (leading to the risk of actors—usually Korman—corpsing on camera), with the improvised sketches often making it to the final edit because they were funnier for their mistakes.

Michael Frayn's play *Noises Off* (1982) is built around the error-filled concept as well, with the show focusing on a group of actors performing the same act of a play at different times during the play's run. Because the audience first gets to see a somewhat professional run (with some minor errors) of the play in act 1, subsequent acts are made funny because the audience knows where mistakes are being made and watches as the characters try to adjust. Mischief Theatre, an improvisational group from the United Kingdom, has made intentional mistakes a cornerstone of its work, starting with its 2008 play *The Play That Goes Wrong* and continuing with television series and specials having to do with various miscalculations in their "live" performances that persist until the bitter end because "the show must go on." In all these cases, the audience is prepared to watch these sketches or shows knowing that the material is purposefully bad, in order to see how it will then be mocked in a funny manner.

Surprising the audience in this fashion and recognizing the theatrical form of the work by having characters point out the very existence of the theater is something that we look on today as "meta." Admittedly, it's a common term heard to the point of wanting to punch people in the face when they use it (and please don't hurt me), but it is a major focus of many works in the theater, movies, and television, and certainly of *MST3K*. "Meta-" is a Greek prefix that means "after" or "beyond"—which works reasonably well for the Metalunas of *This Island Earth* (as seen in *Mystery Science Theater 3000: The Movie*), since "luna" is Latin for moon and thus the aliens get their name from being "beyond the moon." It's also evident that it's a very odd name to call everyone from your home planet, where you're not beyond any moon, and it sounds more like a boy band name that Brack came up with after getting out of the tube one evening. If that is the case, then their annihilation seems justified.

Besides, we tend not to use the term even as a prefix to mean something beyond the noun or verb it is attached to but rather as something reflective and self-acknowledging. For example, physics is the study of physical matter and energy, while metaphysics is the study of why we bother studying matter and energy. Yet its most common use today is as a word by itself. "Meta" frequently refers to something in the media that instantly reminds the audience that the show is self-aware, like an intended "error" or a visual or vocal reference made to something outside of the show. When the series *Newhart* ended by having the main character played by Bob Newhart wake up to reveal that the entire series was a dream by the main character Newhart played in the long-running *Bob Newhart Show*, that was a master moment in meta.

And while it could be seen as navel-gazing to the extreme, when properly used, it can demonstrate to the audience that the production is aware of questions and will resort to meta to get out of tight spots. For example, in the 1942 Bob Hope–Bing Crosby movie *Road to Morocco*, the pair find themselves released by the villain in the middle of the desert with their hands and feet tied. A quick dissolve later and we see them walking through the desert, no longer bound by the ropes. After a brief discussion about their plight, Hope turns to Crosby and asks the question the audience is probably wanting resolved: "How did we escape with our hands and feet tied anyway?" Crosby, pointing out the camera (i.e., the audience), cautiously murmurs to Hope, "If we told them, they'd never believe us." Hope slowly replies, "Well, let's not tell them, then." The pair then move on to continue the story without any further mention of the incident. In providing this acknowledgment by the characters to the audience—a moment of self-heckling at the absurdity of them having escaped their bonds—the film has gone all meta on us. And we, as the audience, accept that moment, because (a) it's a funny joke, and (b) the characters are right in telling us that knowing doesn't really matter to the story anyway. In other words, "Just keep in mind it's just a show."

Yet this type of self-awareness of the performers directed straight at the viewer rather than allowing the audience to be merely observers of the performance in front of them is not something that came whole-cloth out of the movies or even recent theater. Over the years, many scholars in theatrics have even come up with various names to call such self-awareness, from the confrontational avant-garde nature of the postdramatic theater (sometimes achieving a negative physical reaction from the audience as a goal), the "camp" subgenre of films sometimes called paracinema or psychotronic (under which nearly all of the films shown on *MST3K* would fall), and even the theater of the absurd (dramatics that work outside of the narrative norms expected, such as Samuel Beckett's 1953 play *Waiting for Godot*, which purposefully tricks the audience in expecting the title character Godot to arrive, but he never does, leaving the characters with no resolution as the play ends). Yet many of these are simply fancier descriptions of what is enveloped under "metatheatre," a term created by Lionel Abel in 1963 that suggests instances in a play where the playwright directly points out to the audience that it is a play (some critics would say that since a dramatist is creating the work, it would be called metadrama rather than the encompassing metatheatre, but at this point it's really splitting hairs and we only have so many pages to work with here). As suggested above by the instance in *Road to Morocco*, this is fairly common in comedies, but Abel pushes the idea that it is quite acceptable and a long-standing practice in dramatic pieces going back to such ancient Greek authors as Aeschylus, Sophocles, and Euripides. The most readily known version of metatheatre in these plays is that of the Greek choruses, who provide exposition to the audience while also sometimes becoming characters themselves within the plays to direct other characters to perform certain actions. Thus the chorus continually breaks the fourth wall as it speaks to both the audience and the characters who are obvious to the audience, much in the way that Joel/Mike/Jonah/Emily and the bots do on *MST3K*.

What may be unexpected in retrospect is that these ancient Greek authors were not above using metatheatre to insert wry material as winks to the audience in good humor, such as in Aristophanes's *The Wasps*, where the chorus suddenly breaks away from the play at one point in order to jokingly describe the career of the author before the play eventually continues. Metatheatre can also be used to shake up the "rules" of the theater and grab an audience's attention. Robert Lewis Smith, in an article for the *Athens Journal of Philology*, gives such an example in Aeschylus's *Agamemnon*. The play features a secondary character named Cassandra, who is repeatedly asked to speak but does not do so for three-quarters of the play. This may seem a tad odd to us today, but audiences at the time were familiar with plays typically having only three speaking parts, and Cassandra was not one of the three. Yet even with three speaking parts, there would be need for more actors to fill out the stage and be addressed as characters although they would have no lines. Thus, when Cassandra appears silent through most of the play ("for about 300 lines," as Smith notes), even after being asked to speak by other characters, the assumption of the audience is that Cassandra is merely another one of these mute roles. When the character suddenly bursts into song (with a chorus backing her) and monopolizes the play three-quarters of the way in, it is a shock even to modern audiences, who find their expectations flipped and must refocus their attention to a character who seemed like an afterthought up to that moment. Aeschylus knew that audiences would not be expecting the character to suddenly speak and took that knowledge to break a traditional rule of theater at the time, in order to retrain the audience's attention late in the play and create a metatheatrical moment.

Abel's argument for metatheatre, however, really comes into full scope a quarter of the way through his thesis when he focuses on Shakespeare, specifically *Hamlet*. Abel's argument centers mainly on the fact that although *Hamlet* is a serious drama, various critics who talk of the work in hushed, serious tones are forgetting that Shakespeare was writing for a group of rowdy commoners standing in the pits at the Globe in the early seventeenth century. These were people with little patience who would immediately heckle the stage if they were not entertained. Of course, Shakespeare could easily write long plays—*Hamlet* itself can run nearly four hours—but he made sure to include action, comedy, and music even in his most dramatic work to give the people their money's worth and keep their attention. Shakespeare even invites the audience to relieve the tension by reminding them that they are at a play. Critics may sniff at such an approach and focus solely on the dramatics of Shakespeare, but Abel's main purpose in devising metatheatre is to tell such stuffy scholars, "Lighten up, Francis . . . Bacon."

One of the more popular moments that is an obvious nod to Shakespeare's audience is mentioned by Philip Edwards in his introduction to the text of *Hamlet* in *The New Cambridge Shakespeare* edition of the play (most recently republished in 2018). At one point, Polonius discusses playing Julius Caesar and tells Hamlet, "I did enact Julius Caesar. I was killed i' th' Capitol. Brutus killed me." Hamlet replies, "It was a brute part of him to kill so capital a calf there." This is fine by itself, but Edwards's research suggests that actor John Heminges played Caesar in Shakespeare's *Julius Caesar* shortly before playing Polonius in *Hamlet*, while actor Richard Burbage was Brutus in the first play and Hamlet in the second. Since the audience would have seen the previous play performed with these actors, these lines present a moment of metatheatre that would have received a knowing laugh from the crowd.

The most obvious example is Hamlet's use of the play within the play to see his uncle's reaction to the insinuation that he murdered Hamlet's father. The play within the play, also called an induction, is an important element of Abel's definition of metatheatre, since it allows the characters watching the play to become part of the audience as much as the audience is watching them for their reactions (just as we watch these bad movies in *MST3K* so we can see the reactions of the host and the bots). Yet beyond that, there is also Hamlet's directions to the players before the play occurs, where he lectures them to not sweepingly overplay their parts as ham actors are wont to do but to be more natural and get the story across. It is easy to see that this is not Hamlet's advice so much as Shakespeare's professional heckling toward certain actors who he felt went over the top in previous performances. To have Hamlet reinforce these notions of bad acting within the play would certainly have connected with the audience and created a type of metatheatre where they would be looking for such hamminess, and it would have prevented the actors from providing such hamminess, unless their characters were supposed to be performed that way for additional comedic effect.

Hamlet was not alone for Shakespeare in this respect; we get moments of metatheatre in several of his plays, and it was a common dramatic device of the Elizabethan age for many playwrights that continue to this day in both theater and films. Yet the momentum of narrative plays and movies limits outside forces from detouring the material due to lack of empty space for hecklers to use in order to disrupt. Those who worked as masters of ceremonies or as dialogists (like stand-up) in live performances had to and did deal with heckling in a more traditional manner. However, even there, the concept of professional heckling planned within the show was not far away. For example, Fred Karno's Fun Factory of the early twentieth century employed acrobats, clowns, and comedians to perform in music halls and vaudeville. One memorable sketch, "The Mumming Birds," presented performers onstage being purposefully interrupted by other members of the cast planted in the audience as characters, including a clumsy drunk who at one point was played by Charlie Chaplin (Chaplin would revisit some of the material in his 1915 short film, *A Night in the Show*, and Robert Downey Jr. would re-create some of the material early in the 1992 movie *Chaplin*). Such staging of acts with plants among the audience to interrupt the proceedings became a common comedy routine in vaudeville, with the most typical being a faux heckler in the front balcony (the better to spotlight in a stage show) who would trade insults with the emcee for a short time or even throughout the evening ("What's happening behind the curtain?" "Nothing, why?" "Because there's nothing happening in front of it either." "Hey, did you see my last show?" "I hope so!"). This type of insult comedy that usually had the master of ceremonies as straight man was used by comics such as Milton Berle and Bob Hope and is remembered mostly today from *The Muppet Show*, where the popular Statler and Waldorf characters would usually trade barbs with Kermit the Frog or Fozzie Bear and with many of the same gags used by such well-known faux hecklers as Irvin Benson and others in their time.

It would eventually reach the point where the meta of self-mocking was folded back and it heckled itself, such as in 1982, when actor-comedian Andy Kaufman performed onstage for an HBO special celebrating the tenth anniversary of the comedy club Catch a Rising Star. Kaufman announced to the audience in the club that he planned to do his original act in celebration of the tenth anniversary and commenced doing material that was familiar to audiences at the time as his "foreign man" character (and later used as the genesis for his Latka character on the series *Taxi*). Unknown to many people in the audience, however, was that Andy's friend and cowriter, Bob Zmuda, was planted in the front-row table as a faux heckler, continually ruining the act by jumping on all the punchlines. When confronted on falling back on old material and pushed to come up with a new joke, Kaufman instead begins

Milton Berle and Fozzie Bear—two performers that immerse into metatheatre by making careers out of performing with a "faux heckler" or two. INCORPORATED TELEVISION COMPANY / PHOTOFEST © INCORPO-RATED TELEVISION COMPANY

doing a crying routine that Zmuda also points out was part of his old act. Zmuda then pushes into a meta-meta space when he informs the audience that Kaufman knew he had no new material and had paid him to be a plant in the crowd and heckle him, which was just as much of a hack as everything else he was doing. With that comment, Kaufman seemingly slips out of character and begins to directly harass Zmuda just as the camera cuts to black and a card appears stating that something had happened to the video. When it returns, Zmuda is gone, and Kaufman continues his old act to the relieved audience. The heckler had heckled the heckling, and knowing that camera edit was part of the act made the entire affair a form of quadruple-cross with the viewers.

The history of self-heckling had reached a final form for the live act in 1982, thanks to Kaufman, and such mockery continues in a variety of programs, such as late-night television and the form displayed by many performers on streaming services like TikTok and YouTube (not to necessarily say they are very good, but they're evident). Yet the usage of professional mockery of movies in a format similar to what has been discussed so far really kicked into high gear in the 1980s. It eventually led to the emergence of *Mystery Science Theater 3000*, but attempts as far back as the 1930s came before it, as will be seen in the next chapter.

2

Fracturing Flickers
Riffing the Movies through the Years

Phyllis: (shooting at police officers in the 1956 Ed Wood movie, The Violent
Years*) Look at 'em jump! Just like rabbits!*

*Dan Aykroyd: (riffing over the film as Phyllis gets shot by one of the cops)
Yeah, look at 'em shoot! Just like professional marksmen.*

—*It Came from Hollywood* (1982)

Films mocking earlier movies or even themselves didn't take long to begin
hitting the theaters once moviemaking took hold in the early twentieth century. *Mud and Sand* (1922) starring Stan Laurel as Rhubarb Vaseline, an obvious parody of Rudolph Valentino, who had gained fame in *Blood and Sand*
earlier that same year, was an early example of a movie made essentially to
riff off an earlier film. Buster Keaton would parody the D. W. Griffith 1916
film *Intolerance* in his 1923 movie *Three Ages*, with the knowledge that many
people would remember the structure of the earlier film (showing people in
different eras but in similar follies), only with an added comedic twist. Abbott
and Costello would parody the style of horror films in *Abbott and Costello
Meet Frankenstein* (1948) and several of their later films, while comedian Red
Skelton and Bob Hope would parody crime dramas with their respective

Whistling (1941–1943) and *My Favorite* (1942–1951) series of films without any worries, because the formulas of crime dramas and horror films were so well-known that any lampooning would be instantly picked up by the audience. Such films would become more prolific, especially in the latter half of the century, as audiences became increasingly aware of the filming process and familiar with a variety of movie genres (thanks, no doubt, to television repeating so many older films), so a filmmaker could readily parody earlier films in the safe knowledge that the audience would understand the joke. By the 1960s, you had the *Carry On* film series out of Britain, which parodied various genre films, and a dozen or two James Bond parodies floating around. The 1970s saw Mel Brooks's career blossom with various spoofs poking fun of film styles—the western (*Blazing Saddles*) and the Alfred Hitchcock thriller (*High Anxiety*)—leading directly to the Zuckers with *Airplane!* and *The Naked Gun* movies of the 1980s. In more current time, you unfortunately almost expect every comedy to spoof something from an earlier movie, or worse, you see films that simply use various references to earlier movies as the gags themselves rather than coming up with new jokes (as in the endless *Scary Movie* series).

With every type of film genre, there are always certain subsets to the group that are more specific in nature (such as how we have science fiction movies and then ones that are about robots or about aliens invading). The same holds true with parody films, ranging from those that simply put a comedic spin on a dramatic style, such as with the Skelton and Hope movies listed above, to those that are nothing but jokes making fun of genre filmmaking and anything else of popular interest, such as with films like *Airplane!* One subset of the parody film is the narrative edit and overdub, which would become the genesis of what would later be used with *MST3K*. These visual and audio edits are created by taking an earlier movie, usually a serious dramatic film of some sort, and then adding and/or dubbing over the dialogue and sometimes rearranging scenes to re-create the material into a comedy.

As established, talking back in the theater to live acts has been around for many years and would continue as movies came into popularity. At first, there were no worries someone would shout in the auditorium and drown out dialogue, since the movies were silent until the 1920s. Nevertheless, there is clear evidence that patrons were warned in silent-movie theaters to not talk during the movies or risk ejection from the building; thus heckling the movies even then was considered rude behavior and was frowned upon. And while we're talking the birth of a notion here, not the etiquette of it, we do wonder if it was from this type of conduct in the silent-movie halls that the idea came for the first series of films to use the style of "narrative edits," as earlier silent films would be the source for the first fully realized series of parody films using this method.

Pete Smith (1892–1979) was a writer and producer who created over 150 short films, mostly for MGM, that ran in theaters before the main features. These one-reel short subjects, lasting eight to ten minutes in length, were usually listed under the umbrella title of *Pete Smith Specialties*. Several of the shorts would demonstrate interesting sports and stunts while occasionally drifting into advanced film techniques, such as three-dimensional films long before the 3D craze of the 1950s, as seen in his shorts *Audioscopiks* (1935) and *Murder in 3-D* (1941). They were almost always comedic, with Smith himself narrating in an easily identifiable, matter-of-fact, nasally tone, and at times, they featured actor-director-stuntman Dave O'Brien, who played the marijuana smoker who likes his piano playing fast in *Reefer Madness* from 1936, (riffed by *RiffTrax* in 2010). Among Smith's shorts are ten films called *Goofy Movies* that were released between 1934 and 1935. Each one of these shorts (titled as *Goofy Movies* with a number after it) featured bits and pieces from various silent movies, some early talkies, and newly filmed comedic pieces, edited and redubbed to create a stylized "night at the movies" within the ten-minute framework (or as stated in the opening credits, "A Whole Show in One Reel"). Every *Goofy Movies* would start with a "newsreel" showing various preposterous events in the news (such as stock footage from a real newsreel of a skier making a jump that is edited to show him flying halfway around the world) and then a "feature" that was commonly a silent film reedited and redubbed with Smith's narrative. The jokes typically were at the expense of the overacting of the cast and wonky plotting and effects of the films; working best with "serious" melodramas, such as in *Goofy Movies Number Four*, where a boyfriend stiffens in overly dramatic defiance against the local sheriff pestering his girlfriend while Smith narrates, "Peter remembers his school of acting and goes into pose B." This is immediately followed by the girlfriend overplaying the holding back of her angry boyfriend as Smith continues with, "Kate tells him the sheriff proposed to her, and they go into pose D."

The series is a rather stiff watch today, as a lot of the jokes land with a thud and the usage of new footage tends to overplay gags (although a "sporting event" in *Goofy Movies Number One* that shows one person in the grandstands cheering is close to the later *MST3K* recurring gag of "And the crowd goes wild," followed by a bored "Yay" from Joel and the bots). Nevertheless, the shorts did well enough that Smith would return to the form in 1941 with one more, *Flicker Memories*, a repurchasing of *Goofy Movies Number Four* with some new footage to establish the "silent movie" treatment. Unlike some later redubs, the series seemed to face little controversy about the mockery with viewers, although Harrison Carroll commented in his September 15, 1934, column, "Behind the Scenes in Hollywood," that "dozens of letters have been received asking the identity of the stars of the ancient dramas." The publicity department at MGM even pushed a positive spin on the mockery, pointing out that "Smith's series, concocted of fragments of film made seriously about 20 years ago, is playing to more houses and making more money now than the films did when originally released." As Robbin Coons reported in a syndicated column in the fall of 1934, MGM's response naturally suggested a market for such parodies, leading to the question, "Will some Pete Smith of the future take today's screen 'epics' and kid the boots off them for future 'goofy movies?'" It did take a while for that prophecy to come true, but when it did, controversy would follow.

Jay Ward (1920–1989) was a producer of classic animated television characters such as Rocky and Bullwinkle, Mr. Peabody and Sherman, and Dudley Do-Right that had been passed down through the generations due to the level of humor enjoyed by both kids and adults. Ward worked steadily with his partner Bill Scott (1920–1985) on many projects, including a rare live-action series called *Fractured Flickers* (1963–1964), which continues the tradition of *Goofy Movies*. The half-hour series was originally developed as a pilot by writer Chris Hayward, who would later team with fellow Ward writer Allan Burns to create *The Munsters* and write for programs like *Get Smart, Barney Miller,* and the only other live-action attempt from Ward, the pilot *The Nut House!!* (1964). *Fractured Flickers* starred Hans Conried (1917–1982), who had worked as a voice actor for Ward and appeared in many comedy roles throughout his career, typically as a somewhat pompous windbag who struggled to endure the peons around him. Conried played much the same role on *Fractured Flickers,* hosting as a character named Hans Conried who obviously didn't think much of the films he was showing nor even of some of the guest stars who appeared for interviews. And the show certainly had guests, ranging from Rose Marie to Zsa Zsa Gabor and even an appearance from Bullwinkle (in puppet form), who all would appear for a few minutes to be "interviewed" midway through the program, although such interviews were scripted comedy.

The focus of the show, of course, was on the "films" shown before and after each episode's interview, which was demonstrated in the first episode as being reedited versions of silent films, much like with *Goofy Movies.* There were differences, however. Although there were narratives, as in the Pete

A youngish-looking Hans Conried, just a few years away from becoming the host of the memorable redubbed comedy series *Fractured Flickers*. COLUMBIA PICTURES / PHOTOFEST © COLUMBIA PICTURES

Smith series, regular Ward voice actors like Paul Frees (voice of Boris Badenov) and June Foray (Rocky the Flying Squirrel) instead provided dialogue for the characters in the films, allowing more comedic opportunities than with narratives alone, as in Smith's run. *Fractured Flickers* was also more of a grab bag of material, with some pieces running one to two minutes, while others ran much longer, giving the show more freedom to abandon setups when the gags ran their course.

Perhaps the biggest difference was that while Smith chose movies that rarely had actors the public would recognize, Ward was not afraid to use movies featuring stars the audiences of the day would know, leading to Douglas Fairbanks, Lon Chaney, Rudolph Valentino, Stan Laurel, and many others having their movies mocked during each episode. While this helped audiences appreciate the gags more, as they would have had some familiarity with the original movies and actors being mocked, it did not go over well within the acting community. Harold Heffernan, in an article from early 1964, noted that the program was verboten on Thursday nights at the Motion Picture Country Home, a retirement home where "about 25 former stars and featured players still live," as those watching television that night would get agitated at the abuse made of their generation's work. Others were vocal about what they saw as insults to themselves or family members, with Lon Chaney Jr. threatening to sue Ward after his father's famous performance in *The Hunchback of Notre Dame* was changed into (ironically, the most popular comedic short of the series) "Dinky Dunstan, Boy Cheerleader," with Chaney as a cheerleader whose cheers rally the college football team at a time of crisis. "They are making my father out to be an idiot," Chaney Jr. told Heffernan in the article. "They have put silly dialog in his mouth, speeded up his actions until they are grotesque and in other ways have made a fool out of a great and revered screen personality. It is terrible enough to burlesque the stars who are still living—but my father is dead and cannot defend himself." Other stars, such as Mary Pickford, Betty Blythe, and family members of Tom Mix and Theda Bara (who has a mustache drawn on a famous picture of her in the first episode) also were vocal in objecting to the show. The producers would go so far as to parody the controversy late in the series, where in the next-to-last episode, Bob Newhart was interviewed as a protester objecting to how actors were being mocked, only to add his own name to the list by the end of the interview. Ward, who at times seemed to thrive more on people not getting the joke than when they did, blew off concerns, saying that those protesting were "altogether too sensitive," and he promised to go even further in a second season by incorporating footage of Alfred Hitchcock's *Blackmail* (1929) along with footage of Oliver Hardy and Boris Karloff.

Which didn't happen. The show, syndicated through Desilu, Lucille Ball and Desi Arnaz's production company, would only have the one season. While it didn't have staying power to make new episodes, the series itself lasted for years in reruns on stations around the country, up into the 2010s and eventually as a DVD box set of all twenty-six episodes, making it easy for others to be initiated into the concept of talking over movies for the sake of a joke. Many creators who followed in its footsteps referenced it with their own narrative edits and overdub films and programs.

However, a variation on the theme that next appeared helped play a role in many riff-like projects to come, with the release of a short film created by animated film director Ernest Pintoff and comedian Mel Brooks called *The Critic* (1963). Long before his later success as a comedy director, Brooks had been working as a writer for various television programs and found some success in front of an audience with his character the "2000 Year Old Man." That character had been an improvisation that he and actor-director-writer Carl Reiner had started doing in the writing room of Sid Caesar's show, and it developed into a studio album, *2000 Years with Carl Reiner and Mel Brooks*, that was released in 1960 and nominated for a Grammy Award. The 2000 Year Old Man was an old man, sometimes with a Yiddish accent (depending on how Brooks was playing the character in performance), who had seen everything since the beginning of time and had an opinion or two about it. The essence of that character would swing over to *The Critic*, which was the brainchild of Brooks after supposedly seeing an abstract animated film by artist Norman McLaren called *Lines Horizontal* (1962), which is very artistic but is mainly several horizontal lines moving back and forth in time to music. As Brooks watched that film, he could hear an elderly gentleman behind him muttering about how awful and dull it was. Brooks took that real-life incident and asked Ernest Pintoff to do a similar type of animation and then run it for Brooks to improvise off it as an old man not content in simply silently watching it ("What d'ell is this? . . . Oh, I know what it is—it's garbage, that's what it is."). The film, running less than four minutes, earned Mel Brooks an Academy Award for Best Animated Short in 1964 and would later be remembered by Kevin Murphy, in the introduction to the book *In the Peanut Gallery with Mystery Science Theater 3000*, as the first film he recalled seeing that he felt contained "riffing," with the old man's funny commentary on the animation being the focus of the short.

Meanwhile, United Artists (UA) had gotten hold of a movie from Italy that was the latest in a long line of "sword-and-sandal" movies popular for a time in the late 1950s through the early 1960s. The problem for UA was that the film *Arrivano i titani* (*The Coming of the Titans*) had two things going against it. The first was that American interest in such movies was dying out by 1963, as spy movies were the new "big thing," thus making it harder to get theaters interested in picking up such pictures; the second was that the movie has numerous light comedic moments that kept it from being sold as a straightforward adventure film. Such jokey touches, however, led to UA deciding that perhaps comedy was the direction to be taken for the film as a whole and went about redubbing the film with everyone speaking in Brooklyn accents and with some additional cartoonish sound effects. This version of the movie—of which, surprisingly, reviews suggested that the dialogue was straight, only the accents were jokey—was released fleetingly around the country, with reviews remarking that the Brooklyn accents were tiresome after a while.

The ad campaign for the movie, now titled *My Son, the Hero*, attempted to play off this humorous approach with a cartoonish *MAD* magazine style to the poster and newspaper artwork, featuring lighthearted text to describe what audience members would witness ("A Gigantic Spectacle Shot of Location for Peanuts!" "See Hand Maidens . . . Foot Maidens . . . All Kinds Maidens!") To top it all off, Mel Brooks narrated a long trailer for the film in his *The Critic*/2000 Year Old Man voice, suggesting people see *My Son, the Hero*, as if the hero of the movie was *his* son, and then describing scenes as they play out in the trailer, much like how Pete Smith would in *Goofy Movies* ("These are girls. . . . These are ugly men and not afraid to admit it!"). Even with this inventive approach, the movie did poorly in the comedically dubbed version, with reviews being like this one from Barbara Ashford at the *Buffalo News*, who gave the film a one-sentence review: "*My Son, The Hero* is a gratuitous insult to any unfortunate thrust into its company." UA, finding the redub was a failure, quickly reverted to a second dub with proper "unfunny" accents to replace it in theatrical showings and on television (leading to some people to suspect the Brooklyn accent version never existed, although reviews strongly suggest otherwise). What people broadly remembered, anyway, was the ad campaign, especially Mel Brooks a.k.a. *The Critic* trailer, which eventually turned up in the DVD box set *The Incredible Mel Brooks*, from Shout! Factory in 2012, of which some reviews back in 1963 suggested was worth seeing more than the movie itself.

As mentioned, big action films were moving away from the sword-and-sandal movies of the 1950s and instead heading toward spy pictures. James Bond was the big deal, and everyone at a studio somewhere in the world wanted to copy the exploits of a super-secret agent who got the women and used elaborate devices to track down the villains. One such series of spy movies came out of Japan starting in 1963 called *Kokusai himitsu keisatsu* (*International Secret Police*), which starred Tatsuya Mihashi as Jiro Kitami, an agent for the (well, of course) International Secret Police. The series, as would occur with the Bond series, started off as very serious with some humorous touches, only to get sillier with each sequel, and by the time of the fourth film in the series, *Key of Keys*, the humor was starting to outshine the drama. It was around this time that Hollywood producer Henry G. Saperstein worked out a deal with Toho Studios in Japan to export several of its movies to America. Along with obtaining rights to certain Toho monster films, such as some of the later Godzilla movies, he had also gotten the rights to Toho's *Kokusai himitsu keisatsu* series. The problem was that by 1965, just as with sword-and-sandal movies before it, the spy movie genre was starting to look a touch worn out. Further, as with *Arrivano i titani* for UA, Saperstein realized that the humor built into the films could be culturally mystifying to foreign audiences, who probably thought it was unintended, and the stories simply weren't that exciting (*Key of Keys* is a heist movie with approximately three supergadgets in it, and two are electronics built into baggage). Thus Saperstein found himself with a series of movies that he didn't think would work if simply redubbed into English. When a screening of a serious redubbing of the film provided by Toho in early 1966 was laughed off the screen by a test audience, Saperstein decided to go another direction and produced what is considered a classic of the redub genre, *What's Up, Tiger Lily?*

"It was a slick James Bond–type film; very well done; except everyone was Japanese," Saperstein told Donald Liebenson of the *Los Angeles Times* in 1998. Expecting laughs where not intended, Saperstein decided, "You beat them to the punch. I decided to do our own spoof." Taking a cue from *Fractured Flickers*, Saperstein thought of having the film redubbed with funny dialogue and contacted comedian Lenny Bruce. Bruce's response upon finding out that the dialogue would need to be appropriate for an all-age audience was to turn it down. When Saperstein asked, "Who's a clean you?," as an alternative, Bruce recommended Woody Allen.

Allen, after having spent years writing for television and doing stand-up, was fast becoming a well-recognized figure on television, had completed work on the movie *What's New, Pussycat?* (1965), was working on the James Bond spoof *Casino Royale* (1967), and had signed to make his first movie on his own, which was eventually released in 1969 as *Take the Money and Run.* To get him would be a catch for Saperstein, and the producer (as per John Baxter's biography about Allen) offered the writer-actor $66,000 to redub the movie, which Allen accepted. Setting up a projector in a hotel room at the Stanhope Hotel in New York, Allen and several friends (including many who did voices in the film, such as Allen's soon-to-be-second-wife Louise Lasser and early Allen cowriter Mickey Rose) began work in early 1966. "We had pens and pencils," Rose told Liebenson. "We ran the projector for a scene, then stopped and tried to figure out something. Finally, we thought to get the script of the film to see what the actors were actually saying." The film, originally featuring our dashing hero agreeing to work with a crime boss to steal money from a terrorist group that had stolen the money from a struggling new country, instead found our jabbering, Broadway song–bursting hero (who may be an airplane) trying to steal back a recipe for the world's best egg salad from gangster and football coach Shepherd Wong. He gets help from mom-hitting gangster and so-so impressionist Wing Fat, along with two sisters, Suki and Teri Yaki, who admit to being "great pieces" even if taking off jewelry may cause parts to fall off.

Supposedly Saperstein promised Allen the results would be an hour-long television special and then realized he had a better chance of making back his investment if the film was released as a feature film to theaters, leading to Allen threatening to sue. However, as editor Richard Krown pointed out to Brett Homenick in 2021 for the online site, Vantage Point Interviews, Allen took part in additional shooting to help extend the film when it was realized that at less than seventy-five minutes, the movie was not long enough to gain film distribution. "I remember sitting in several meetings in Hank Saperstein's office with Woody [asking] how are we going to length this picture up?" This was accomplished with a long opening sequence showing part of the climax of an earlier movie in the series, *Kokusai himitsu keisatsu: Kayaku no taru (International Secret Police: Keg of Gunpowder)*. It then cut to Allen being interviewed by Len Maxwell, explaining the redubbing process in a humorous manner. Also added were two musical numbers by the Lovin' Spoonful, featuring the band performing the earworm "Pow," named after the initial title of the repurposed movie before changing to its eventual title, along with joining in on the joke with Japanese dancers in an orgasmic trance while the band performed the quaint, upbeat song, "Fishin' Blues." Other additions were a late break in the film, where a projectionist's romance becomes an onscreen affair, and then the ending credits sequence, where Allen lies back on a couch and eats an apple while dancer (and comedian Mort Sahl's wife) China Lee does a striptease, ending with Allen stopping her to tell the audience (with editor Krown's voice being dubbed in) that he promised to put her in the film "somewhere." There is also an alternate vocal track with some different gags used for dialogue, which has been suggested was done for possible use for television airings and has been commonly heard more recently on streaming channels, suggesting that Allen's involvement was more extensive than previously thought. (The alternate dialogue works to a lesser, disappointing effect for the most part, although switching Wong's "rack of meat" gag while reviewing his prostitutes into one where he's giving them a halftime pep talk during a football game is comedy gold and leads to a callback joke later in the movie that's a solid payoff.)

If Allen had any reservations about the movie, it was the way the film was promoted as *Woody Allen's What's Up, Tiger Lily?*, a title he hated, as it was a hacky play off the earlier *What's New, Pussycat?* The personalization also soured the stance that the upcoming *Take the Money and Run* would be his first official film. When word of mouth from audiences and critics showed that *What's Up, Tiger Lily?* was to be a hit, however, Allen was convinced that any thoughts of a lawsuit would not be good for his emerging film career and decided to let it go. Even so, he rarely has discussed the film over the years and does not consider it as part of his filmography.

No matter how Allen views the movie, *What's Up, Tiger Lily?* went on to be many people's introduction to the concept of comedically redubbed movies, thanks to frequent reruns on television during the 1970s and 1980s. The success of *What's Up, Tiger Lily?* was also a springboard for various independent—especially nonprofit, college-oriented—radio stations across the United States to experiment with the redubbing process during the 1970s. This was commonly in a form of audio guerrilla attack, with a DJ on late-night radio suggesting listeners tune to a program on a local television station and turn off the television volume in order to listen to improvised dubbing by the DJ and others at the station in real time. Occasionally such practices were even scheduled, such as one in November 1978 at the public radio station WYSO in Yellow Springs, Ohio, for a station fundraiser, where a live redubbing of *Little House on the Prairie* was done and went over well—that is, until the cast at the radio station began parodying the advertising during commercial breaks, causing the redub to be briefly halted and then only segments of the drama allowed to be spoofed from that point onward. One can make fun of the programming but not of the companies forking over the money for the show, it seems.

Although released in 1975, there's no denying that the emerging cult success of *The Rocky Horror Picture Show* by 1978 helped to introduce not so much the concept of talking back to the screen but the permission to do so on a much larger scale. The movie, based on a stage musical that briefly hit Broadway, has had so much written about it that there's not much need to cover it here; of main concern is how the movie became part of the midnight movie experience that spread over the United States in the 1970s. Larger cities, especially those with college kids looking for something to do on a weekend, commonly had at least one theater (sometimes more) that ran late-night "cult" movies, and *Rocky Horror* quickly emerged as one of the most popular. Fans came back again and again to see the movie, and as their familiarity with the film grew, so did their need to entertain themselves by making the experience new. This was partially done by audience members dressing up and even performing part or all the movie in front of the audience as it played. Others, and the ones that are of more interest here, began trying to outdo each other by setting up callbacks to the screen to coincide with dialogue or actions (e.g., the audience warning Frankenfurter when he wishes to explain his actions right before being shot, "This better be good. Remember what happened last time."). There were regional changes in certain callouts, and some were discarded over time for overuse, yet this type of audience participation became so incorporated into the "feel" of the movie that when the film was eventually released to DVD, an alternate audio track featuring an audience responding to the film was offered. While attempts to replicate this phenomenon for other movies failed (such as with *Mommie Dearest* [1981] and even *Rocky Horror*'s sequel *Shock Treatment* [1981]), this type of crowd participation would be reflected in how *MST3K* incorporated the theater setup and talk-back to the screen.

Elsewhere, Peter Bergman and Philip Proctor of the satirical radio-performance group The Firesign Theatre ventured into the *Tiger Lily* arena in 1979 with *J-Men Forever*, a film featuring several clips from old Republic Studio serials from the 1930s (such as the *Commander Cody* and *Undersea Kingdom* shorts that ran on *MST3K* in its early seasons), and showcasing Captain Marvel, Captain America, Spy Smasher, and Commander Cody, but renamed as the Caped Madman, the Lone Star, Spy Swatter, and Rocket Jock, respectively, if not respectfully. Like *Tiger Lily*, *J-Men Forever* had new segments filmed to help establish the new story, although in the case of the Proctor-Bergman film, such scenes do not introduce the concept; instead, the pair appear in character as the chief and his assistant of the J-Men. Their segments mainly allow them to introduce the characters in the older clips as fellow J-Men being assigned to a dangerous mission. Their mission: to squash the plans of the "Lightning Bug," stationed on the moon, who plans to take over the world through the power of rock and roll music—with artists like the Tubes, Billy Preston, Head East, and Budgie heard on the soundtrack— which you can tap your foot to. ("But don't tap the brakes, because they don't work! Bwa-ha-ha-ha!")

J-Men Forever only got a very limited theatrical run, typically in the "midnight movie" circuit across the country. However, with its jokey sex and drug references ("Yes, the Bug's into drugs!") and musical references, it was picked up by Stuart S. Shapiro for the USA cable network's new edgy rock-music program *Night Flight* in June 1981. *Night Flight* played every Friday over a seven-and-a-half-year period and featured various oddball clips from movies, interviews with rock stars, blocks of music videos, and typically a cult movie, with *J-Men Forever* being a favorite. As the program aired from 11:00 p.m. until 3:00 a.m. and then immediately repeated from 3:00 a.m. until 7:00 a.m., stoners, I mean, viewers became very familiar with what was programmed during the show, which only helped reinforce the cult following of *J-Men Forever* over the next few years.

Bergman and Proctor must have felt comfortable with the format, for even if *J-Men Forever* didn't do well when released to theaters, the duo was soon back with the 1979 HBO special *Madhouse of Dr. Fear* and with Firesign Theatre alumni David Ossman and Phil Austin in tow to help. The star of the hour-long television special is none of them, however; it is comedian and actor Don Adams, who plays a "Walter Mitty"–type schmuck who dreams of taking off with his employer's money only to end up at a haunted mansion belonging to "Dr. Fear." Using additional clips from the Republic serials, travelogues, early exploitation films, and a heavy reliance on Ed Wood's *Glen or Glenda*, Adams's character imagines various things that have or could happen to him (almost as a predecessor to the later HBO series *Dream On*, which used various movie and television clips to accentuate the humor in scenes). Getting to see The Firesign Theatre working on film is fun, even if it feels somewhat iconoclastic to have them defer to Don Adams as the hero. But the special isn't quite on the level of high results as with *J-Men Forever* (a laugh track doesn't help matters). There are some solid moments even in the wraparound material, however, which isn't always the case in these programs, and it is a shame that the special has essentially disappeared unless you were lucky enough to have recorded it back during the early 1980s when HBO re-aired the program a handful of times.

The Firesign Theatre group (minus David Ossman) got back together for one more reflection on the old Republic serials and exploitation films with the 1983 film, *The Firesign Theatre Presents Hot Shorts*. Released on VHS and laserdisc, the seventy-five-minute program featured more narrative edits and overdubbed footage to create nine different stories, usually focusing on sex or politics ("The Mounties Catch Herpes" and "The Last Handgun on Earth" are two such examples). Creating several shorts out of the footage allows for the writers to regroup and go in a different direction every eight to ten minutes, but without a story line—such as with *J-Men Forever* and even *Madhouse of Dr. Fear*—to tie everything together, the material starts to feel a bit repetitious after a while.

What's Up, Hideous Sun Demon (a.k.a. *Revenge of the Sun Demon*) was a 1983 project started in order to *Tiger Lily*-fy an old horror film written, produced, and directed by and starring actor Robert Clarke called *The Hideous Sun Demon* (1958). Clarke, who owned the rights to the film, sold it to producer Wade Williams—a name that will appear again later—who then agreed to the redubbing of the movie. Craig Mitchell, working with Allen and Mark Estrin, created the redubbing script, along with new footage added to the beginning of the movie that shows college guys eating disgusting food as they sit down to watch the movie (a segment that has no payoff or connection to the movie itself), and some additional insert shots that set up dirty jokes throughout the film (such as an old woman reading a bondage magazine and later a large dildo being presented as a gift to the femme fatale). The best new bit is an altered ending that allows the creature to survive and have a somewhat happy ending, although even that lands with a large thud before the final credits.

The movie's original premise, about a scientist who pulls a reverse-werewolf by turning into a monster only when exposed to the sun, thanks to a radiation accident, was changed to an oral suntan oil inventor who turns into the creature and goes on a scaring spree through most of the picture. Robert Clarke was not happy with the results and quickly went on record with magazines such as *Psychotronic* and *Fangoria* that he felt left out of the loop in the process, telling Anthony Petkovich in *Psychotronic*, "It's not very good. Wade thinks it's funny. I don't think it's funny, I think it's dirty. Real low-grade humor." It probably didn't help that Clarke found his name in the ending credits, as if he voiced himself in the redub. There were actually two attempts made for the redubbed film, the first featuring a different actor doing Clarke's character that was rejected as not being good enough, and a second that featured comedian Jay Leno playing the lead. Leno, who was already making a name for himself by this time and probably realizing the material was not very good, requested his name not be listed in the credits, leading to Clarke's name being used instead. While Leno's request was granted, that didn't stop the filmmakers from making people aware of Leno's presence in the film in promotional material and interviews, making the absence of his name a rather moot point. *What's Up, Hideous Sun Demon* bounced around for some time without finding distribution but eventually made some very limited theatrical appearances around 1990 before finally being released on VHS tape under a new title, *Revenge of the Sun Demon* in 1998 and then eventually on DVD in 2003.

Repurposing older movies for comedic effect continued in the 1980s and to better effect, with the Steve Martin–Carl Reiner 1982 movie, *Dead Men Don't Wear Plaid*, although with a slight twist. With a top-line cast and a major studio behind them, Reiner and Martin were able to dip into the vaults of various major studios and create a new movie taken from bits and pieces of classic film noir movies (*White Heat, The Big Sleep, The Postman Always Rings Twice*, and more) instead of B movies to tell a new story. What sets it apart from *Tiger Lily, J-Men*, and *The Hideous Sun Demon* redo is that the film clips were not redubbed; instead, Martin and other actors were inserted into the footage so that only the lines spoken by the new characters would change the subtext of the earlier footage and help create the humor (e.g., a scene from the 1941 movie, *Johnny Eager*, which has Edward Arnold menacing Robert Taylor as Johnny by demanding he pick up something from his desk, becomes Arnold demanding Martin pick up the mess just made by a puppy Martin brought into his office; "But it's all hot and steamy," Martin whines). Steve Oedekerk's 2002 movie *Kung Pow! Enter the Fist* would go one step further by taking footage from the 1976 Hong Kong movie *Tiger & Crane Fists* and restaging those scenes by inserting himself into footage—by having his head superimposed over that of *Tiger* actor Jimmy Wang Yu—while new redubbed dialogue and other insert shots were created to turn the film into a comedy.

Other attempts continued into the 1980s, some better than others. Troma's *Tiger Lily* rewriting of an Indonesian action film about a woman forced to become a professional wrestler in an illegal wrestling syndicate, *Perempuan Bergairah* (*Passionate Girl*), became *Ferocious Female Freedom Fighters*

(1984). One interesting aspect difference from previous movies mentioned here, however, is that *Ferocious* features a movie largely unaltered except for the redubbing, which was done in a variety of ways in search of humor, such as heading back to *My Son, the Hero* territory by giving the male lead a voice like Elvis in hopes the accent alone would make the dialogue funny. The response was a moderate success in the video market, but it created some bad blood between the spoofers and the original creators. The head of Troma, Lloyd Kaufman, later showed the movie to the producer of the original film and, as reported by Mike White in *Cashiers du Cinemart*, "He was, to say the least, overcome with great emotion and told us that if, by chance, the actors from Indonesia ever came to New York and saw the *Ferocious Female Freedom Fighters* we had created, they would kill us. Literally, we would be dead."

Included in the voice actors for *Ferocious Female Freedom Fighters* were members of a comedy improv team from Los Angeles that would pretty much dominate the market for redubbed comedies in the 1980s and into the 1990s: the L.A. Connection. In 1977, Kent Skov helped form the group, and it soon began doing improvisational shows at their own theater. In August 1982, the group was asked to do a live *Tiger Lily* version—or "Dub-A-Vision" as they called it—of the 1958 movie, *Attack of the 50 Foot Woman* at the Fox Venice Theater in Los Angeles. This went over so well that they began to do other live redubs in theaters for movies such as *Wrestling Women vs. the Aztec Mummy, Andy Warhol's Frankenstein,* and *Cat-Women of the Moon*. By 1983, the troupe had gained enough interest that they began appearing on a regular basis for the short-lived *Thicke of the Night* talk show, starring Alan Thicke, doing a segment of short versions of the Dub-A-Vision, with additional help from people like Gilbert Gottfried, Richard Belzer, and Charles Fleischer. *Thicke of the Night* didn't last long, but the national attention for the L.A. Connection and their movie parodies would lead to a syndicated half-hour television series, *Mad Movies with the L.A. Connection*, which ran for twenty-six episodes in 1985–1986.

The group had managed to work out a deal with Four Star, a distributor of many older films for theatrical and television airings, some classics and some not so much, to use their library for the program. They first put together a pilot called *Mad Movies with the . . . Dungeon Women*, which had a premise where, as Skov described it to Mike White for his book *Mad Movies with the L.A. Connection*, "Judy Landers [is] tied up by her sister in a dungeon. She was shackled to the wall and forced to watch bad old movies." Oddly enough, the concept of a host being forced to watch bad movies would be independently used by *MST3K* a few years later, but with *Dungeon Women*'s reliance on a "Bettie Page–approved" bondage scenario, the pilot was considered "too kinky" when shown to a Los Angeles station. Restructuring the show to have Skov in a more traditional "movie host" role instead was enough to get the show green-lit.

Mad Movies followed a setup similar to the one seen in *Tiger Lily*, with Skov in wraparound segments introducing each episode's movie, but one element that was unique to *Mad Movies* was the higher-quality films made available to the team thanks to access to Four Star's library, including *Santa Fe Trail*, *A Star is Born*, *D.O.A.*, and *The Inspector General*, among others. Unlike redubbed films by other groups that would try to name the films something humorous, *Mad Movies* stuck with the original film titles, although all were drastically altered into eighteen- to twenty-minute-long films for the show (e.g., the Shirley Temple movie *The Little Princess* from 1939 becomes a story about a girl possessed by her doll to do terrifying things to the rest of the cast). The films were then broken up at commercial breaks by various skits, occasional interviews with people connected to the films, or even home movie footage that is given new narratives, like the *Goofy Movies* of old. Over the course of twenty-six episodes, the series picked up a following across the country, but budget issues kept the series from continuing into a second season.

After the series, the L.A. Connection continued as an improv group with occasional excursions into Dub-A-Vision over the years, including dubbing a Basil Rathbone Sherlock Holmes movie, *The Woman in Green*, for the A&E cable network in 1993. Most importantly after *Mad Movies* came *Blobermouth* in 1991, which was its redubbing of the 1958 science fiction/horror classic, *The Blob*, starring Steve McQueen in his first lead movie role as a teenager who must band a town together to stop a growing alien mass that eats everything in its path. The L.A. Connection had done a live redubbing of the film several times up through 1988 to enthusiastic response, when the film's original producer Jack Harris offered the team the film to redub as a permanent record of their performances and to perhaps make some money off any interest the 1988 remake of the movie would achieve. Kent Skov, Stephen Rollman, Bob Buchholz, and Steve Pinto wrote the script based on the earlier live performances, with the new plot having "Steve" (McQueen, voiced by Buchholz) now portrayed as a stand-up comic who has his one-man show interrupted by an alien comedian who tells nothing but bad one-liners (voiced by Henny Youngman doing many of his old jokes). In the end, instead of defeating the blob, the blob goes on to national fame on *The Tonight Show*, while Steve ends up delivering pizzas at the North Pole. The finished product was not considered the success hoped for, however. "*The Blob* was one of my favorites, the live version," Buchholz told Mike White in his *Mad Movies* book. "*Blobermouth* was good, too, but there was an example of where I think we fine-tuned it too much. We polished it too much and lost some of the spontaneity we had [when performing] live." Although the crew had access to the real Henny Youngman for the production to play the Blobermouth, his schtick works against the film, becoming more annoying with each utterance rather than endearing, and you grow to really hate every

Watch out! A "rap" number is on its way if you're watching the redubbed Mad Movies version of *The Blob* (1958), starring a young Steve McQueen and redubbed as *Blobermouth* (1991).
PARAMOUNT PICTURES / PHOTOFEST © PARAMOUNT PICTURES

appearance of the monster ruining what is a consistently amusing movie. Attempts to add musical numbers to stretch out the film time slow it down as well and are grating. Even with those misfires, the finished product has some very good writing and, as with the *Mad Movies* series before it, shows that the team could be tight and funny when focused. *Blobermouth* did get some theatrical distribution, mainly on the festival circuit, in 1991 and 1992, before finally being released on VHS in the 1990s and on DVD in 2007.

The festival trend also helped with other redubbing attempts in the 1990s, such as with the James Riffel films made between 1991 and 2011 that circulated with fans, having taken earlier movies and redubbed them with some brief footage added to create new comedies on the very, very cheap (typically less than $100 to create). The first one that many people heard of was *Night of the Day of the Dawn of the Son of the Bride of the Return of the Revenge of the Terror of the Attack of the Evil, Mutant, Alien, Flesh Eating, Hellbound, Zombified Living Dead Part 2 (in Shocking 2-D)*, which was a redubbed *Night of the Living Dead* (1968). Parts 3, 4, and 5 were later released, redubbing *The Brain That Wouldn't Die* (1962), *The Most Dangerous Game* (1932), and *The Andy Griffith Show* mixed with *Bonanza*. While on the lower end of recognition in the field of such redubbed movies, they still garnered attention and are well remembered by fans of the genre.

Festivals were about the only place Americans got a chance to see a movie that was a return to the style of improved redubbing that earned the L.A. Connection its reputation: the Australian comedy, *Hercules Returns* (1993), which—much like the L.A. Connection—came out of an improv group's live shows. The group was a duo called Double Take, Des Mangan and Sally Patience, who would perform live redubs in theaters using B movies such as *The Astro-Zombies* (1968 and later riffed by *RiffTrax*) and *The Bees* (1978). One of the movies done in these live shows was *Ercole, Sansone, Maciste e Ursus gli invincibili* (1964), commonly known as *Samson and His Mighty Challenge*, and the Double Take's live version was seen by a businessman, Philip Jaroslow, who pulled together money in order to get a movie made of their take of the film. *Hercules Returns*, directed by David Parker and written by Des Mangan, featured a wraparound story where Brad (David Argue), a man who quits working for a major movie theater chain, buys a broken-down theater and plans to show classic movies in it. When the premiere movie, *Samson and His Mighty Challenge*, turns out to be the Italian print with no subtitles, Brad, his girlfriend Lisa (Mary Coustas), and his projectionist Sprocket (Bruce Spence, best known in the United States for his appearances in the original *Mad Max* movies as a pilot) must improvise the lines from the projection booth, with their improvisations winning over the audience and saving the day. Interestingly, while Argue, Coustas, and Spence are shown as doing the voices, it is the Double Take team, Mangan and Patience, who do many of the voices in the film for the actors. The movie did well in Australia and played in theaters in the United Kingdom but did not really gain notice in the United States until it was eventually released on video in 2006, even with a promotional campaign stating it was "Funnier than *Gandhi*! Sexier than *The Little Mermaid*! Shorter than *Dances with Wolves*!"

As these attempts continued through the decades, there was another outlet for the occasional narrative edit and overdub excursion through local television and the late-night movie shows, and mainly thanks to the old horror movie hosts and their camera crew. When Kent Skov became the movie host of the *Mad Movies* series, it made sense, as the concept of the movie host on television goes back to the earliest days of television itself, when movies first began airing on stations around the country. Sometimes such a host would simply be an announcer at the station talking over a still, stating it was "Channel 4 Midnight Movie" and then giving the title of the film and naming a star or two to attract viewers to stay tuned, perhaps even coming back at the commercial breaks to restate the movie for people just tuning in (*Amazon Women on the Moon* contains a running gag using this image, for example). At other times, it involved a host appearing onscreen to do the same and throw in a few live ads for local businesses at some point, much like how Drs. Forrester and Erhardt did an ad for a real Minneapolis pizza place called Pizza 'N' Pasta in the middle of *Phase IV* during the KTMA season of *MST3K* ("Mmm, yummy noise"). The concept really hit its stride in 1957, when fifty-two Universal horror movies and thrillers were packaged for television syndication under the title of *Shock Theater*, a title that would also commonly be used as the name of the program each local station aired to show the films. And since at the time, you couldn't do a movie show without a host, why not have your announcers at your local station get some overtime by putting them into Dracula makeup and having them do a "scary" voice and introduce the movies for the kids watching?

Thus started the tradition of seeing some poor dope station employee on a Friday or Saturday night dressed up like a mad scientist or vague Dracula clone who would tell kids about the movie appearing on *Shock Theater* that night (a good example/parody of this phenomena can be found with Joe Flaherty's newscaster Floyd Robertson on *SCTV*, who periodically would be seen as "Count Floyd" announcing bad movies on *Monster Chiller Horror Theater*). Surprisingly, individuals who got stuck with such jobs usually grew to like the position, as it gave them some local fame with kids and families, created outlets to make personal appearances (local drive-ins, store openings) that put some money in their wallet, and guaranteed their employment at the station for a few years because of their fan base. But the weekly program could be a chore, because B movies (so called because when such movies played theaters in programs featuring two movies, they were never the main feature—the A picture—but second-string, and thus "B") were on average between seventy-five and eighty minutes long. These short movies meant there was a lot of time to kill in a two-hour time slot on television and only so many commercials you could run. This invoked creating a lot of fresh material to eat up time between commercial breaks, which led many of the hosts to slip into doing comedy segments with cheap props and visual effects that mocked the movies they were airing.

Fortunately, such shows were usually run by people who were "let loose in the candy store" to do what they wanted at the station and typically ignored by the station manager unless there were complaints. And sometimes the complaints did come in, as these programs were given over to young college-aged people willing to work odd hours at the station and an announcer who may have felt a bit of an outsider to management at the station. Shenanigans and goings-on were possible, such as Ernie Anderson out of WJW in Cleveland as the popular horror host Ghoulardi nearly burning down the studio when exploding plastic model kits with firecrackers live on the program. Such risk-taking could lead to these personalities becoming well-known to people in their region, sparking memories for fans in certain cities. Others, however, would become famous on a national scale, such as the already mentioned Ghoulardi, Zacherley (a.k.a. Roland, played by John Zacherle), and Vampira (Maila Nurmi, who is best remembered from *Plan Nine from Outer Space*), thanks to syndication of their shows to other areas or to simply being in a city that allowed them to gain interest on a larger scale. Even as the general interest in local programming died out in the 1980s, the interest in *Shock Theater*–type shows continued with national programs that played some of the same horror films as of old, such as with Elvira (Cassandra Peterson), Joe Bob Briggs (John Bloom), and Svengoolie (Rich Koz). While Briggs's program had a somewhat more traditional tone to it, as he introduced movies and did interviews, albeit with a slight "jaded film geek" vein (appearing on pay channels where there were no commercials and limited chances for hijinks during the actual films), Elvira and Svengoolie would lean toward the more traditional horror movie host setup of making sure there were plenty of gags between commercial breaks.

The 1986–1987 series *Canned Film Festival*, starring former *Saturday Night Live* actor Laraine Newman, was an attempt to do a similar program like Elvira's *Movie Macabre* series (airing from 1981 to 1986), but for bad movies like *Santa Claus Conquers the Martians*, *Bride of the Monster*, *Rocket Attack U.S.A.*, and others that eventually made their way to *MST3K* over time. In the case of *Canned*, there were wraparound segments, which featured Newman as the usher and manager of the Ritz, a rundown theater trying to regain interest by showing bad movies. Actors who played regular characters attending or helping at the theater would also be featured in segments that related to the movies being aired (much like how Tom and Crow would participate in some type of sketch between commercial breaks that were extensions of things they had just seen in the movies). The series, really made to help promote the Dr Pepper soft drink, would only last thirteen episodes, but it showed that the concept of a host-driven series still had commercial possibilities.

With each of these many shows over the years, whether local or national, most of them were consistent in one element, and that was to gently mock the very movies they were airing that day. Some of the earlier hosts gave it the old college try in supporting the movies (Bob Shreve out of Cincinnati avoided the issue by calling every movie playing "a fine movin' picture" while mumbling the name of the film and the stars with his hand over his mouth to show he probably had already forgotten what was playing). After a while, however, it was hard to keep being upbeat over a movie like *Pillow of Death* (1946, and an actual movie in the *Shock Theater* package) and not want to have some fun at the expense of such a dull thriller. Thus many of the horror hosts, with the support of their young crew, began to place video or audio inserts of the host into scenes of the movie. One tactic would be for the program to cut from the movie to show the host and others doing something in the studio; then cutting back to the movie would make it appear the film's characters were reacting to them. Sometimes the programs would even superimpose the host into a scene to make the host part of the movie in a silly way. There would even be occasions where the programs would go completely *Tiger Lily* and have cast members redub dialogue for a portion or even for an entire movie, such as when Svengoolie did (and still does) an episode in "Svensurround." (When Svengoolie would later air *What's Up, Hideous Sun Demon*, Svengoolie introduced the film by essentially apologizing for the airing and making sure viewers knew it was not a Svensurround production and that the show wasn't to blame. Sometimes the chance to play around can come back to haunt you.)

The narrative edit and overdub continued over the next few years, such as with the *Night Flight* series, *Dynaman*, that appeared in 1987 and featured various episodes of *Kagaku Sentai Dynaman* (what would later become known in the United States as *Mighty Morphin Power Rangers*) with episode content rearranged and redubbed to turn out six episodes of a new *Tiger Lily*–like series. Each episode was introduced by a man who supposedly was the producer of the program explaining the dubbing process (a made-up procedure that supposedly created new English translations instantly as the episodes were simulcast in Japan and the United States) but seemingly more concerned about business than the show. The programs themselves didn't shy that far away from their roots as being a group of people given powers (thanks to the snazzy watches they got from their leader, who runs a laboratory/day care center, according to the new dubs) in order to fight monsters. The show, featuring Mark McKinney of the Kids in the Hall comedy troupe as Dynablue, was fondly remembered by *Night Flight* fans who had hung around from the *J-Men Forever* days, although Toei, the production company of the original series, was rumored to not be happy about the changes and requested the series be terminated. That didn't stop the Nickelodeon network from repeating the six episodes in 1988 for its series, *Special Delivery*, however.

MXC, alternately known as *Most Extreme Elimination Challenge*, didn't appear to have any issues with the parent company that produced the series it mocked, *Takeshi's Castle*, which ran from 1986 to 1990 on TBS (Tokyo Broadcasting System), and that probably was due to the original show not being taken seriously either. *Takeshi's Castle* was a reality-based game show that had contestants perform in a series of silly physical games, with the show centered around an imaginary theme of a count (played by famed comedian and actor Beat Takeshi), who owns a castle, and his minions, who try to keep the contestants from advancing across dangerous terrain to invade it. Helping the contestants was General Tani (Hayato Tani), along with various other supporting individuals. The program would start with nearly one hundred contestants, sometimes more, and if someone failed to make it through a game, they were eliminated, leaving typically only a handful left to invade the castle at the end. The series did not take itself seriously, and much of the show was done in good humor and self-mockery (much like how *Key of Keys* or *Arrivano i titani* were not to be taken quite so seriously before any redubbing by Americans occurred). This made the later changes in *MXC* so much easier in a way, as the series was already over-the-top and loose in its presentation before the redubbing process even started.

While the series would feature comedic commentary when dubbed in other countries, the Americans involved in the *MXC* version, Paul Abeyta, Peter Kaikko, and Larry Strawther, edited episodes so that it became a more traditional "us versus them" obstacle-course game show, with Takeshi's character becoming announcer Vic Romano (voiced by Vic Wilson) commentating alongside his coannouncer Kenny Blankenship (Chris Darga) about the contestants' performances, with General Tani now becoming Captain Tenneal (voiced by John Cervenka), who encouraged the contestants along their way. Although there were over 130 episodes of the original series, those making *MXC* only had limited access to a certain number of episodes and began to repeat footage with new dialogue in later seasons. The program also had to severely edit an episode down in reruns that featured various copyrighted creatures ("Real Monsters vs. Commercial Mascots"). Nevertheless, the series was amazing in its ability to wring continual laughs out of similar material, if risqué at times (a game featuring contestants wearing giant hand costumes was named "Hand Job," for example), and well worth seeking out for some of the best redubs from over the years.

There were other attempts to do narrative edits and overdubs, but many fell below the level of the examples listed above. Interestingly, most of the filmmakers mentioned with the projects listed in this chapter felt the need to set up a premise for the redubbing within the framework of the redubbed comedy; some as simple as Woody Allen explaining the technique in *What's Up, Tiger Lily?*, up to the involved plot that lays out why a redubbing has to occur in *Hercules Returns*. Even something as straightforward as *Dynaman*—a silly half-hour redub show—showed us a "producer" to explain what was going on, while *What's Up, Hideous Sun Demon* prefaced the shenanigans of its redub with the pretext of it being a movie that "gross, funny" college students were watching. It would be an element that would continue into *MST3K*, once it began, and not the only one borrowed from these sources, as later chapters will show.

Yet of all these projects, the one that comes closest to being the parent to *MST3K* is not really something as old as *Goofy Movies* or *The Critic* nor the redubs of the 1970s through the 2000s. The movie that really captures the feel of *MST3K* episodes to come is the 1982 documentary, *It Came from Hollywood*. Produced by Paramount Pictures, the movie was created by Andrew Solt and Malcolm Leo, who had first gotten together to create the excellent (and hard to find) ABC documentary on rock music, *Heroes of Rock and Roll*.

The hosts of *It Came from Hollywood* (1982), a celebration of bad movies that was panned by critics and fans, would set up the method of riffing soon to be used by *MST3K*. © PARAMOUNT PICTURES

Their work pulling together rare film and video material of many artists into a thorough twenty-five-year history of rock music led to similar duties with *This Is Elvis* in 1981. The two branched off after *It Came from Hollywood* to do similar documentaries about music, movies, and television over the years, such as Solt working on various Ed Sullivan compilations. Many of these subsequent documentaries had good critical and fan reviews. *It Came from Hollywood*, not so much.

Some of the backlash *It Came from Hollywood* faced came from where Solt and Leo no doubt saw as inspiration to their work: *The Golden Turkey Awards* book and their various forerunners and offspring (*The Fifty Worst Films of All Time*, 1978; *The Hollywood Hall of Shame: The Most Expensive Flops in Movie History*, 1984; and *Son of Golden Turkey Awards*, 1986) by Michael and Harry Medved. The Medveds' *Golden Turkey Awards* and its subsequent volumes became a popular film book series because it was one of the few works available in everyday bookstores at the time that addressed movies we all knew of but certainly did not consider "classic" by any means. Instead, many were the types of films broadcast on *Shock Theater*–style programs or at 2:00 a.m. on a Thursday night for those of us unable to sleep with a cold. Films that didn't even rise to B-movie levels had moments of dreamlike quality that stayed buried in your head long after your cold was gone. Who could turn away from a movie with a title like *They Saved Hitler's Brain* in hopes of seeing Hitler's brain at some point? (It paid off, as you got to see his whole head in that one.) As much as everyone ridiculed *Plan Nine from Outer Space*, who among us wasn't somehow charmed by the oddball dialogue? ("The saucers are up there. And the cemetery's out there. But I'll be locked up in there.") Who could forget sitting through the Japanese monster movie without monsters, *Attack of the Mushroom People*, and yet be stunned by the downer ending?

While some cult movie fans who dismiss the book would have a hard time admitting it, *The Golden Turkey Awards* gave us one of the first opportunities to learn about these movies, their creators, and cast. The advancement of home video released in the 1980s and the need for products to fill the void of people wanting to watch anything led to new awareness among the public as well, but without the success of the book series, many of the books, magazines, and video releases that have followed over the years would most probably not have happened or would have been slower in coming. No doubt, the Medveds' book brought up titles of movies and plot descriptions that compelled many of us to seek them out, to learn more about the filmmakers and how they could have made such odd movies. It was a building block for a generation of movie fans.

The problem was that although it gave us tantalizing details about these movies, the writing leaned toward a smirky superiority over them. We gained some knowledge—the chapter on Ed Wood was an obvious revelation for many readers that has been expanded upon in other forms, such as Rudolph Grey's *Nightmare of Ecstasy* (1994)—but we were supposed to be dismissive about the work done by the filmmakers and to treat everyone involved as deficient in intelligence and creativity. And because the books were meant to be a quick, funny way to learn about the films, there was limited information available in them beyond certain details. Further, placing an unfunny review for a fake movie, *Dog of Norway*, didn't help matters, as it made some readers question the authenticity of the text elsewhere. Once other books came out that placed a more serious tone and extensive research to the movies and their creators, readers quickly turned on the *Golden Turkey* series as being meanspirited fluff.

And in the middle of that revolt there was *It Came from Hollywood*. Leo and Solt edited together snippets of over one hundred movies that had elements easily made fun of, as was done in *The Golden Turkey Awards*. The film was broken down into ten segments, much as how the Medveds' book was broken down into categories, focusing on specific elements of movies, with each segment introduced by comedians well-known to viewers at the time: Gilda Radner, Dan Aykroyd, John Candy, and Cheech and Chong (Cheech Marin and Tommy Chong). What infuriated some viewers was not that the clips shown were there to make us laugh over how goofy they were but that additional narration by the hosts was added to each segment. In some cases, this gave us some information about the movies, but much of it, primarily written by Dana Olsen, who later found success as the cocreator of the Nickelodeon comedy series, *Henry Danger* (2014–2020), was there to mock the scenes as they played out. It became comedy poking fun at comedy and set some viewers' teeth on edge. Michael Maza for the *Arizona Republic* in November 1982 put it best when he said, "There's a lot to laugh at in *It Came to Hollywood*. Just be sure to close your eyes and stick your fingers in your ears whenever the 'hosts' show up."

Yet once you got used to the construct and ignored the few moments where clips of classic science fiction movies, such as scenes from *War of the Worlds* and *The Incredible Shrinking Man*, were used, there were some solid laughs from the hosts. More importantly, the additional dialogue was a decided break from the redubs of the past. Earlier attempts like *Goofy Movies* were all narrative and commentary-like, while most attempts from *Tiger Lily* onward have been 100 percent dialogue overdubbing, but *It Came from Hollywood* went in a new direction: it let scenes play out as they did in their original films, or in only slightly edited form, which threw some viewers (more than one reviewer complained the giant ape giving the finger in the movie *A*P*E* had to be edited for a cheap gag when it was actually a cheap gag ripped straight out of *A*P*E*). More importantly, it let the original dialogue stand without any changes, allowing the hosts' comments to play off it in traditional faux heckler form. This was a radical departure from the norms of traditional comedic overdubs and was closer to that of the horror movie hosts and the performers stationed at showings of *Rocky Horror*.

Everything was closer to the bone of the original text, and any type of joke was now possible. The impossible-to-ignore racism exhibited in the blackface "Goin' to Heaven on a Mule" musical number from *Wonder Bar* from 1934 gets commentary from Radner reminding viewers, "Even this we owe to Hollywood," while Aykroyd fills in as the announcer telling people fleeing from a monster that "parochial school will remain in session," as you would expect from a traditional redub. Further, there was no pretense of hiding the mockery of the movies by giving them phony titles or creating new plots, as for previous movies. For example, Nan Peterson's character of Trudy Osborne may have been made silly as Bunny in *What's Up, Hideous Sun Demon*, but in *It Came from Hollywood*, it is clearly Peterson's performance and her "slow right-hand" piano playing that is the target. The faux heckler was now straight out in the open. There was one segment with John Candy in a serious tone reminding viewers that the people who made the films worked hard with little money, much as Mike Nelson as Hugh Beaumont as one of the four horsemen of the apocalypse sends a similar message in a skit from the *Lost Continent* episode of *MST3K* (season 2, episode 8). It even featured members of the cast, Cheech and Chong, sitting in a theater and riffing on movies as they played out on the screen, as Irvin Benson would with Milton Berle (or audiences at most college and inner-city theaters would do on a Saturday night).

It Came from Hollywood did not do well at the box office. The critics were rarely positive, and while a popular critic like Roger Ebert gave the film three stars in his review, he was not alone in stating that the commentary by the hosts was annoying ("That should be left for the paying audience to make," Ebert quipped in his review). Ebert also commented on the lackluster advertising campaign for the movie, which only drew attention to the new cast and not to the "bad movie" concept of the film, misleading audiences at a time where action movies and dramas were drawing dollars at the box office. Even as essentially a clip show, the movie made about half of its budget back, and its usage of movie footage from a variety of sources has led to copyright issues that kept it from being reissued in more recent years. It did have a strong run on cable television during the 1980s and 1990s, however, leading to many fans still remembering lines from the movie, such as the one opening this chapter.

It Came from Hollywood wasn't alone when it came to low returns at the box office. Except for *What's Up, Tiger Lily?*, none of the programs made a large financial impact, and even *Tiger Lily* is mainly remembered now for its many late-night airings on various television stations over the years. *Goofy Movies* ran for a year, as did *Fractured Flickers* and *Mad Movies with the L.A. Connection*. Movies like *What's Up, Hideous Sun Demon, Hercules Returns*, and *Blobermouth* managed to hit the festival circuit in the United States and then spawn lukewarm video sales. *My Son, the Hero* is so obscure that beyond Mel Brooks's commercial, no one is sure if it even exists in its original over-dubbed form. The concept appears more enjoyable to the filmmakers than to the audience. Even when done, the general rule was that the movies had to be edited down and sometimes with scenes out of order or new footage inserted, while plots were completely reworked to make them "funny." Mocking the original material as-is was for local horror movie hosts and couldn't be done on a continuing basis—certainly not for the length of an entire movie. It was just not workable.

Yet all these elements and others would find their way into the mix when the time came for *Mystery Science Theater 3000*. That was still in the future, however, and as *It Came from Hollywood* was about to hit theaters in October 1982, a young man from Green Bay, Wisconsin, was heading out west to LA to seek his future, only to find it in his own backyard. Okay, actually in Minneapolis, but that's getting ahead of the story.

3

Comic, Magician, Spy

Joel Hodgson before MST3K

Correction: Ventriloquist Joel Hodgson's dummy is incorrectly identified in a story in today's issue of CloseUP *magazine. The dummy's name is Stanley.*
—Correction in the September 24, 1978,
issue of the Green Bay Press Gazette

Joel Hodgson at one point in his stand-up career would bill himself as described in the chapter title: "comic, magician, spy." That type of multi-tasking has turned out to not be far from reality, with the possible exception of the spy part. Or so the government would have us believe. Hodgson has gone through a staggering number of careers in the entertainment field—magician, puppeteer, comedian, writer, producer, visual effects inventor, creator of a certain long-running television series, and many of these jobs all at the same time—but what is nearly as impressive is that his is not your standard Hollywood story. After all, he has come to the crest of fame twice in his career and walked away. That typically would be a troubling sign standard to many Hollywood tales, with tales to fill up an episode of standard celebrity documentaries, full of divorces, drugs, bizarre industrial accidents, and joyful recoveries with revelations and redemption.

And that's not Joel Hodgson's story. People would like to paint him as an enigma when it really comes down to a guy who is simply not interested in doing anything other than what he wants to show us—and better yet, who has the skill, determination, and perhaps luck to be able to do exactly that. And all the dicey, materialistic things that make it into the gossip columns never seemed to be part of his makeup. His story is more that of an extroverted introvert: he creates things to entertain the public, hopes they enjoy it, and then just disappears into the crowd to be happily left alone to concentrate on the next thing he wants to put together for the audience. "I think that was always complicated to me," Joel told Benjamin Nason for *The MacGuffin* in 2013, "people who just stood up there alone and did a talent like told jokes or sang. I'm not that kind of person. Anything I've ever done has been kind of like I stand to the side and show things. I showed magic, or did ventriloquism, or even *Mystery Science Theater* where I spent eighty percent of the time in the audience watching a movie. I always had

Joel Hodgson in his role as Joel Robinson from *MST3K*. COMEDY CENTRAL / PHOTOFEST © COMEDY CENTRAL

things I was demonstrating or showing, that I felt were more interesting than me."

Born on February 20, 1960, in Stevens Point, Wisconsin, Joel and his family would soon move to Fort Atkinson, where he developed an interest in ventriloquism at the age of eight. "I used to watch this ventriloquism show out of Madison," Hodgson told Carol Bizzardi, for the *Green Bay Press-Gazette*. "Like every little kid, I thought the dummy was real." Saving up his allowance, Joel bought a ventriloquist dummy when he was in third grade ("Actually, it was more a doll than a dummy," Joel told the paper, which is what it was: a doll with a painted wooden head whose only mechanism was a simple string-pulled jaw to move the mouth) and began working with other kids in school to do shows for younger students at Rockwell Elementary. Seeing his interest, his parents paid to have him take a correspondence course and then a thirty-lesson master course in ventriloquism. As a teenager, he would eventually get himself a professional dummy, a penguin in a top hat whose eyes and feet could move as he "talked," that Joel would name Stanley and begin to incorporate into his performances.

Hodgson's family next moved to Green Bay when he was ten years old, and they quickly found community in an evangelical church in the city. It was at that age when Joel saw a man named Charley Fairchild perform a magic act in church, and while a number of the tricks were easy to figure out even for a young child like Joel at the time, what mesmerized him during the performance was Fairchild's use of various professional magic props in his act. Hodgson was fascinated with the mechanisms involved with these "toys for grown-ups," as he described them to Benjamin when reflecting on the event. "And I remember asking him where he got them, and I think he thought I just wanted to find out how it was done, but I really just wanted to know, 'How do you get that stuff?'" Told that the props were bought out of a place in Colon, Michigan, called Abbott's Magic, Joel discovered the magic supply shop had a catalog, and he began ordering various tricks.

As his interest in the mechanics of magic percolated, Joel also was drawn toward creating his own inventions and using comedy in relation to them. A novel assigned in school about a boy inventor led to an assignment where the students were told to invent something to show in class. "I got really enthused," Hodgson told Nason, "because I remember that I had this idea for an invention which was called the Cracker-Cracker, which was a thing that would sit on your counter and was like a cutout of a hand and an arm, and it had a spring, and you'd put a rubber band on it, and you'd put crackers on the counter and it would smash them by karate chopping them." With his father's help, Joel brought his device to school along with a pile of crackers. "When it went off it just shattered these crackers, and they went flying all over the room. And all the kids laughed, and then walking back to my desk I ate one of the crackers, which I knew you were not supposed to do, right? And that got a laugh, so I think that kind of started me thinking about that."

Although Joel has argued that he had little interest in being the center of attention, events such as that of the Cracker-Cracker and others made it clear that he was definitely not a wallflower. By the mid-1970s, Joel's picture or name popped up quite frequently in the *Green Bay Press-Gazette*. In May 1975, he was seen presenting an award as president of his high school's Youth Against Dystrophy club, which helped organize events to raise money for the Muscular Dystrophy Association. He was listed in the cast of the Ashwaubenon High School's production of *The Music Man* (featuring sibling Julie Hodgson) in February 1976, was shown as doing well in a series of forensic competitions in March of that year, and appeared in a group photo meeting with town supervisor Jim Kuhn as part of the school's Key Club (a civic duty club designed to help students become future leaders) in May.

May 1976 was also a big moment for Joel as he was crowned "Junior Magician of the Year" by the Green Bay magicians' union. He had been doing his act since the age of fourteen, after a summer in Bible camp, where he learned some new tricks from a fellow camper, and soon afterward signed up with the International Brotherhood of Magicians. The honor allowed him access to certain tricks and devices but mainly gave him the chance to promote himself as "Junior Magician of the Year," which was helpful in getting gigs around town. His act would begin with a bit of ventriloquism with Stanley and then progress into the magical portion of the act. Incorporating Stanley into his set as a means of introduction allowed him to present "outside" of himself, with Stanley getting the laughs and Joel playing straight man, which he saw as a good icebreaker even as a sixteen-year-old when discussing the process with the *Green Bay Press-Gazette* in 1976: "If you want to explain it psychologically, people think of the ventriloquist as the establishment and the set ways of people. The dummy is rebelling against this, so people tend to like the dummy." It was a message remembered many years later with the robots of *MST3K*.

After graduating from high school, Joel would attend college at Bethel College in Saint Paul, Minnesota, in the fall of 1978 as a drama student, and at first, he gladly put aside his earlier dedication to ventriloquism and magic. "It's tough to find new material," Joel remarked in 1978 to Warren Gerds of the *Green Bay Press-Gazette*, after mentioning that his last major routine written for Stanley was already three years old at that point. "That's one of the reasons I slowed down a bit." The block for Hodgson appeared to be how he could incorporate everything he wanted into one act in a logical manner. While studying at Bethel, things suddenly fell into place. "I just happened to take a Theatre of the Absurd course in college," Hodgson told Rob Turbovsky for the *Boston Phoenix*, "and that's where it really started for me. It had this great little device, which is that if you perform absurd material, you can't really fail. No one can say, 'Hey, that wasn't absurd.' It gave me permission to try all the things I wanted to show people: it was inventions; it was bad magic tricks, weird concepts." Using his already near-professional talents as a

magician, a dash of puppetry, and his love of invention, Joel began performing to audiences again in 1981, and within four months, he won a comedy
competition on campus that featured over twenty other contestants.

Thanks to the growing boom of comedy clubs in major cities by the
early 1980s, Joel started getting regular gig in clubs; preferring places like the
Comedy Cabaret and the Comedy Gallery. "It really started as a club called
Mickey Finn's," Joel told Dylan Dawson in 2010. "The guys that were there
were really hard-assed guys—like Louie Anderson, Wild Bill Bauer, and Jeff
Gerbino. They were prepping for Hollywood by being kind of harsh to each
other. I went there one day, and I just knew I wouldn't survive it." Fortunately, the Comedy Cabaret was more relaxed and catered to Joel's style of
humor. The pairing worked well; Mike Steele for the *Star Tribune* in Minneapolis happened to see Joel as the headliner in a showcase at the Comedy
Cabaret in September 1981 and described Joel as "a comic magician and your
prototypical apathist, a master of inaction. Absolutely deadpan, a bit dopey
with a punk haircut and an ill-fitting white tail coat, Hodgson sort of decides
to do a trick or two." While the initial description does not sound promising,
Steele concludes by saying, "I don't know where Hodgson can take this act,
possibly into something more zany, more magical and more daring, but he is
genuinely funny." By the time he was a senior, he was performing over two
hundred shows a year, becoming a headliner in the Saint Paul-Minneapolis
area, and opening for musician B. J. Thomas in the fall of 1982.

Graduating from Bethel with a BA in speech communication, Hodgson
continued getting plenty of work in the Minneapolis area. "It is not that I
am talented at changing my routine to fit the audience," Joel mentioned in
a brief interview in September 1982 for the *Marshfield News-Herald* when
asked about how he shapes his show for different clubs. "I just present a show
that is designed to be acceptable to a lot of different people." Then came the
Twin Cities Comedy Invitational in mid-September of that year, where Joel

competed against eighteen other comics in a multiday showcase where comics were eliminated every day until only a handful were at the finals on September 26. As such showcases were seen as a good way to be noticed in the industry, the field of comics was diverse, with many comics from the two coasts appearing, to the point where one of the local comedians, Jeff Cesario (later a writer and producer for *The Larry Sanders Show*, among other programs), called the local contestants "the no-name division of the competition." Joel had found that he had lost so consistently to the major players that had "ten or more years of experience" in the semifinals that "I set my sights just on placing," he told the *Star Tribune*. Instead, he would come out on top in the finals, winning $500. Oddly enough, while some comedians would have seen this as a motive to head out to the coast themselves for bigger opportunities, Joel didn't need the sign. "I had been planning to move for a long time," he told Jeff Strickler. "I had decided to move at the end of September. The contest didn't have anything to do with it. It just worked out that way."

For a time, Hodgson bounced between LA and Minneapolis, performing gigs at his usual Minneapolis haunts besides getting a gig at the Magic Castle in Hollywood a week after arriving in the area. He soon moved on to one of the hottest comedy clubs of the 1980s, The Comedy Store, where fellow Minneapolis comic Jeff Cesario joined him. While at the Magic Castle, he made connections that allowed him to send a tape of his material to the producers of *Late Night with David Letterman*, and by February 1983 he made his first appearance on the program. Things slowly snowballed from there, with Hodgson beginning to perform shows in other parts of the country, such as Detroit, San Francisco, and Kansas City, but mainly he stuck with LA or Minneapolis in 1983 and into 1984.

During this period, he had a run-in with Gallagher, a very popular comedian of the 1980s who was known for using a large number of props in his performances and probably best remembered for his "Sledge-O-Matic," which was a giant mallet that he would then smash various things with, ending typically with a watermelon that would spray bits out into the audience. Gallagher became a continuing butt of jokes later on *MST3K*, as when zombified people in *It Conquered the World* (season 3, episode 11) said, "Now I understand, Gallagher IS funny," and in the idea of Gallagher floating in space as not only "unfunny" but "extremely unfunny" in a skit for *Rocketship X-M* (season 2, episode 1). The reason for this came out of an encounter at a show where Joel found Gallagher digging through his props. Not thrilled with the uninvited intrusion into his stuff but excited to meet a fellow prop comic, Joel happily introduced himself by saying he did "prop-comedy too!" As Joel remembered to Mr. Beaks on *Ain't It Cool News*, "And he said, 'You call them props? When a surgeon goes in to work on somebody, do you think he calls his instruments props?' And I just kind of went, 'Whatever, man. They're props!' He was kind of a dick, so any chance I had to take a shot at him, I would."

Television appearances picked up in November of that year, with a couple of spots on *Thicke of the Night* (mentioned in chapter 2 for the L.A. Connection's Dub-A-Vision movie appearances) in November before popping up on *Saturday Night Live* on November 12, 1983. At this time in the show's history, the series would feature a segment to showcase up-and-coming comedians, and it was not uncommon to see comedic magicians like Penn & Teller and Harry Anderson in such segments. Hodgson's appearance was popular enough that he returned to perform three more times on the program, up through May 1984, although he was originally asked to return immediately for the next episode in November. To many comics, this would have been an amazing request, but Joel declined for reasons that make sense in retrospect.

One popular laugh in Joel's act played around with the audience's knowledge that comics would only be given x number of minutes onstage before they had to get off. The same held true for comedians when they performed on television, with comedians given three to seven minutes to perform before quickly saying, "Thank you!" and bolting from the stage. Near the beginning of Joel's act, he commonly asked an offstage person how many minutes he had left. When told he had something like "three minutes left," he would then pull a fake time bomb out of the bag or box he had with him for props, set the time for the minutes given, sit the bomb down, and say, "I guess we all have three minutes."

Hodgson decided to do the bit in his first appearance on *Saturday Night Live*, but the show's prop department didn't think Joel's time bomb looked authentic enough and built one for him to use in the show. Once the show was over, he was gifted the prop to use and took it back to the Berkshire Place hotel where guests of the show stayed during the week. Finding that even after taking the prop apart he did not have room for it in his duffel bag, Hodgson left it behind in his hotel room and went to the airport to fly back to California. As one could expect, when a maid came in to clean up the room and found what looked to be sticks of dynamite and a ticking clock, it caused concerns. Three floors of the building were evacuated as a bomb squad was brought in, only to find the bomb was not real. When it was discovered that the room had been vacated by Hodgson, who had just appeared on *Saturday Night Live*, the assumption was that it was some showbiz elitist trying to cause trouble and thinking it funny to scare people by leaving the bomb there. The police demanded Hodgson return for questioning, while the Berkshire Place was threatening to sue him and the show over the incident, and multiple newspapers had picked up the story with headlines like "comedian bombs" and such other amusing puns.

Hodgson was mortified that the incident had gotten so far out of hand. The staff at *Saturday Night Live* however saw it as a gold mine for free publicity and asked Hodgson to come back the following week for a cold-opening sketch that would feature Hodgson accidentally leaving bombs all over the place in the studio where the show was shot. Joel refused. "I told them no 'cause I needed to be home with my family to get a bearing on things," he told Jon Bream of the *Star Tribune* in March 1984. Even with his dismissal of the skit, Joel appeared on the program again in December of that year, made four appearances on *Letterman* in the coming months, and also appeared on *The 8th Annual Young Comedians Show* that aired on HBO in December 1983 (hosted by John Candy and featuring up-and-coming comedians like the Amazing Jonathan, Carol Leifer, Paula Poundstone, and Bill Maher).

At this juncture for most comedians, the objective would be to push to do more television, get a series, make a movie, or have their own show on a network. Maybe all those things at once, if possible. Other comedians that had made the shift to LA around the same time as Hodgson were attempting just that. Louie Anderson saw initial payoffs quickly, with movie roles and pilot scripts sent his way, while others would take a bit longer, like Jeff Cesario, who eventually achieved his goal of writing and producing. Joel was doing well enough that he had gained an agent and was getting jobs at clubs, but the allure of working on a regular series or doing a movie simply wasn't the same for Hodgson as it was for the other comics that made it out west.

"I had this [track] record that I was really proud of," Hodgson told A.V. Club in 1999 when discussing those days in Hollywood. "Of doing these shows and doing exactly what I wanted to do, and the idea of going on a sitcom and having to do jokes whether they were funny or not just didn't sound very good." Things came to a head in the fall of 1983, when Joel was offered a part in a pilot for a possible series called *High School U.S.A.* The one-hour pilot made for NBC was a continuation from a television movie that had aired on October 16, 1983, which did mildly well in the ratings thanks to a gimmick where the cast was made up by younger (Michael J. Fox, Todd Bridges, Nancy McKeon) and older (Angela Cartwright, Tony Dow, Dwayne Hickman) television faces who were currently playing or had in the past played teenagers in other series. When the pilot came around, Joel was given the script and offered a part in the show. "It was . . . a rip-off of *Fast Times at Ridgemont High*," Joel told the *Star Tribune* in October 1984. "It was [then NBC Entertainment president] Brandon Tartikoff's baby, but it was terrible. So I turned it down."

Expecting his dismissal of the offer would be enough, Joel was surprised when the network came back with a counteroffer that was three times the amount of money offered the first time. Or maybe not that surprised. "Here's this kid, a nobody, turning them down. And they had to go back to their boss and say, 'This kid doesn't want to do your show because he doesn't think it's funny.'" Thinking further on it, Joel saw exactly what the problem was: "To them, it didn't mean much that the show was bad. They figure exposure on any show is good. But if I'm going to trade my face and my image to help someone else accomplish something, I want to believe in what I'm doing. And I couldn't believe in that show." The hour-long pilot eventually aired in May 1984 and disappeared due to low ratings, never going to series.

Two other problems were rearing their heads for Hodgson the longer he stayed in Hollywood, mainly that he wasn't advancing with his comedy either on a professional or personal level. "I've always been convinced that I was in comedy for a different reason than other people," Hodgson continued with Jeff Strickler in 1984. "I never felt that I needed the stage as much as they do. While they were up there striking in the dark, I was a speech-communication major in college. For my senior project, I broke down my act according to Nancy Harper's Paradigm of Communication." Isolated from how others saw comedy and their careers, Hodgson was also concerned that he wasn't coming up with new material for his act. And although he was working on material for a possible Showtime special in March 1984, he knew things were getting creatively dim out in LA. "The only thing left," Joel told *Ain't It Cool News* several years later, "would be to do a [solo] special. I suppose if I would've hung around, I could've done that, but I had burnt all my stuff on *Letterman* and *SNL*. . . . I was genuinely out of ideas. I had gotten to do as much as I could do with my stand-up, and I couldn't think of anything else."

The thought of possibly leaving his emerging career behind took time to fully form, although in March 1984 he was planning to spend at least another year out in LA. He filmed an episode of the Nickelodeon series *Out of Control* in the summer of 1984, playing a bad magician who works with the cast to do various tricks, while continuing his commitments to the *Letterman* show in April and June of that year. Yet as the summer wore on, Hodgson knew he was never going to be completely accepted until he conformed to be what Hollywood wanted. He also began feeling that people were praising him for his act but not for himself. "And if enough people come up and tell me I'm good, I start to believe it. Or at least I have to make them believe it so they will relax. You have to accept the lie—and I don't feel I could do that." Friends he trusted thought that perhaps his issue was that of burnout and suggested that new material would help snap him out of his funk about LA. For his final appearance on *Letterman* in September 1984, he decided to prove to himself that he could come up with fresh material and did an act full of new inventions, such as a mice-powered wheelchair, an accordion-driven vacuum cleaner, and a time machine that was a box large enough to change into a costume representing the time period he "visited" (Forrester and Frank are shown using a similar idea for the invention exchange in the Mike Nelson–era episode of *MST3K* for *Outlaw*, season 5, episode 19, although Hodgson is not listed as a writer on the episode). To some, it proved Hodgson was wrong to want to stop, but Joel saw it another way: "It proved that I could break away from my club material. It proved that I could keep going. I wanted to feel that it was my decision [to quit], not theirs." Although in July 1984 he was telling the *Star Tribune* that he planned to continue to work on his act once he returned, by October he was announcing his retirement. When Jeff

Strickler asked him what his plans were after his last shows at the Comedy Gallery that October and into early November, Hodgson mentioned possibly writing a book about magic or creating a few new magic tricks, but his main goal seemed to get a regular job. "I've never been a good worker—a regular normal worker. I would like to be a good worker." His props were auctioned off to the fans after his final show that November to show definitive closure to that part of his life.

Yet Hodgson did not stay dormant for long after returning to Minneapolis in late 1984. By early 1985, he was creating one-of-a-kind "robot" figures to sell at a store called Props. He also spent time working in a T-shirt factory, created Halloween masks, and even fixed Gobot costumes for a Tonka trade show. He never strayed far from the clubs either, especially the Comedy Gallery, although at first as an audience member rather than as a performer, which gave him a better perspective on the club process. "Comics make the audience out to be some kind of club that hang out together and judge comedians," Joel told Colin Covert in 1987. As a member of the audience, he felt he came to understand that the audience was more of a natural current that the comic must ride, like a surfer: "The audience is the wave." He was even enticed back to Hollywood briefly in order to read for the role of Woody on the popular sitcom *Cheers* in 1985, showing that his time away was hardly the "wilderness years" as they are sometimes portrayed by fans.

At the Comedy Gallery in November 1985, Hodgson met Jerry Seinfeld, who was performing at the club, and the two hit it off so well that when Showtime signed Seinfeld to an hour-long special in 1986, he turned to Hodgson to write the special with him. Coming up with gags and utilizing various new props Hodgson had created since returning to Minneapolis, the pair came up with *Jerry Seinfeld: Stand-Up Confidential*, which aired in September 1987 and featured Hodgson in a cameo. The special, set up as a demonstration to viewers to get a better understanding of what it was like to be a comedian, including special glasses to "wear" during portions of the show, had the obvious Hodgson touch. It also helped Seinfeld in selling his long-running sitcom to NBC when network executives saw the segments of the special where Seinfeld proved that he could act.

By spring 1987, Hodgson was getting the bug again to perform after spending the past two years watching, advising, and making props for others. He even had begun teaching a class about being a stand-up comedian that was called "Creative Stand-Up and Smartology," which is where he would meet a teenager name Josh Weinstein who was looking to do stand-up and would quickly come back into play for Hodgson's projects. "After a while, it dawned on me, I'm writing stuff for other people, I'm building stuff for other people, I'm teaching people creativity and helping them assess their acts; I'm doing everything but going up there and doing it myself." His lifelong pursuit of demonstrating and then standing back to see the results was now forcing him to not share in the immediate reaction his work was producing. He decided to jump back in at the end of May 1987 by performing a handful of shows he called "Heavy Levity" at the Ha Ha Club (which was the Comedy Cabaret before switching ownership in 1985) in Minneapolis, featuring all new props (several that would eventually turn up on *MST3K*, such as the motorcyclist air-bag helmet), a band called "Los Joelos" to support him, and members of his class given the opportunity to perform as the opening act.

Hodgson hoped that the show would be successful enough to lead to being able to pull off doing similar shows once or twice a year, and he followed up Heavy Levity with "Spook Fest 87" in October, although first-night production errors (from gags that refused to work, to a sheet covering a guillotine refusing to come off when the time came for it to be unveiled) led to the club refunding the audience's money and Joel announcing from the stage that it was a "run-through" and later claiming it to be one of the worst experiences of his life. Nevertheless, Hodgson continued with looking

Before the series *Seinfeld* shot him to superstardom, Jerry Seinfeld worked on a Showtime special with Joel Hodgson, *Jerry Seinfeld: Stand-Up Confidential* (1987). Hodgson would become acquainted with Stu Smiley in the process, leading to bigger things down the road. PHOTOFEST

to do larger semiannual shows, such as an "All My Best" series of shows at the Comedy Gallery in April 1988, but the pull of doing more frequent one-off performances continued, such as opening for Seinfeld in March 1988, and by the fall of that year, he was appearing regularly as the "Gizmocrat" at the club.

Hollywood began calling again as well. "Weird" Al Yankovic had written a script for his first movie, later to be released in 1989 as *UHF*, that featured a bizarre character named Philo, a worker at a television station, who seemed somewhat detached from everything going on around him as he worked in his lab inventing various gizmos. As one can guess, Yankovic had Hodgson in mind for the role. Meanwhile, fellow Minneapolis comic Louie Anderson had gotten a deal with NBC in late 1988 to create his own sitcom and was hoping to entice Joel to appear in the pilot as his wacky "building superintendent." Joel readily passed on *UHF.* He did commit to help Anderson with the pilot of his NBC show, which he fulfilled in March 1989, but in December 1988, he had told the *Star Tribune* that "it could only be one show" and probably nothing that would keep him out in LA, which was fine by him.

After all, there was no need to be a second banana when he was preoccupied with his own local project. In 1984, Hodgson had left the stage saying that he wanted to go back to Minneapolis to relax, recharge, and create "video comedy." By 1988, he was about to do exactly that, and no outside projects could sway him. In doing so, he was about to create a cult television series and reshape the way redubbed movie comedy was done. All he needed was a group of people as passionate as he was, a lot of spare parts to make robots, a bunch of bad movies, and a television station no one watched.

4
I'll See You on the Other Side
The KTMA Year

In the not too distant future, TV23 will present a startling new show so bold,
so innovative, it will launch television comedy into the next millennium.

—NARRATIVE FROM SALES TAPE MADE FOR POTENTIAL ADVERTISERS

BEFORE THE SERIES PREMIERE ON KTMA IN NOVEMBER 1988

It's not like Jim Mallon was chopped liver, of course. Nor that chopped liver is so bland or forgettable that you should be using it as slang for something that is, uh, bland and forgettable. When's the last time you had chopped liver, after all? I don't see it on the drive-through menu at McDonald's. You want chopped liver, you've got to search for it and order it, probably in person and after waiting in line behind other people ordering a Reuben or some decent brisket. That makes it a bit more important, doesn't it? Maybe it's a side dish? Okay, but without the side dish, do you have a meal? No, you've got to have a side dish to make a decent dinner plate.

So, in the greater scope of things, maybe Jim Mallon is chopped liver. But he came by it honestly.

In all seriousness, Jim Mallon did have comedic chops of his own beyond his technical knowledge as he was moving his way through his career in television production during the 1980s, making his association with Joel Hodgson in 1988 and thereafter understandable. Born March 19, 1956, in Rochester, Minnesota, Mallon was like most kids who wanted to be involved in making films and was lucky enough to be at the right age to get in on the ground floor on both video and cable access. "I started making comedy movies in the fifth grade. I was inspired by *Laugh-In* and my friend had a regular 8mm camera," Mallon told the Official *MST3K* Info Club website in 2009. Having a father who was an engineer for IBM, Mallon had an aptitude for electronics and noted, "When I was in the seventh grade, Sony came out with the first inexpensive black-and-white reel-to-reel video gear. Our junior high bought one, and I was hooked." Comfortable with the equipment, he would go on to create, while in school, his own parody of *Mutual of Omaha's Wild Kingdom* that was featured on what would have been early public access television.

Even so, his parents were hesitant to have Jim go into media, and it took him until his junior year at the University of Wisconsin–Madison before he decided to pursue his communication major. It was the same school year where he also achieved some of his earliest publicity when he joined up with Leon Varjian (1951–2015), a known prankster who had previously run for mayor of Bloomington, Indiana, with the promise to turn downtown into a giant Monopoly board. Varjian had graduated from Indiana University (IU) with a master's in mathematics, but his heart was in off-kilter and often improvised street-level comedy. Mallon would first meet Varjian when the group he started, the Pail & Shovel Party, was trying to petition the student body to have the college's name changed to the University of New Jersey, since New Jersey didn't have a university with its name, while Wisconsin had several. Soon afterward, Mallon joined Varjian and others to perform "street theater"—staging spontaneous improvised skits—on campus whenever possible. Eventually, the pair would run for student government, and surprisingly they won, leading to Jim Mallon becoming president with Varjian as vice president of the Wisconsin Student Association. With the funds that came as part of running the student government, the Pail & Shovel Party began staging elaborate pranks to help raise awareness and funds for the student government. This included hosting the "World's Largest Toga Party," where over ten thousand drunk students in sheets turned up; planting 1,008 pink flamingos on Bascom Hill in 1979, which is now an annual fundraising event; and scheming to bring the Statue of Liberty to the university. The Statue of Liberty idea would have an elaborate payoff, with people arriving one morning to see the tip of the statue's head and part of the arm holding a torch "sticking" out of frozen Lake Mendota, with the story that the statue had sunk in transport (in actuality, it was a constructed model of just the head and arm placed on the ice to give off the illusion). The statue was so well done that it earned national news in the papers and on television for the pair and the Pail & Shovel party, with Mallon being especially proud that it made NBC News' David Brinkley, a man known for telling the news stone-faced, smile.

Mallon would continue his connection to Varjian with a public access cable show called *The Vern & Evelyn Show* that ran from 1980 through 1984. The program, a comedy-variety series that starred two real mice (Vern and Evelyn, who typically were seen grooming themselves as the opening credits ran), was done in a guerrilla-camera style that was only accentuated by the black-and-white cable access video footage and editing used. Those videos eventually led to Mallon moving to work at the CBS affiliate WISC, where he began producing and directing other programs for the station. He then moved over to WHA, a PBS station in Madison, Wisconsin, where he headed the film/video department. It was at WHA that Mallon would meet up with Kevin Murphy, who was working in production at the station.

Kevin Murphy, born November 3, 1956, in River Forest, Illinois, had gone to the University of Utah and earned a BA in journalism before moving on to the University of Wisconsin–Madison to study stage, television, and film in order to get a master's degree and feel like he was actively involved in film and television production. "It's wonderful and they had a public TV station right there on campus," Murphy remembered to Ken Plume in 2007. "And so, it seemed like the perfect place, and as it turns out it was a great place to finish my undergraduate education and get a master's degree in the process." After graduating, Murphy briefly moved to California in an attempt to get into professional television production on the ground floor but found he had no inclination to "work as a grunt on *Simon & Simon*." So he returned to Madison to begin working at WHA as part of the remote truck crew. It was there that he met up with Jim Mallon and, having gone to the same university and pursuing similar careers, they found that they had mutual friends and began hanging out together.

It was while Mallon and Murphy were working together at WHA that Mallon got involved with an old friend by the name of David Herbert to film a low-budget slasher movie based on a home movie they had made when they were nineteen called *Revenge of the Hill People*. The new project was to be called *Muskie Madness*, and Mallon invited Kevin Murphy to join the crew as a key grip along with other people Mallon knew from WHA and WISC. The movie was shot in Hayward, Wisconsin, during July and August of 1985, with a professional crew and a low budget, meaning everyone—cast and crew alike—dug in to make sure sets were up and equipment was running. "We didn't have any money," Kevin told Plume, "because it was an incredibly low budget thing, but we camped out at a local old-fashioned hotel and would shoot day and night and just . . . I learned so much about the filmmaking process in one shoot, because we had to do everything with nothing."

The horror movie with some comedic elements is about a group of young people visiting a small town having a fishing festival called "Muskie Madness" and stumbling upon a serial killer who uses his victims to create bait. The movie was offered to thirty-five distributers before being picked up by Troma (the same studio that released *Ferocious Female Freedom Fighters*, discussed in chapter 2), and renamed *Blood Hook*, as no one outside of Hayward seemed to know that a muskie was a fish. The film then faced further delays after the Motion Picture Association gave the film an X rating due to the violence and gore. Finally, after pruning the film down, the movie premiered on May 15, 1987, in Minneapolis and was eventually released for a brief time to theaters in 1987 before making a bigger splash on the video rental market of the 1990s. The movie would be rereleased on Blu-ray in 2018 in its original uncut form.

After shooting the movie, Mallon worked on the editing process for *Blood Hook* in an office he had rented at the Colonial Warehouse in downtown Minneapolis. Adjacent to Mallon's office was a space that Joel Hodgson had rented to work on his various projects, including tricks, art pieces, and puppets made of found material. The two met there and took mutual interest in each other's projects and ideas, but it was all casual in nature with no immediate thoughts of working together.

While in Minneapolis working on completion of the editing, Mallon discovered that a station in town called KTMA was looking for a "film director." At first, he thought this meant that they wanted someone to direct films for the stations, but the job was to be a director of the station's film library. As it happened, Mallon's resume impressed anyway, and instead of the film director job, he was offered a job as production manager. "I grabbed the job," Mallon told the Official *MST3K* Info Club Web Site, "because aside from paying the bills, it provided access to production gear." The opportunity was too big to pass up, and he contacted Murphy to join him with an ulterior, albeit not sinister, motive in mind. As Murphy told Plume, "He brought me out there pretty much telling [me] that the reason to have this job—we have to shoot the commercials and we have to do the local hosted matinee movies and we have to do the public relations programming—but we have access to tools and we can do anything we want with them. That was the appeal to me. We could make a TV show and we could actually get it on the air." And at KTMA, it wasn't like anyone was really paying too close attention anyway.

KTMA had a long history in the area as not so much the "little station that could" but rather the "little station that can't." An application was filed for the station back in 1966, but various construction issues and failed conceptual ideas led to a sixteen-year delay before the station finally began broadcasting in September 1982. KTMA was initially to be set up as being independent, in that it was not connected to one of the three major networks at the time (NBC, ABC, and CBS). Eventually, the station was conceptualized to be an early pay channel, delivering sports and movies in a manner that turned out to be a short-lived alternative to satellite television (much too expensive for people in 1982) or to the standard concept of cable television with phone-line services that were still in the early stages of becoming the norm throughout the country. Instead, at the time, there were services like ON-TV and SelecTV, where a low-wattage UHF station could have regular "independent television programming," such as old sitcoms, movies, and shows like the *PTL Club* until sometime in the afternoon. After that time, the station would send out a scrambled signal that only a box rented out by the company and connected to the television set could then descramble, allowing one to watch sports or movies airing on the service, similar to channels like HBO, but without the cable. Spectrum TV (not the same television service that was started in 1993) was just starting in the Minneapolis area and had worked out a deal with the Minnesota Twins baseball team and Minnesota North Stars hockey team to air their games on the scrambled channel that would become KTMA TV-23. The charge for the service was $19.95 a month for only sports, or $29.90 for sports and movies.

The main issue was that there was never enough interest to make the system a success, and antitrust claims by fellow station WCCO-TV over how the sports games were set up for subscribers only were causing headaches. By August 1985, the Twins and North Stars had decided to not renew with Spectrum, which was a problem as many of the subscribers they did have were there for the sports. Without that, the movie package was not enough to keep the company going, especially considering how many consumers were adopting cable television, and the subscription-television experiment was abandoned after September 1985, leaving KTMA as a station with not just a big hole in its programming but a vast desert with nothing to air. As the owners put the station up for sale, KTMA switched to a music video format, with the "K-Twin Sound" in October 1985 that featured eighteen hours of "Jazz & Pop Television" each day. As one can guess, "Jazz & Pop Television" was hardly grabbing the kids and shaking up the place, leaving the station a ghost town.

Bought by a group called KTMA-TV Acquisition Corporation, the new owner and general manager was Donald H. O'Connor, who purchased the station for $13.8 million and began updating the station at a cost of another $2.5 million, as well as hiring staff between July and October of 1986. O'Connor told the *Star Tribune* in October 1986 that he had hopes of seeing "a 4 or 5 percent share of the market in the first year, maybe 6 to 8 percent in the second year, then settle in somewhere around 10 to 12 percent when we mature." The programming was nothing out of the ordinary for the most part—shows that had been in perpetual rerun for many years such as *Love, American Style*, *The Flying Nun*, and *Gomer Pyle, U.S.M.C.*, along with old movies and four hours of wrestling on Saturday mornings—hardly the stuff that was going to shake up the ratings. The one upside was getting Elvira's *Movie Macabre*, which caused issues when TV-23 placed large ads on buses showing Elvira's cleavage with the slogan, "Features that will scare you to death," raising complaints in some areas of the city. Yet even there, *Movie Macabre* was in its last season by the time KTMA had picked it up, so there was a general feeling of entering into the business without a strong rudder to guide the ship. The staff hired on seemed to be on alert that things could only get worse, as Mallon recalled to the Official *MST3K* Info Club Web Site: "It was just crazy. For example, the chief engineer had been given the vending machine concession, so he made sure those machines ran perfectly while we did not even have frame-accurate editing in our edit suite. Also, the sales staff worked so much out of a certain saloon that the bar put up a plaque commemorating that 'satellite' office."

And this is what Mallon and Murphy had entered into when signing up with KTMA in 1986. Their days were spent, as Murphy put it, "half in the field, half in the studio or control room putting together ads," then doing promos, and filming local programming, like the wrestling show. The "half in the field" part was traveling around the city to various car dealerships, pawn shops, travel agencies—mainly anyone who thought advertising on the station would be worth the trouble. "The salesmen, the ad force, decided that a cool thing to do was if you bought a certain amount of ad space, you'd get a free commercial," Murphy told Plume. If out in the fields was rough, being in the studio wasn't much rosier, according to Murphy, thanks to having to do promos. "They called them donuts, because it'd be the same on the beginning and the end and then you put in something about the episode in between, and that was the hole that you'd fill. That stuff was a grind. The commercials were a grind. Doing the Ax-Man Surplus Store or the Blaine Flea Market, or the endless used cars and discount furniture places."

One bright spot for the pair was that O'Connor was very open to the idea of local programming, especially if done cheaply. Mallon and Murphy began putting pieces together on their own time that could be aired by the station, including a parody of *60 Minutes* called *15 Minutes*. The show starred Murphy as Bob Bagadonuts, based on a local newscaster, a slightly too-serious news reporter who did reports on various goings-on in the area. Their most famous story dealt with sound barriers that had been built between the Twin Cities of Saint Paul and Minneapolis to damper highway noise. The *15 Minutes* crew took it a step further, filming the barriers as if they were like a Berlin Wall to separate the two cities, leading to some people sneaking over the wall. Mallon, Murphy, and individuals such as Vince Rodriguez and Todd Ziegler, who later helped on the KTMA episodes of *MST3K*, were also involved in one-off programming in 1986, 1987, and 1988 (along with Hodgson and Weinstein in the 1988 broadcast) that staged an annual event on New Year's Eve called the Melon Drop. These were surreal annual events broadcast live on KTMA and hosted by Kevin Murphy as Bob Bagadonuts that gave questionable historical basis for a watermelon being dropped and smashed on the ground at the stroke of midnight, while other events dealing with watermelons, including a marathon with runners carrying melons, would occur. Although only produced for those three years with Mallon and Murphy's direct involvement (there was a "best of" program in 1989, but without the participation of Mallon and Murphy), the annual shows were so well remembered that the station, now WUCW, revived the event in 2015 and 2016.

The 1987 Melon Drop event had a large ad in the December 27, 1987, issue of the *Star Tribune*, calling it the *23rd Annual New Year's Eve Extravaganza*, although every year's special was called the "23rd Annual" event. Along with photos of the cast and mention of what would be occurring, the ad had a logo that read, "Team23—It's the best we can do," further showing the extent to which Mallon, Murphy, and others could get away with things that commonly would not have been accepted at other stations. "It was probably the first time the station got any press outside of just the local business columns, the business pages," Murphy said to Plume while discussing Don O'Connor's feelings about their work. "It was in the entertainment pages and the guy loved the show, so he wrote something really nice about it. That's currency for a TV station, I think."

Even with this work, however, Mallon and Murphy realized that there was no way they could continue to come up with the amount of material needed to help fill up the holes in the station's schedule—especially when in August 1988 the station couldn't pay the syndicators, and certain episodes of their standard "old sitcom and movie" schedule couldn't be aired until new investors could be lined up. To help, the pair began turning to local entertainment, various comedians working at the clubs in the area, for possible projects to air. This led back to Mallon reaching out to Joel Hodgson, who had been on national television and had been doing more and more local club events after what some saw as a sabbatical.

The issue was that there wasn't much creative thought emerging from the comedians, who typically wanted to do either their act for a solo half-hour special or be part of a variety show where they performed their act, which didn't satisfy the long-term needs of the station. Mallon himself was to the point where he thought one of the best ideas would be to have a weekly program where comics come on and compete against each other, such as was done years later with the reality series, *Last Comic Standing*. Going to lunch with Joel, Mallon presented the idea to him, who was very unenthused about doing another run of stand-up on a regular basis, especially on a program that he saw as a variation of *The Gong Show*. Instead, he offered to think about it and get back together with Jim on any ideas he had.

Joel Hodgson has mentioned over the years several ways that *MST3K* came together in his head, and each added its own aspect to how the show was formed. For instance, anthology television series like *Death Valley Days*, *Thriller*, and others that were still running in syndication featured hosts who not only introduced the stories but then would on occasions turn up in the shows as characters in the stories. Even Rod Serling would do so on *The Twilight Zone*, albeit as a brief punchline to a gag in one story. To impressionable minds like those of children, the idea would naturally turn to every host having this ability. Thus it was no wonder that a young Joel had watched a movie host begin a film and then be disappointed when that host did not turn up in the movie itself but only reappeared during the ad breaks to help sell stuff. Further, Joel had grown up on programs like *Beany and Cecil*, where the show would feature puppets talking directly to the kids in between cartoon segments featuring those same characters (Cecil looked like a dragon as a sock puppet because that's basically what the puppet was in the live-action portions of the show). Joel also admitted to a fascination with a series called *CBS Children's Film Festival* (1967–1984), which aired films from several other countries aimed at a child audience and had Fran Allison and puppets Kukla and Ollie (with the trio known better as Kukla, Fran and Ollie) hosting for

A picture of Kukla, Fran and Ollie from 1952. It shows the essential setup for the *CBS Children's Film Festival*, best remembered from the early 1970s, and the look Joel wanted to incorporate into *MST3K*, featuring a human host and two puppets. NBC / PHOTOFEST © NBC

the first ten years of the program. The program started with Fran standing in front of a balcony where Kukla and Ollie appeared, and the three would introduce each movie, appear briefly at the commercial breaks, and then wrap things up in the final segment of the show. The concept of a human host with puppets assisting—one that was not completely alien to some of the horror movie hosts over the years as well—stuck in Joel's mind.

Another element that Hodgson had often thought about, and one he usually refers to when discussing the initial concept of the show to come, was taken from the inner sleeve of the Elton John album, *Goodbye Yellow Brick Road* (1973). Printed on the sleeves were the lyrics for the album, along with photos and drawings to represent each song. For the song, "I've Seen That Movie Too," is artwork showing a silhouette of a couple in a row of theater seats watching what appeared to be Rhett and Scarlett in *Gone With the Wind*. "It was an idea I'd had tucked away in the back of my mind since high school," Joel told *Wired* in 2014. "I remember going, 'Someone should do a show like that. Run a movie and have these people in silhouettes say stuff.'" In a way, it was going back to fulfilling his younger self's wish of seeing the movie hosts actively take part in the movies they introduced, even if it meant only sitting and watching it with the audience.

When pulling his ideas together to form the core of the program, Joel's initial concept for such a show was admittedly bleak. Remembering the Charlton Heston movie *The Omega Man* (1971), Joel pictured his movie show for KTMA as having the same setup. In the movie, Heston plays a character who may be the last man on Earth, with zombielike creatures stalking him at night, trying to kill him. To pass the time of day when there is nothing to do, Heston's character goes down to a deserted movie theater and watches the rock documentary *Woodstock*, where he, having seen it so many times, is shown reciting dialogue along with the screen as it plays. Joel fleshed out the idea initially as the human character living within a television station after the end of the world and desperate to locate other humans still alive by broadcasting movies. "It's not a great premise for a comedy," Joel admitted to Benjamin Nason in 2013. "It's during the apocalypse, like a zombie uprising." (One can see a remnant of this idea in the *MST3K* pilot, with Joel attempting to reach anyone via transmitter until he realizes that he is being watched and so directs his attention to the camera in relief.)

Then Joel remembered something he said to Jerry Seinfeld after doing *Stand-Up Confidential.* "In fact, my first idea of a show after I did Jerry's show was a show for Jerry which was about him in outer space," Joel told Euan Kerr for MPR News in 2012. "As stupid as that sounds. And I pitched that to him, and he goes, 'Yeah—no!'" Yet now space is the place, as Joel realized. "I thought of this movie *Silent Running*, which is about a guy in space with robot companions. So, I just transposed that idea and that's what I pitched Jim Mallon. This idea about a guy in space forced to watch bad movies." Joel met with Jim and showed him a yellow pad with a handful of drawings; the first showed a guy in a type of lab suit sitting behind a counter, with a crazy-looking wall behind him, two dinosaur-like robots to his left, and one flying over his head. The image shows the stage set devised in such a manner that when the door behind the human character opened, so, too, would the counter, splitting the entire stage in half, as the subsequent vault doors behind the first were full-sized, tailored in different styles (sketches for these show one door with a zipper down the middle, another like a window blind, and a third like a tumbler lock), and opened as the camera would go down what was meant to look like a tunnel with locked doors opening, ending at the theater set. The sketch for the theater showed the silhouettes at the bottom of the screen with the human figure in the middle, two robots to the right of him, and one to the left. There is also a series of names listed for several possible robots that could appear, matching up with Joel's comment in the pilot to Crow that there were twenty-plus robots on the space station,

"Are you really from the Internal Revenue Service?" Heston riffs his own movie *Omega Man* (1971), which featured a scene of Heston alone in a theater watching a movie—an image that stuck with Joel Hodgson when putting together *MST3K*. WARNER BROS. PICTURES / PHOTOFEST © WARNER BROS. PICTURES

as Joel initially pictures various other robot creations turning up to partake in the program over time. (This concept was dropped soon after the show was being put together, since establishing Crow, Gypsy, and Servo for viewers to identify over the course of many episodes made sense and there was too much work to do to keep building more robots for the show. When the show came back in the 2010s, however, the idea of more robots would get another chance, as will be seen.)

Mallon looked over the sketches and heard Joel out on his concept of the human movie host sitting in a theater watching bad movies alongside his robot friends. Mallon's response was that it was worth a shot, and they would go ahead with a pilot to get a feel for what the show would look like. With that, Joel began work on the puppets and the set, while Kevin Murphy was brought in to create the illusion of seats by outlining the row in foam and propping it up against a chair for Joel to sit in. Murphy also created the doorway sequence, which for the pilot was simply a series of real doors opening as the camera pulls into them to give the effect that the camera is entering each one until it gets to the theater. Joel then needed to recruit two individuals to play the three puppets he created for the pilot.

His attention turned to two men whom he had been frequently seeing as part of a comedy writer's group in Minneapolis called Writer's Block, named as such because "we never got any work done," as Trace Beaulieu recalled in 2007. The group met on Tuesday nights, first at a restaurant-bar called the Green Mill and then in the basement of a nearby library when it was realized that the only thing getting done at the bar was drinking. As the group had no certain membership, it was common to see people come and go from the group, with Joel becoming a regular in 1987.

One member, Josh Weinstein, Joel already knew from the Creative Stand-Up and Smartology class he taught. Born May 21, 1971, Josh Weinstein was only fifteen when he started doing stand-up at the Ha Ha Club. "Standup is really what made my high school years endurable," Weinstein told the Star Tribune in 1999. "Having a passion got me through the prison-like daily life of high school." With a physical appearance that defied age, Weinstein toured the Midwest during school breaks and was seldom carded. By the time most people caught on he was underage, he had been around long enough that people just ignored it and went on with their business.

The other member of Writer's Block that Joel remembered was Trace Beaulieu, whom Joel had seen perform as part of musician and improviser Eugene Huddleston's improv group and who had worked with Weinstein on the road as a stand-up, although it wasn't Beaulieu's preferred career. Trace was born November 6, 1958, and had already seen and done much by the time he would meet up with Joel in the 1980s. Working at a display company off and on since high school, Trace had just finished a year at the University of Minnesota when a friend returned from traveling with an ice show through the Far East and Australia. Deciding to take a shot at trying something new, Trace turned up just as the show needed someone to work as part of the staging crew, "building props and moving the show from town to town," Trace told Plume in a 2007 interview. It seemed a good fit to Trace: his family had always been creative, and his brother Bryan is a mechanical engineer who has twenty patents in structural systems, including having built a hydrogen-powered house in Arizona, so building things seemed right up his alley. "So I showed up one day thinking, 'Hey, if I get a job, that'd be great—and if I don't, that's okay too.' And I hung around for a while and they said, 'Okay, we just fired a guy, so you're in.'"

The tour went well, with the exception of an incident where Trace psychologically scarred a monkey after putting too much gasoline on a flaming hoop that the monkey was supposed to jump through (the monkey backpedaled off the stage in fright when the hoop went up like an inferno). When the ice show moved on to South America, Trace decided to stay on in Europe, seeking work in other shows, but as 1980 approached and with places in Europe becoming increasingly antisocial to Americans, he returned home and back to working at the display company. He also began hanging around the comedy clubs, where he became part of an improv group, and doing performance pieces at the Comedy Cabaret, such as one that started with him playing a saw in a musical number only to end up using the saw to cut what appears to be his own leg off in a frenzy. Over time, he found himself slowly working his way into doing stand-up, although with reluctance. "It was really bad," Trace told Plume. "I never really wanted to do stand-up, it was never my goal, but it sort of happened. I was hanging out with all those guys in Minneapolis doing improv, and I liked that much more."

As Hodgson himself had stated, he usually pivoted to people who were serious about the craft they were doing and had initiative to do something more than tell jokes and get laughs. "They were both really talented," Joel told Ain't It Cool News. "They had lots of ideas themselves, and they're both really funny. . . . I had a vague idea of us making comments and talking about the movie during the breaks and stuff like that, but those guys really deserve credit for helping me figure out the toolbox of movie riffing." Contacting the two of them, he asked them to turn up at the KTMA studio to help him with a pilot he was working on. It was upon arrival that Weinstein and Beaulieu found out that their roles would involve actively pulling the strings of the puppets as they voiced their dialogue, as Joel told them to go over and "pick up a puppet." Trace told the Official *MST3K* Info Club Web Site, "On the matinee movie host's set there were a couple of bright colored piles of plastic. Josh went to one pile, and I went to the other. I guess I liked the look of Crow. I'm attracted to shiny things." One advantage for Trace in the process as well was that he had done puppet voices before as part of his display company job setting up material for trade shows. "I had done a stint operating a remote-control robot at trade shows. I'd walk around speaking into a coffee cup and go up to people and be a smart ass." With the people, puppets, and stage in place, the pilot was ready to film on October 3, 1988, with Joel, Josh, and Trace in front of the camera, and Kevin and Jim behind it.

After the pilot was recorded, it was clear that it needed a lot of changes before the series could start. The setting of the show was changed from an abandoned television station to a space station orbiting Earth. That was the

Satellite of Love (SOL), a name taken from a song of the same name from Lou Reed's 1972 album, *Transformer*, while also commonly used during the Jerry Lewis muscular dystrophy telethons to describe the television satellite carrying the broadcast. The change to a space station was done to feed into the idea of Joel and the robots being in a similar situation to *Silent Running* and also to reinforce the concept that the host of the show was truly trapped into watching the movies, while the television station idea meant he could readily leave whenever he wanted. In the pilot, Joel tells the viewers that he created the space station himself, while in the series and thereafter, it was created by Dr. Forrester (Hodgson in early interviews would always state that his character was accidentally shot into space, but it is clear from the first theme song onward and in dialogue that his bosses intentionally sent him there). While we do not see SOL in the pilot, the *Mystery Science Theater 3000* wiki points out that the KTMA sales tape for the program, made after the pilot, shows Thunderbird 3 from the old *Thunderbirds* television series as the station is mentioned, while the KTMA season filmed after the pilot would show us a SOL that looks more like a traditional satellite (hastily put together on a dime-store budget but clearly a satellite). When the series went to the Comedy Channel, SOL was changed to the bone-shaped station that we all came to love as much as the Demon Dogs that attack the ship in *The Robot vs. the Aztec Mummy* episode (season 1, episode 2). Although the pilot suggests that the show takes place sometime in the distant future and Joel questions whether anyone is even still alive besides himself at the beginning, Joel also references "your president" Ronald Reagan, setting the timeline as current. Later episodes would pretty much confirm that the original series with Joel as the host always took place "next Sunday, A.D." This confused some people, as the show was called *Mystery Science Theater 3000*, leading people to think the "3000" was the year, as in *Space: 1999* or *2001*. Joel would tell the Official *MST3K* Info Club Web Site that he intentionally placed this misinformation into the title to throw people off. "If you notice, any of the press from when I was with the show, I would always deny it being the year 3000. I thought of it more as a series number, like the HAL 9000 computer or the Galaxy 500." (However, according to Jim Mallon, in an interview with Looper back in 2017, the "3000" really was to represent the year. He stated that when he asked Joel for a show title, "Without blinking he said, 'Mystery Science Theater 2000.' But since we were so close to the year 2000, we decided to shift it up one thousand years." Hodgson in the same article agreed with Mallon's recall, saying, "The 3000 was a joke on all the people that were attaching the year 2000 to various programs. In the late '80s it was everywhere: 'America 2000' was something George Bush was talking about a lot, so I thought, 'Wouldn't it be cool if I name it 3000 just to confound people?'")

Joel had three robots ready for use for the pilot, which were made from found parts: Gypsy (sometimes referred to as Gypsum, but this may have been simply a nickname), which was made of baby car seats to form the head, a flashlight for the eye, and a PVC hose for the body. In the pilot, Gypsy appears to be designated as male, although in the series it is strongly suggested that Gypsy is female and often referred to as "she" by Joel and the other robots. Gypsy tended to seem a bit dim, grunted a lot, was fixated on *Voyage to the Bottom of the Sea* star Richard Basehart, and sometimes came off more as a pet than another humanized bot in the early years of the shows. During *Wild Rebels* (season 2, episode 7), it was established that this inability to communicate fully was due to Gypsy running most of the higher functions on the SOL and when Joel shuts them down for a brief time, she can think and talk clearly. Her level of intelligence and ability to communicate grew as the series continued. Because of her function, she is actually the smartest of the bots—perhaps the smartest being altogether—on the ship and uses her abilities to protect Joel (and later Mike) and the other robots from the Mads ("bad guys") and each other. Josh Weinstein played the voice of Gypsy in the pilot and through the KTMA season, while Jim Mallon took over for season 1 through half of season 8, followed by Patrick Brantseg (October 10, 1967–, who was a set designer and occasional actor on the show) from that point on until the series ended in 1999. Joel told the Official *MST3K* Info Club Web Site that "Gypsy" was the name his brother gave to a pet turtle, which struck Joel as odd. Since bot Gypsy was designated as slow-moving and talking, the name given to a pet turtle seemed logical. Gypsy is in the theater for part of the pilot and also appeared there in the opening credits of the KTMA season, although this would be a rarity in the original series (she would begin to pop up in the theater once or twice an episode with the Netflix series onward).

Beeper is another bot seen in the pilot and mentioned in the first episode of the series but never seen again after that. His silver body is pretty much that of Tom Servo in embryonic form, only instead of the gumball head of Servo, Beeper had a large, clear, detachable hood to protect the small head inside. Josh Weinstein also did the voice for this character, who spoke in beeps and buzzes that only Crow could interpret, leading to an R2-D2–C-3PO from *Star Wars* relationship (and, considering Crow's gold body, probably wasn't that far off from where the characterizations originated). Even from the pilot, it was clear as to why Beeper didn't last long. "It wasn't all that fun sitting there going 'BEEP BEEP BEEP' and I'm sure I made some wise-ass remarks about it, but I don't remember having to convince Joel of anything. We all just thought a character that didn't talk was a waste," Weinstein told the Official *MST3K* Info Club Web Site years later.

Crow was the final robot seen in the pilot. His name was revealed in the *Hanger 18* episode (episode 19 of the KTMA season) as meaning "Cybernetic Remotely Operated Woman," but that turns out to be just a gag that Joel built into Crow from the start. Joel told the Official *MST3K* Info Club Web Site that the name came from several sources: "I thought it would be cool to have a robot with sort of a Native American feel to it. I had a friend in college who had a friend named Tommy Crow he had all these adventures with. I always thought that was such a cool name. Also, the Jim Carroll Band had a song called 'Crow' on the album *Catholic Boy*." Crow is built out of a variety of pieces, including a plastic bowling pin for his head, a hockey face mask for his "hair," a soap dish and ping-pong balls for the eyes, desk lamp arms for his arms and legs, and an upside-down Tuppercraft floralier for his body, all painted gold. Trace Beaulieu did the voice from the pilot up through 1996, when he left the series, although there were a couple of occasions when Josh Weinstein did the voice (e.g., in the fifth episode of the KTMA season, *Gamera*, where Beaulieu was unavailable, Weinstein does a couple of lines as Crow). After Beaulieu, Bill Corbett took over for the rest of the original series. One element that Beaulieu brought into the show in the first episode that had not been anticipated was that of having Crow physically react to the movie, which instantly clicked with the others as a vital piece of the puzzle to make the experience work. After all, what'd be the point of having the silhouettes if they didn't visually respond to what occurred in front of them?

Although Trace started with a voice for Crow that was like the one he had used in the trade show for the remote-control robot, he told Collider in 2008 that there were good reasons to change Crow's voice early on: "Originally Crow was a very staccato, machine, more classic robot. It got kind of hard to speak that way. It was hard to riff like that because it was locked into one intonation. I think as we did it, I got tired of doing it." Crow's early speech pattern was also dictated by an in-joke where Crow spoke like the robot on *Lost in Space* and referred to other characters by their full names ("Danger, Will Robinson, danger!" [Robinson was the name of the family in the television program]), which led to Crow constantly referring to Joel as "Joel Hodgson." In his early appearances, he was slightly confused but

It's Gamera! Quick, get the camera! Gamera would inflict a lot of pain on Joel and the bots over time, but several of the turtle's movies first appeared in the KTMA era of the show. WORLD ENTER-TAINMENT CORP. / PHOTOFEST © WORLD ENTERTAINMENT CORP.

somewhat knowledgeable and attempted to do puns on many occasions to impress Joel. Although Joel seems at first to appreciate the puns, the series will make it clear that both he and Mike become tired of them pretty quickly—not that it stopped Crow. In the *Gamera* episode, Crow is put into suspended animation (a process he didn't like) and spends this episode and the next as SOL's Christmas tree. Once he is released, his personality becomes more like the sarcastic, sometimes bitter, and typically confused Crow remembered best from the series, with a voice that moves closer to Groucho than is robotic. He even drops the whole "Joel Hodgson" gimmick from his speech pattern.

And, yes, the character Joel played was that of "Joel Hodgson," and he continued to be that character through the rest of the KTMA season. When the series jumped from KTMA to the Comedy Channel, Hodgson decided to change the character's name from his own to Robinson for two reasons:

Robinson was easier to pronounce than his own name, and he liked the idea of referencing back to the old *Lost in Space* series. No doubt he also wanted to put a bit of distance between the character on the screen and himself, who was much different from how the real Joel was. For the pilot, Joel had been putting in hours on his own to get the set, costume, and robots ready while still fulfilling his stand-up appearances, so he arrived on set with almost no sleep. Because of this, in the pilot he stumbled upon the portrayal of the Joel seen in the series that is a bit sleepy in his speaking pattern, which helped set him up as the straight man role the character needed to be for the puppets that surrounded him. He kept that characteristic for the role into the series, although he began to insist on being allowed to have fun as well, as the show moved into seasons 2 and 3 of the Comedy Channel/Comedy Central series, such as when Joel snaps at the bots for ruining his Colossal Man sketch in the middle of *The Amazing Colossal Man* (season 3, episode 9).

The pilot film is not a full episode featuring an entire movie, nor did it need to be to get the concept across. There wasn't even much emphasis on the theater in the pilot, and even riffing the movie is not the emphasis. As Mallon and Hodgson both mention in later interviews, the idea was that Joel and the robots would spend their time in the theater talking general trivia and their reactions to the movie rather than just making fun of it. This can be seen in the pilot, when the first thing Joel mentions as the MGM movie *The Green Slime* (1968) begins to play is that the movie was made the same year as *2001: A Space Odyssey*. The comment makes the rather charming special effects look instantly (and perhaps unfairly) antiquated but is hardly a "riff." The main thrust of the pilot, however, is to get across the host segments, with Joel talking to the robots and propelling a story line that involves the robots and Joel all catching a virus from a flower that grows on the ship, which would be done again in the first episode of the KTMA season.

It's a rather clumsy affair—the type you'd expect from a group of young guys on short notice with no money—and clearly scripted at the last minute, leading to lulls in the dialogue and moments where Joel can be seen holding back laughs due to the improv nature of the work. Even so, the groundwork showed that the program would work. Some changes would be made before going to series that were perhaps cosmetic but still improvements. The first was fixing the doorway sequence, as while Murphy's montage of various real doors was amusing enough for the pilot, it didn't accurately set up the "space station" look, even for a series that was supposed to look like it was made with spare change. The cast worked on the doorway to give the illusion of multiple doorways down a tunnel to get from the area in the SOL where Joel and the robots did their host segments and the theater. At first, the KTMA season implies that Joel can't go through the tunnel himself and thus pulls away as Cambot brings the camera into the tunnel, telling viewers that he will see

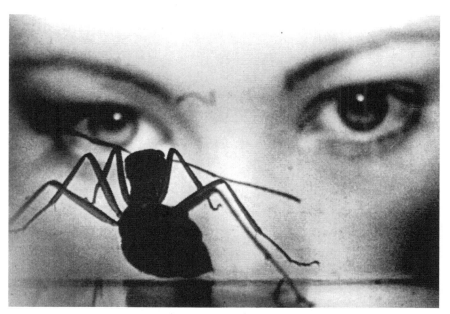

An odd choice for the show, KTMA or not, the Saul Bass's artful *Phase IV* (1973). PARAMOUNT PICTURES / PHOTOFEST © PARAMOUNT PICTURES

them "on the other side." Later episodes show Joel and the robots entering the tunnel, however, starting with episode 9 for *Phase IV* (1974), so there's not much of a story premise behind Joel not taking the tunnel; it just looks better for the show.

Another update was to create a couple of new robots for the series. One, Cambot (mentioned above), was a simple redress of Gypsy with some facial do-das. In the KTMA season, it appears that Cambot uses a camera and is not the camera itself, as seen in later seasons. There is no stated gender for Cambot, but since Cambot is a variation of Gypsy, it is implied Cambot is female. Cambot doesn't talk but will on occasion show emotions, such as crying for the cameras killed in *Danger!! Death Ray* (season 6, episode 20) or even making a joke as the onscreen scorecard during *The Side Hackers* (season 2, episode 2).

A replacement was also needed for Beeper, as a second robot in the theater helped with the flow of dialogue and neither Gypsy nor Beeper fulfilled the job. Instead, Beeper was redressed so that the head was a gumball machine, giving the puppet a workable mouth, and it was renamed Servo. "The name Servo came from a vending machine at the Southdale shopping center in Minneapolis. They had this great vending machine that was shaped like a robot called Servotron. I just pulled Servo from that." Josh Weinstein experimented with voices for the character and, much like Trace with Crow, found that the goofy voice he started with was a strain on his vocal chords. In episode 6, *Gamera vs. Gaos*, they decide to do a story line with Joel adjusting Servo's voice as he sings "Lucy in the Sky with Diamonds." Eventually they land on a voice that sounds like a midmorning radio DJ, which Joel isn't crazy about but Servo loves. With his new, confident "mighty" voice, Servo is set to be Tom Servo; "Tom" was added by Weinstein on a whim as it seemed to suit the radio DJ voice. His version of Servo was an overconfident, clueless guy, like when he tried to hit on a blender before mistakenly doing the same with Mr. Coffee (a gag later reworked in an episode during the first Comedy Channel season).

The biggest change was the opening of the show. After completing and editing the first two episodes, there was a general feeling that something was missing. The concept wasn't quite coming across, and they feared that viewers would get lost as to why Joel and these robots were watching the movies. "Then a friend of Jim's suggested we make a theme song to explain the story, and this is where the Mads came from," Joel told the Official *MST3K* Info Club Web Site. "Josh and I wrote it into the theme song, 'His bosses didn't like him so they shot him into space.' Then when we shot the theme song, we dressed up Josh and Trace and had them mouth the words." Although Joel would still frequently kick off each episode with an explanation, the *Gilligan's Island*–style theme song made it clear what was occurring.

The theme song also set up the premise of the Mads who were back on Earth sending movies for Joel and the bots to watch. The initial idea was simply Joel and the bots having to watch bad movies, and the pilot goes the further step to make it appear that Joel initiated the whole scheme himself (perhaps not intentionally, but after whatever occurred on Earth that sent him packing to space, the movies were his way to pass the time stuck up there). With the premise of the "bosses" sending this guy from the Gizmonic working bay to the SOL because they "didn't like him," there is an additional spin where he's forced out there for some reason. Even at that point, though, it is not quite clear why, as the song does not state they are forcing him to watch the movies but merely sending him movies that are the "worst ever made," and in the first episode, Joel even states that it is a movie that "the guys at the station" sent instead of some type of mad experiment. The sixth episode, *Gamera vs. Gaos*, is the first time we even learn the names of the bosses: Dr. Clayton Forrester (Beaulieu) and Dr. Laurence Erhardt (Weinstein), and even that is simply a snapshot of the pair from the opening credits with their character names superimposed. Beaulieu's character is named after the scientist in the 1953 classic film version of H. G. Wells's *The War of the Worlds*, produced by George Pal. The naming of Weinstein's character is more ambiguous, with Weinstein stating that it was based on Werner Erhard, the founder of EST, which the *MST3K* staff knew was popular among some of the comics in the Minneapolis area at the time.

In the seventh episode, *Gamera vs. Zigra*, viewers finally got a chance to see and hear the "bosses" talk. As per the *Backlot* documentary done by Shout! Factory, Forrester and Erhardt are dressed in what the pair wore to the studio that day, along with matching lab coats, so there was still work to be done in getting the pair looking as "mad" as they would get in season 1 from the Comedy Channel. Joel had asked Trace to use his "killer [Gregory] Peck" impression (Trace will revisit it a few times in the series, especially in *Space Travelers* [season 4, episode 1], which was a retitled and shortened version of the 1969 movie *Marooned*, starring Peck). This was toned down as the season went along, and it settled into something closer to Trace's own speaking voice, with a slightly more upbeat tone. Weinstein decided to contrast the deep "mighty" voice of Tom Servo, which was established by the seventh episode, by giving Erhardt a high-pitched, squeaky voice. About a third of the way into the KTMA season, the voices of four of the other major characters were pretty much set, with Beaulieu's Crow and Forrester and Weinstein with Servo and Erhardt.

Although the bosses reveal in episode 7 that the movies are part of an experiment, it's still not quite clear what the purpose of the movies are. Forrester and Erhardt point out in episode 8, *Gamera vs. Guiron* (and yes, they certainly did start things off with a bang by showing five Gamera movies early on and, better yet, not in the proper order), that the rockets on the SOL are powered by ratings. Low ratings mean the ship's orbit will decay and Joel will die, and they are concerned that the movies aren't pulling in the numbers needed. Then again, episode 9, *Cosmic Princess* (the weirdest Gamera movie yet; okay, actually not a Gamera movie but rather two episodes of *Space: 1999* slapped together) did so well that ratings went up, which also upsets the mad scientists. When Joel asks them why they are upset over good ratings, it simply comes down to the fact that they are mad. Mad! In other words, we don't really know what the heck their agenda is. They do at least offer Joel the chance to be brought back down in episode 7, but only to be submerged three miles down in the ocean and to do what he's doing out in space, so Joel passes.

The first full episode was done at the beginning of November 1988 (a title card that appeared at the beginning of the official release of the episode states November 4, 1988) for the movie *Invaders from the Deep*, which has a 1981 copyright notice but is really four episodes of the old Gerry Anderson puppet series, *Stingray*, from 1964 strung together to kinda-sorta tell a full story. When the episode aired on KTMA, the scheduled *MST3K* episode in the television grid of the *Star Tribune* states that the movie scheduled was *Thunderbirds in Outer Space*, another 1981 compilation movie made from a Gerry Anderson series. A marketing ad done for *MST3K* as the series was being produced also mentioned that the program would air *Thunderbirds to the Rescue* (another compilation movie) at some point. What it comes down to is KTMA's access to a film package in 1988 called *Super Space Theater*, which featured thirteen compilation movies of various Anderson series, of which *MST3K* would use three for the first season and two for episodes 1 and 2: *Invaders from the Deep*, *Revenge of the Mysterons from Mars* (a compilation from the series *Captain Scarlet and the Mysterons*), and *Cosmic Princess* (as mentioned previously, two episodes of *Space:1999* strung together). It appears that both *Thunderbirds in Outer Space* and *Thunderbirds to the Rescue*, along with an advertised mention of *The Green Slime*, were considered for the season but eventually dropped for more promising movies. This suggests that even five Gamera movies in a row and movies like *Superdome* and *The*

Last Chase were considered better than the Gerry Anderson compilation, but Anderson fans could take that to mean the Anderson films were too "good" to make the cut and therefore not necessarily a bad thing.

After the opening theme song, the show starts with just Joel telling us about the movie and giving it a positive spin by mentioning it is done by the same people who did *Fireball XL5*, which was a popular series in the 1960s. What's interesting in this first episode, besides seeing Hodgson with really long hair, which will last until episode 4, is that the movie plays for about two and a half minutes before Joel makes his entrance into the theater, and nearly four minutes before Joel responds to something on the screen. Further, it is not until the second theater segment and about a half hour into the movie when Crow (in this rare instance, voiced by Weinstein) joins Joel in the theater. Tom Servo, who will become part of the trio seen in the theater and appears in the opening theme song, will not make his first appearance until episode 2.

The first episode, along with the second, *Revenge of the Mysterons from Mars* (making it an all-puppet night for *MST3K*'s debut) aired on November 24, 1988, which was Thanksgiving. Like many stations on a holiday like Thanksgiving, the day's programming was different than normal, and in the case of KTMA, the emphasis was on running science fiction movies all day. To promote the experience, the station ran a one-sixth ad on the television grid page of the *Star Tribune*, with a picture of one of the aliens from *Invasion of the Saucer-Men*, a movie that was not part of the marathon of films played that day (*Invasion of the Saucer-Men* was later remade as *Attack of the The Eye Creatures,* which aired in season 4, episode 18 of *MST3K*). The ad states that the channel would begin showing "classic sci-fi movies starting at 2 p.m.," but it really began at noon with *Gamera*, followed by *Gamera vs. Barugon* and *Fugitive Alien* (three films later to appear not only in the KTMA season but in later seasons of the series as well). Starting at 6:00 p.m. came the first two episodes of *MST3K*, which were promoted as being hosted by "comedian Joel Hodgson." This was then followed by Elvira's *Movie Macabre* at 10:00 p.m. that night, with *Night of the Zombies*.

By the time of the third episode, a phone line had been set up, and phone calls were played during episodes, some positive and some obviously not so much. The show was being filmed on a weekly basis at the time, but the production schedule was flexible at first, usually completed within a twenty-four-hour period two days before it aired on Sundays at 6:00 p.m. Mallon, Hodgson, Beaulieu, Weinstein, and Murphy were the core group at the time, and the process typically went as follows:

1. The group would arrive on Thursdays in the afternoon and dig through what movies were available in the KTMA film library.

2. Once a movie was picked, the group watched the first ten minutes before deciding if it would work.

3. If the first movie fit the bill ("We'd screen them, and say, 'This looks dumb,'" as Murphy told Plume), the work was done for the night, and everyone went off to do their own things.

4. Friday morning around 8:00 a.m., the group would get together and write the host segments for the show. This was credited to all five members of the group, including Brian Funk for six later episodes in the KTMA season.

5. The group would then head to the *MST3K* set to film the host segments before breaking for lunch. Everyone jumped in to make sure things were prepared, including other members of the KTMA staff.

6. Lunch (this is sometimes remembered as occurring before filming the host segments, so no doubt it was all dependent on how long it took to write the material beforehand).

7. Everyone would return to shoot the movie segments in the "theater."
8. The group would be done by 5:00 p.m., as the camera had to be turned around to film wrestling in the other part of the studio.

Camerawork was easy for the first season (since the camera didn't move), with just a zoom-in to the back of the set when "movie sign" indicated the movie portions were to start. Additional staff during the KTMA year included Vince Rodriguez, a holdover from the Melon Drop and *15 Minutes* days, as technical director and associate producer, while Todd Ziegler, another holdover, did audio. Faye Burkholder did makeup and would do Gypsy's "Marilyn Monroe" voice in episode 14, *Mighty Jack*. Faye most famously appeared in her final season with the show as a person holding a clipboard and rocking out to "Idiot Control Now" in the *Pod People* (season 3, episode 3). Lisa Erickson was the color consultant in the editing department. Finally, there was Alex Carr, who was production manager and postproduction supervisor from the start of the show up through 1992. Carr also helped run the fan club, played Sylvia the mole person in season 2, episode 1, *Rocketship X-M*, and—most importantly—played Magic Voice in season 2 through the first half of season 4. Charlie Erickson cowrote the theme song music with Joel, while Josh Weinstein helped with the lyrics alongside Joel. The music is credited to "Joel and the Joels." The final credit in each episode, after one showing that Crow had done everyone's hair, listed KTMA and Hair Brain Productions (the predecessor to Best Brains Productions that would come with the subsequent season).

Early episodes were very sparse with riffing, with Joel sometimes left alone in the theater with nothing to do but watch the movie in silence before one of the bots, usually Crow, would wander in several minutes into the movie or even in a later segment of the feature. "We all had our good days and bad," Weinstein told the Official *MST3K* Info Club Web Site. "It really had to do with how many opportunities the movies provided. We didn't know what was coming, since we hadn't watched the whole movie before taping. Sometimes we'd get sucked into the movie and there'd be long silent patches." This started changing with episode 4, *Gamera vs. Barugon*, where Joel and the bots entered the theater as the movie began. Even then, it wasn't until episode 7 when the riffing began to gel a bit more. "We had a sort of mission of trying to get better and better at improving these movies," Josh told Plume in an audio interview from 2010 (still available [in 2022] at http://asitecalledfred .com/2010/03/09/j-elvis-weinstein-ken-plume-chat). "It started out with a few comments and then you start to feel the absence of comments, so you start making more comments." It became clear to the team around the time of episode 14, *Mighty Jack*, that filming their improvisations while the movie played was not giving them the biggest return. It was decided to spend the Thursday watching the full movie instead of just the first ten minutes so they could think on it a bit and be more prepared to have funny responses the next day. "We eventually realized, hey, this might be funnier if we had some jokes in our back pocket," Weinstein told *Wired* in 2014. Things could have been helped as well if the group picked a movie earlier in the week, which was an option available to them, but they decided Thursdays worked just fine. With the additional foresight, the shows began to be more consistent in the laughs, earning more fans as the season continued.

Things were still evolving on the show as well, with cast members having to disappear for an episode here and there. Trace could not be there for episode 12, *Fugitive Alien*, so Forrester was written out as attending a convention in Vegas while Crow had been disassembled by Servo and Gypsy. Episode 18, *The Million Eyes of Sumuru* (featured in season 13 and as a *RiffTrax* release), has Servo leaving midway through the movie "in order to bake brownies for the Pinewood Derby," as Weinstein had to leave before recording the episode could be completed. Episode 17, *Time of the Apes* (another movie that was returned to in a later season), went on with only Servo and Crow in the theater, as Hodgson had committed to help Louie Anderson with his sitcom pilot. To explain his absence, the show came up with the ludicrous idea that Joel had somehow gotten himself locked out of the ship wearing only his "BVDs." When he returns the following week, Crow asks how he was able to survive in space without oxygen or a spacesuit. This merely leads to Joel playing acoustic guitar and singing the final part of the theme song to remind everyone that "it's just a show."

In the first two episodes, Joel announced a phone number that was hooked up to a machine to take messages, and when the tape was full within two hours of the first night's broadcast, the group knew they may be on to something. By mid-December, the show received strong publicity with a large story in the *Star Tribune*, leading to more people checking the show out. After a time, letters with drawings from people of all ages were being read at the end of each episode, while a fan club started with episode 12 had just reached one thousand members by the end of the season. *Cosmic Princess*, which was programmed against the Super Bowl on network television, saw the ratings actually improve. All of which made it a rare success for KTMA at a time where things were looking bleak, so the station let them do what they wanted. "The station manager," Murphy recalled to Plume, "would come back and see the mess we'd made out of Styrofoam and junk and jingle his keys in his pockets and shake his head and chuckle and say, 'You crazy guys, what are you up to now?' Then he'd walk away. I don't think he ever saw the show."

Yet even with that success, the guys creating the episodes were not seeing much in return financially. Jim Mallon and Kevin Murphy were on salary at KTMA, so *MST3K* was just part of the job, with no additional money involved. As to Beaulieu and Weinstein, it was "gas money." "Our budget for the show was microscopic," Beaulieu told *Wired*. "I think Josh and I were pulling down $25 a show, and I think Joel's budget was a little higher, because he had to build props." Weinstein, in his interview with Plume, said he believed Joel was earning about $100 to $125, but "even then, still, you're getting pretty much nothing for it."

But there was recognition. After completing the first season, Josh Weinstein and Joel Hodgson managed to sneak their way into a premiere showing of Tim Burton's 1989 movie, *Batman*. After the movie was over, a local television station was interviewing some of the people who attended, including Josh and Joel. When the news segment aired, the pair were mentioned onscreen as being "among the celebrities at the event last night." June 1989 also saw Joel, Josh, and Trace do two performances of a live version of *MST3K* at the Comedy Gallery, with Jim Mallon showing the pilot and the cast doing a Q&A with the attendees at the sold-out shows. It was clear that *Mystery Science Theater 3000* was a local success, and the cast received positive feedback. Everything was looking good for the show.

It's just a shame that the television station that helped produce it was about to go under.

5

He Did a Good Job
Cleaning Up the Place

Going National

Trace once said a really clever thing: "The movies are Margaret Dumont, and we're the Marx Brothers."

—JOEL HODGSON IN A 2014 INTERVIEW WITH *WIRED*

KTMA was in trouble and had been for some time. The incident in August 1988 where the station lost rights to run episodes of *Hawaii Five-O*, *The Andy Griffith Show*, *The Untouchables*, and certain movie packages due to a lack of funding had made it into the newspapers, giving the station a black eye. The station found other investors and moved forward, as everyone at the station put their head down and kept working, but it was clear that something was up. "Basically, the station existed as a get-rich scheme," Jim Mallon mused to the Official *MST3K* Info Club Web Site in 2008. "The owners bought the place and attempted to juice up its ratings so they could flip the station and make a fortune." If true, the major problem with that scheme was the station was losing money, with only *MST3K* as a positive beacon on a schedule full of third-tier reruns. Viewers could even see it by way of *MST3K* when the "bad" movies it made fun of were airing on KTMA as part of the regular film schedule just a few weeks before.

Yet KTMA general manager and owner Don O'Connor was not quite ready to give up hope. In December 1988, O'Connor began eyeing fellow independent stations in the area in hopes of creating a network of stations that would combine their antenna power, resources, money, and even programming to combat other stations in the area that had more of everything. In hindsight, it was an innovative idea that could have led to a groundbreaking cooperative or, perhaps, the inkling of creating a superstation-type structure with several stations under one leader. But various delays and concerns about how it would work kept pushing the project back until finally, in July 1989, O'Connor admitted defeat. At the end of that month, KTMA filed for bankruptcy after less than three years in service. The station had a total of thirty-seven employees at the time.

KTMA continued with standard programming during the bankruptcy, until it was finally bought by a Christian broadcasting group that changed the call letters of the station to KLGT and attempted a Christian-oriented schedule for a time before finally moving back to a generic independent station format when ratings did not improve. As with many independent stations in the early 1990s, KLGT teamed up with a new television network, the WB. The station was then bought out by the Sinclair Broadcast Group in 1997, and the call letters were changed again to KMWB, and when the WB merged with another network, UPN, the network became the CW, leading to a final (so far) call letter change to WUCW. This version of the station drew upon the old Melon Drop concept for new specials in 2015 and 2016, while its website links to older KTMA footage, including *15 Minutes*.

That was all in the future in 1989, however. The guys putting *MST3K* together could tell the wolves were howling outside the station and it was time to start thinking of what could be done to save the show, or at least save their jobs. Murphy recalled, "It was actually after we finished the show that we started hearing the rumblings, and that was when Jim and Joel shopped it up to New York and tried to get it going, because Jim was saying, 'We'd better get this going because we're not going to have jobs in another six months,' and that's what it turned out to be."

The *MST3K* group were feeling pretty good about the show's chances that another station in the Minneapolis area would take an interest, thanks to the attention it was getting locally through fans and the press. Joel also had name value, thanks to his earlier work on *Letterman* and *SNL*, and Joel was not afraid to allow references to his past be used if it meant attracting attention to *MST3K*. But the dream was to go even bigger. "I remember doing an interview way before *Mystery Science Theater* saying, 'The way to do it is to make the show locally, and then sell it nationally.' I know that's what we wanted to do, it just wasn't that clear," Joel told Ain't It Cool News. Going national was not an impossible dream at the time either; KTMA's showings of Elvira's *Movie Macabre* was a perfect example of how such a show could start off small and gain national attention as part of a syndicated package. That show was ending its run, so there was a chance stations could be looking for something to replace it.

The first step was to see if he could get the rights to the show, since the production had been a joint venture between KTMA and the Hair Brain Production company. Mallon was unsure how Don O'Connor would take to the idea of selling the station's rights over to Mallon and Hodgson and was prepared to offer all types of negotiation tactics to win O'Connor over. Fortunately, O'Connor—perhaps knowing that he wouldn't be able to keep the show going at KTMA and feeling that it was a fad that would burn out quickly—had no qualms and gave the copyright to Mallon without any issues. With the show theirs, Mallon and Hodgson agreed to work together to keep the show going, as Joel remembered to *Wired*: "He said to me, 'The only logical thing is for us to be 50-50 partners, so we're not working for each other.' And I shook his hand and said, 'I'll run the creative; you run the business and the technical.'" According to the April 1991 article titled "The Million-Dollar Sight Gag," in *Corporate Report Minnesota*, Mallon and Hodgson agreed to start a new production company for the program, to be called Best Brains, Inc., with the pair each owning 45 percent and Murphy and Beaulieu owning the other 10 percent.

As Mallon and Murphy finished out their days at the station, Trace, Josh, and Joel followed through on their onstage gigs at the clubs in town. Joel also participated in other television projects after the KTMA season ended, including cohosting a pilot for Hubbard Broadcasting in March 1989 called *Seriously Weird Magazine* and later had a long stand-up segment in a comedy special for KTCA called *Land O Loons III* that aired in October that year. The most interesting announcement for Joel, however, was one that seemed to only make the press in the May 31–June 6 edition of the *Twin Cities Reader* (a local free paper), where, besides noting that KTMA had put *MST3K* "on hiatus," it mentioned that Joel was heading off to New York to do a "writing stint with HBO." There were no other details, but it soon became clear that the "writing stint" would lead directly to the next phase of *MST3K*'s evolution.

In April 1989, the news began to filter out that cable movie and special television giant Home Box Office (HBO) was looking to start an ad-based sister channel that showed comedy twenty-four hours a day. The official announcement came on May 1, 1989, that the Comedy Channel would be a comedy version of MTV, only instead of music, the programming would center around funny clips from movies, television shows, and stand-up specials. A few days later, MTV's parent company, Viacom, mentioned that it, too, planned to have a twenty-four-hour comedy channel starting on April 1, 1990, that would be called HA! Oddly enough, HA! was publicized as carrying old sitcoms and movies, perhaps to be different from the already

With the move to the Comedy Channel, both Crow T. Robot (alias Art) and Tom Servo were spiffed up to look sleeker. COMEDY CENTRAL / PHOTOFEST © COMEDY CENTRAL

promoted Comedy Channel's stance of a comedic MTV but also because such a formula had worked for the parent network when it added Nick at Night, which was an adult-themed portion of the Nickelodeon channel, featuring old sitcoms. Part of this Comedy Channel versus HA! rivalry came about due to Viacom—the then-owners of Showtime—feeling that HBO was attempting to muscle Showtime out of business through intimidation of cable systems, and it had been suggested that Viacom immediately piggybacked off the Comedy Channel concept to create trouble for HBO. It would be a simmering problem that would not be resolved for a couple of years and cause confusion for fans searching for *MST3K.*

The Comedy Channel's concept of cheap clips making up its schedule had some promise, but creating such clips from movies turned out to not be as easy as they assumed. Many comedy bits from movies needed setup that took too long or would have needed editing from other parts of the movie to really pay off (a procedure the channel wanted to avoid), while other clips were simply not laugh-out-loud funny. A further problem developed when a member of the Directors Guild of America balked at the network running excerpts from movies on the channel (Art Bell, one of the originators of the channel, suggests in his book *Constant Comedy* that the member who complained was *What's Up, Tiger Lily?*'s director Woody Allen). The network had a workaround that allowed them to use a certain number of clips from movies currently on HBO's schedule, but a good number of clips already created were verbatim, and the initial core of its twenty-four-hour programming had centered around using those clips. Suddenly, in a near-repeat of KTMA in the summer of 1988, the Comedy Channel's programming disappeared, something was needed to fill that space, and it needed to be available as quickly as possible, as the channel was already promoted to start November 1.

Hodgson and Mallon didn't know this was the case back in April when they first heard about the channel; they only knew this was a golden opportunity to present the concept of *MST3K* to a new national cable channel and maybe get some attention. They needed a promotional reel to send to HBO. Looking through the KTMA episodes for the best moments of the show, Joel and Jim edited together a demonstration reel of the funniest moments from the season. Out of twenty-one episodes and a pilot, the "best of" from the mostly improvised series was less than ten minutes long. As Joel reminisced in a conversation at the Museum of Broadcast Communications (MBC) in 2013, "The moment where I realized we had to write was when we cut together a sell tape from KTMA to show to the Comedy Channel and it was our funniest moments of the show and that's when I go, 'Oh I get it. The whole show has to be like that.'" The concept of a show with occasional trivia and jokes during the movie parts, which was Joel's original intention with the KTMA series, had been steadily reshaped into a more consistently funny series in the second half of the season when they prepared more gags ahead of time. Even with that, there needed to be much more prepared material if they wanted to get national attention. It was a much-needed moment of clarity, as Joel went on to say in the MBC discussion: "And I remember that conversation with Jim Mallon, because he was starting to do the numbers to see how much it would cost, because 'now we're going to improvise this, right?' And I said, 'I don't think we should. Let's just write it now, because we're getting paid and let's just take our time to do that, and so that's when that started.'"

The tape, which included bits from several host segments along with excerpts from the movie-riffing on *City on Fire*, *SST: Death Flight*, and *Phase IV*, was sent off to Hodgson's manager, David Campbell, in New York, who then passed it on to the staff at HBO. According to Art Bell, it had already been decided to program the channel in two- to three-hour blocks, with a separate comedian and production team to front each segment. One program idea tossed around at the new channel, specifically from head writer Eddie Gorodetsky, was to do what he called a "watch-us-watch" segment, where viewers would tune in to see a comic commentating on some television show or movie as it aired. Just a few days later, the tape for *MST3K* came in the mail for their review, as if it was made-to-order. It had its own production team, ran two hours, and fulfilled one of the concepts being tossed around at the channel. Best of all, it wasn't just an idea waiting for money to be handed over to see if it worked, which helped locked in the show as is. "If we would have just brought them an idea, they could've changed it all around," Hodgson told *Corporate Report Minnesota*. "But *Mystery Science Theater* worked, and it had a track record—1,500 pieces of fan mail at Channel 23 was really convincing to them. Fortunately, the Comedy Channel was just getting started and they needed to fill 24 hours of programming a day, so I think we also got lost in the shuffle before anyone could mess with us."

Further, Joel's comedy success from earlier in the 1980s to help sell the show was a plus. "It wasn't like he was some guy off the street," executive vice president of the channel John Newton told *Corporate Report Minnesota*.

"Besides, he had something to show us." It was also helpful that Joel was already known to the vice president in charge of original programming at the Comedy Channel, Stu Smiley. Smiley had met up with Hodgson a few years before at (ironically enough) Showtime and asked Joel for any ideas he had for a program. "I came up with this concept of a combination between a talk show and *The Prisoner* [the 1960s science-fiction spy series about a former secret agent forced to live in a small village because of his knowledge]. The host would be in a controlled environment, and guests would come in and leave through a portal. It was too weird; a fifteen-minute variety show." Too weird, but memorable, and thus when the tape came to the Comedy Channel, the *MST3K* group already had an insider chance, thanks to Smiley.

That led to that summer trip to New York for Joel, as discussed in the local Minneapolis paper back in May. Heading to New York with Jim Mallon, the pair went to discuss with Stu Smiley the possibilities of the channel purchasing the show for the Comedy Channel. Having spent the past year with virtually no money at a small independent station, the trip to the Comedy Channel's headquarters was intimidating. "The whole place was art-directed like a 1930s newsroom," Mallon remembered to *Corporate Report Minnesota*, while Hodgson pointed out the smoked glass everywhere. "They must've spent millions to meticulously refurbish this period furniture. Our eyes just went wide. Here we were, back at Best Brains sitting on chairs we borrowed from Kevin's dad's basement." Such intimidation was standard operation for the HBO staff, who were hoping to make a cheap deal with these corn shuckers from Farmland, USA. They didn't expect, however, that Hodgson would bring along his New York agent, Rick Leed, to the meeting. Leed would go on to be regularly praised by the *MST3K* cast over the years for his ability to (loudly) talk back to network negotiators when everyone from the show would let their midwestern tendencies come into play and want to back off and avoid a fight. Smiley wasn't quite prepared for needing to butt heads with the legal pitbull the quiet Hodgson and his partner from Minnesota had brought with them and told them so. "I do remember a very somber Stu Smiley saying that we needed to straighten out our agent if we wanted this deal to happen," Mallon told the Official *MST3K* Info Club Web Site in 2008.

Fortunately, the Comedy Channel was hungry for the show to fill out its schedule. There were concerns about a two-hour length being too long and the thought that perhaps the program should concentrate on excerpts of movies and television shows instead of a full feature, since "they did not believe that audiences would sit still for real-time riffing of a feature length movie," as Mallon told the Official *MST3K* Info Club Web Site. But these worries were quickly brushed aside, and the Comedy Channel agreed to let the show be produced without any changes to the concept, cast, or crew. What it did want, however, was for the show to move from Minneapolis to the Comedy Channel's studios in New York. This was a problem, as Mallon saw it; he told *Wired*, "Some of us had families and none of us wanted to just drop everything and move." There was then a suggestion that the channel fly the cast up to New York during the week to film an episode on Mondays and then fly them back on Fridays. This, too, was looked upon as a major inconvenience. The real deal breaker on the notion of working at the New York studios, however, came when they were given a tour of the studio space: cramped quarters situated between offices, with ten-foot-high ceilings that would make performing the professional puppet show they had designed virtually impossible to pull off.

Negotiations continued, and finally a deal was worked out where the group could stay in Minneapolis and send in the episodes. "That was great," Mallon mentioned to Joshua Murphy in an interview for the JM Archives (which can be heard in full on YouTube at https://www.youtube .com/watch?v=SWMDzjhSgGc&t=1728s). "Because they didn't want to come out here. It's just flyover territory to them. So we were left alone."

In retrospect, it was also probably a big reason the show stayed on the air, as Kevin Murphy discussed with *Wired*: "If we had done the show in New York, it would have been cancelled within a season or two. There would have been people in there sticking their fingers in it, and the reason the show got to grow was because nobody wanted to come out to Minnesota." The opportunity to do what they wanted was ideal. The money, not so much: "[Rick] got into screaming matches with them and he said, 'If you're gonna pay these guys dirt,' which is what they wanted to pay us, which was $25 grand [per] thirteen episodes," as Mallon continued with Joshua Murphy, "'you can pay them dirt, but they get to keep the copyright.'" It should be noted that reporter Dave Itzkoff in a *New York Times* article from 2008 states the production company got $35,000 per episode, but the *Corporate Report Minnesota* article from 1991 had its license fee from HBO and the Comedy Channel for the first season as a total of $344,000 for thirteen episodes, which breaks out to a little over $26,000 per episode. According to the article, this was paid out in portions, with $123,000 up front, which went to help pay for production space, setting up staff, and building sets. The remainder was then $17,000 per episode, with $8,500 paid when a script was delivered and the remaining $8,500 paid when the completed episode arrived at the Comedy Channel "four days later." Even at the time, this was a remarkably low amount for a two-hour program for a major cable network, especially when production costs of around $50,000 to $75,000 was not uncommon for a "cheap" half-hour television program. As surprising as it was to Mallon when O'Connor at KTMA had given him the copyright to *MST3K*, it was more shocking when HBO agreed to let the show keep its copyright, even though the channel would be investing all the money into the show. "I believe the network thought the show was only going to last one season anyway," Mallon told the Official *MST3K* Info Club Web Site, "so they granted the copyright to us."

With a deal in place, Mallon and Hodgson returned to Minneapolis with the good news and a lot of tough work in front of them. Kevin Murphy had left to get married and travel to Central America for the honeymoon, arriving back in time to hear that the Comedy Channel season was a go. With KTMA out of the picture, the priority was to find a place to film the show, and this concern was quickly resolved when Bryan Beaulieu offered the group warehouse space that he had in an industrial park out in Eden Prairie, twelve miles southwest of Minneapolis. "The Best Brains office was in this industrial park in a second-ring suburb, by all these medical-equipment buildings," Bill Corbett, later writer and second voice of Crow on the show, commented to *Wired*. "It could not have been more generic-looking. When people took the Best Brains tour, they were often shocked: 'Is somebody going to kidnap us and kill us?'" In July 1989, the crew began building at the location that would bear the name Best Brains, Inc.

Moon Zero Two (1969) was a late entry in the first Comedy Channel season, and a chance to see a color movie, although a very dull western in space. WARNER BROS. PICTURES / PHOTOFEST © WARNER BROS. PICTURES

Joel was working on a second project at the same time, having landed a developmental deal with the Comedy Channel for a show that would become well remembered from those early days of the channel. "When I first approached Comedy Channel with *Mystery Science Theater*, they also rolled out this development deal that they handed to twelve or fourteen people. They said, 'Create shows for us. We want your ideas.'" Taking the money, between $4,000 and $6,000, Joel got in contact with a comedy trio he knew from Los Angeles called the Higgins Boys and Gruber, made up of David Anthony Higgins (*The Wrong Guys, Ellen, Malcolm in the Middle*), Steve Higgins (*Saturday Night Live, The Tonight Show Starring Jimmy Fallon*), and Dave "Gruber" Allen (*Bad Teacher, The Naked Trucker and T-Bones Show*, and who came up with the acronym of *MST3K* for the show to use), and put together a pilot for them to show the Comedy Channel. "I think most other people just wrote a synopsis and took the money," Hodgson told *Alibi* in 2014. "But I felt like you had to experience the show." The pilot led to the show being picked up, and the Higgins Boys and Gruber would become a weekday fixture on the channel for the first couple of years. The two- to three-hour program centered around the guys as a type of mixture between the Monkees and a children's morning show, featuring them at "the ranch," their supposed home, playing music or doing sketches in between an assortment of oddball cartoons, such as *Clutch Cargo*, episodes of *Supercar* (the multiple usage of *Clutch Cargo* and *Supercar* explains why the early seasons of *MST3K* refer to them several times, as viewers would have been familiar with the shows), and even old episodes of shows by comedians Bob & Ray. Both it and *MST3K* would also help anchor the look of the Comedy Channel in those early years, with the wry but calmer style of comedy without a laugh track that played out in both programs giving the feeling of funny acquaintances whom you'd like to know better. It's a tone that seeped into other early programming, such as *Night after Night with Allan Havey* (late-night talk show that usually featured Havey in a darkened office area, trading jokes with his crew) and *The Sweet Life* with singer Rachel Sweet (an excellent singer, whose hours on the channel probably came closest to the look and feel of MTV programming).

That was slightly in the future at the time, however. Back at Eden Prairie, the guys began building the two standing sets for the new version of the show: an area for Forrester and Erhardt that would become known as Deep 13 and the newly expanded (and definitely cleaner-looking) bridge of the Satellite of Love. The bridge of the SOL, usually referred to as the location for the "host segments" that surrounded the movies, would look less like a slime-covered dungeon and more like a sleek "spaceship," with hexagon shapes for the walls—a carryover from the way the interior of the ship looked in *Silent Running*. A waist-high desk, as seen in the KTMA season, remained at the center of the bridge, and eventually a new pad with lights was added for "movie sign" that Joel could hit when the time came to go into the tunnel and to the theater.

One of two interesting features added to the bridge was the "Hexfield Viewscreen," which was added to stage right of the desk as a means for Joel and the bots to communicate with other characters from outside the SOL and open up the means to set up skits rather than just being Joel and the bots. As mentioned in *The Mystery Science Theater 3000 Amazing Colossal Episode Guide*, it was easy to see that the viewscreen was just a box built on the other side of the "viewscreen" with actors inside it, usually Mike Nelson in various roles during the Joel years. It first employed a blind to open and shut the viewscreen that Nelson had to operate by hand on camera in its first appearance in season 2, episode 1 (*Rocketship X-M*). The effect got better with an iris setting to open and close the viewscreen in later episodes, although it could easily be seen that the actors inside the "viewscreen" still had to avoid movement as the screen went dark, since they were slightly visible even when the screen was closed.

The other interesting addition, although rarely used, was a portal placed on stage left with a bar above it that allowed Joel to jump feetfirst through it (reminiscent of how the pilots in the Gerry Anderson series *UFO* would be transported to their ships). In season 2, they explicitly demonstrate this in *Ring of Terror* as the means Joel uses to get directly to the theater, suggesting once again that the tunnel that Cambot (and possibly the other bots) uses to get to the theater was unsafe for humans. Yet in later episodes, the portal had other functions, including how Joel disposes of Timmy, the evil entity that looks like Crow, in the *Fire Maidens of Outer Space* episode in season 4 or received supplies from Deep 13 in other episodes; plus Joel and Mike both have direct access to the theater tunnel in various episodes, so it was a cool feature that wasn't relevant to the program. Speaking of the tunnel to the theater (which Joel actually calls the "Mystery Science Theater" in the seventh episode of season 2, *Wild Rebels*), it was completely revamped from the KTMA season, with a newly made tunnel that was about four feet in height and with doors that were manually opened from the outside as a camera was pushed through the tunnel to achieve the effect needed.

The robots, listed in the early credits for the first Comedy Channel season as "Joel Hodgson's Puppet Bots," were given an update as well. Crow's look stayed the closest to how he appeared in the KTMA season, only with a sleeker build that smoothed out the edges and allowed them to move, giving him more personality. Gypsy—now voiced and controlled by Jim Mallon—was fleshed out, and while she was still built from baby seats for her head, the seats were now solid rather than the stripped-to-the-steel-base look of the KTMA season, and she was given lips to make her more feminine. The lamp on her head that is her eye was also demonstrated in one episode as being detachable to allow her to see in tight areas. Tom Servo was given a new torso, using a "Money Lover Barrel" coin bank, and a new skirt that made it appear he could hover if he wished, although beyond the later theatrical movie, he rarely used this talent visibly in the original program (the series explained in-story that Joel and later Mike had to carry Tom into the theater because a ventilation grate at the entrance of the theater made his hover skirt inoperative, although it was clear that creating the effect in the original series to make it look like Tom could hover three to four times an episode just wasn't worth the headaches to film). His hands and arms remained mostly for display and were repeatedly referred to as nonfunctional. Cambot was changed to look more like the Gypsy of the KTMA season, only with a football-size tube in her mouth to represent the camera. This was refined in season 2 of the cable network series, when Cambot begins to look more like a video camera with a flashing light on her head.

The SOL was completely redesigned for the new series, going from the cheap metal satellite of the KTMA season to a spaceship design reminiscent of the Discovery One in *2001: A Space Odyssey* (1968), a movie also featuring a transitional scene where a bone thrown up in the air cuts to a long spacecraft. The idea of the bone-shaped SOL came about as the writers knew they would eventually use the "demon dogs" seen in the opening credits of the KTMA season and would even give one away as a prize that year, for a story line for *The Robot vs. the Aztec Mummy* episode (season 1, episode 2). Thus a bone shape for the SOL was needed, and Trace built the ship using foam pieces with "a lot of stuff glued to them," according to Beaulieu on the Official *MST3K* Info Club Web Site. Trace also created the *MST3K* logo that appears in the opening and ending credits, along with certain commercial breaks, throughout the series. The Guthrie Theater in Minneapolis had used a giant plastic orb in a production of *A Christmas Carol* (although it seems unlikely that giant plastic orbs are typically featured in productions of *A Christmas Carol*), and Trace had bought it when the theater had an auction of props. It then sat for a time before it was decided to turn it into the logo for the show on the Comedy Channel. Joel and Trace used Styrofoam letters

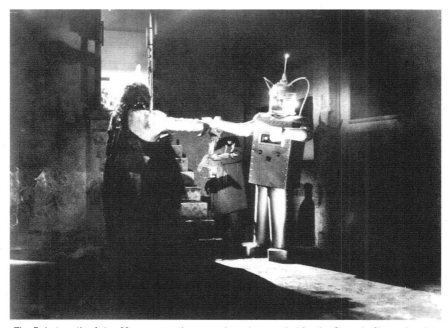

The Robot vs. the Aztec Mummy was the second movie recorded for the Comedy Channel series, although there is some speculation that it was the first episode aired. AZTECA FILMS / PHOTOFEST © AZTECA FILMS

glued to the orb and covered it all in spray-foam insulation to give it a "lunar landscape look."

The story line of the series was set up as a continuation of the first season but with major changes. Joel no longer appears under his own name, but rather as Joel Robinson (see chapter 4 for more details as to why). The opening credits and theme song are also updated to showcase the new look of the show. Ironically, with the change in name and the footage of "happy in his work" Joel being updated, as well as the look of Joel's departure from Earth and the clear mention in the song of the "bosses" being able to monitor his mind as part of the experiment (something never mentioned in the KTMA season), the program is pretty much an alternate-universe version of the Joel, bots, SOL, and Mads from the KTMA seasons. If this was from DC Comics, the earlier Joel would be from Earth-KTMA, while the new one would be from Earth-CC. One could extend that into the Mike-hosted era, with the later theatrical movie—thanks to its scenery changes to Deep 13 and the SOL that disappeared when the series returned to television—would represent Earth-Gramercy (named such mainly to irritate *MST3K* fans). While the return from being higher life-forms to an altered SOL (with differences in the bridge, tunnel, and the whole "nanite" setup) in the Sci-Fi Channel years could be seen as merely an extension of Earth-CC that is in the far future (in the year 2525, if those apes didn't lie), it could instead be another alternative universe called Earth-SF. If so, that would certainly explain why Joel from Earth-CC could be seen as living on a SOL orbiting Earth in the year 3000 during season 13, even though we also know the "destroyer of worlds" Mike Nelson helped blow up Earth in the year 2525 (if woman still—ugh, no, let's just drop that gag) in season 8, episode 4, *The Deadly Mantis*. If so, that means the Earth-CC Mike and the bots are still pure energy, having fun out at the end of the universe, leaving the SOL to not be destroyed in season 10, episode 13, *Diabolik*, and that somehow the SOL made its way back to Joel. Oh, and let's not forget Earth-10.2, where Mike never temped at Deep 13, meaning Joel never left the SOL, Tom has a new voice, TV's Frank never ascended to Second Banana Heaven, and Forrester never became a space-baby-whatsit, leaving the only constant in all universes to be that *Godzilla vs. Megalon* still accidentally gets released in a Rhino DVD box set in 2008 and Frank must clean up the copyright issue.

Or it really is just one big continuity mess, and I should just relax.

Elements of the story line morphed for the "bosses" as well. This time around we see what the Gizmonic Institute looks like from the outside in the opening credits. It is also established in the first episode of the season that Forrester and Erhardt had moved their operations in secret to the pits of the institute in an area called Deep 13 (explaining the cave-like walls), which is supposed to be dangerously radioactive, although the mad scientists aren't feeling it. The dynamics between Forrester and Erhardt also change slightly from the partners in evil of the KTMA series to that of Erhardt increasingly coming across as an assistant to Forrester as the Comedy Channel season plays out—a development vastly expanded upon in the second season once TV's Frank (Frank Conniff) replaces Erhardt in the show. And while Joel would occasionally show off inventions he made in the KTMA season, it is with the first season on the Comedy Channel that the display becomes an expected part of the show, with Forrester and Erhardt taking part in showing off their own inventions for what is now called the "invention exchange."

What many of the people who had been involved with the KTMA season have said about this season is that they really don't believe people should watch it. It is even blatantly stated as such in the *Amazing Colossal Episode Guide*. For a long time, that wasn't the easiest thing to do anyway, as the only way to see any of those episodes was to find fellow fans who had recorded them off KTMA when the show aired, usually leading to fans getting a copy of a copy of a copy. It was even thought for years that there were no copies of the first three episodes of that season, until prints of the first two were eventually discovered and released as a streaming premium (leaving only the host segments from the third available if one hunts for them on the internet). Then as various video sites on the internet evolved and allowed for fans to push those episodes out for everyone to see, we soon discovered . . . that they weren't that wrong about needing to see them. To be fair, the writers' feelings aren't completely off base in the early part of the KTMA season—those episodes are slow goings. Yet if you're in the right mood on a rainy Saturday night and view them in the spirit of the old *Shock Theater* programs, they are a nostalgic reminder of watching such monster shows from our youth, even if they're not that funny. As noted in the previous chapter, however, the series did improve by midseason, after the cast began to write ahead instead of improvising. As Joel later stated, viewing the KTMA episodes may be beneficial from a historical standpoint because they had twenty-two times to "workshop" the program and figure out how to do it.

With that type of setup, especially with a show where no one outside of Minneapolis would have seen the first season, it was easy for the writers to go back to the first season for bits and pieces to redo in the Comedy Channel version. This included a few of the inventions seen in the KTMA season reshot in a more effective fashion, such as the motorcycle airbag helmet seen in episode 2 of the first Comedy Channel season (*The Robot vs. the Aztec Mummy*), as well as sketches, such as Servo trying to talk up the blender. The results were improvements on the KTMA season along with several movies revisited with better jokes in the first two years of *MST3K* on cable. It reaffirmed the notion that the KTMA season was best left behind in the memory of a handful of fans. Over time, Hodgson became more appreciative of the idea of people watching the early episodes but, at best, only on the level of studying them to see how the process developed, as he told Flavorwire in an interview in 2013, "That's really where we figured it all out: the theme song, the story, and even movie riffing, which wasn't super clear when we started, because I remember thinking, 'Man, how much can we do? At what point is it gonna become a big distraction to the audience?'"

At first it seemed that the easiest element would be getting movies, since it was assumed that HBO had a film library of which the show could then pick movies from, but that was not necessarily the case. HBO licensed movies for a set period, and while the Comedy Channel would send them boxes of movies and shorts to review (with the instructional shorts mostly picked from the Rick Prelinger Archives, some of which had previously appeared in episodes of *Night Flight*), nine times out of ten, the movies were not proper for the show. As described in various interviews over the years by many of the writers, there were certain requirements needed for the movies:

- Movies had to be appropriate for family viewing or could easily be trimmed to make them appropriate. For example, *Robot Holocaust* in that first season has a scene with nudity and suggested sex, which did not do anything to propel the story forward. A well-slotted commercial break in the program allowed the show to simply discard the scene without looking like an edit. This approach was agreeable to both the *MST3K* crew and Comedy Channel at the time, as Mallon related to *Corporate Report Minnesota* when HBO chairman Michael Fuchs came to Minneapolis to see the Best Brains layout: "He said we were exactly what Home Box Office was all about: G-rated, but with an edge."

- Movies had to be short enough to fit within the time allotted. Shorter movies were less of a problem, as the series had several movie shorts that easily could fit into the slot. This is one reason why so many B movies of the 1940s and 1950s were used. The program was approximately ninety-five minutes in length without commercials, and host segments and credits took up about twenty minutes of those ninety-five. A standard B movie of the black-and-white era usually ran sixty to seventy-five minutes at most, making it easy to fit without having to do much editing. On the other hand, longer movies needed to be trimmed, and this unfortunately led to some movies becoming somewhat incoherent. *Mitchell* (season 5, episode 12) had this occur when John Saxon's character simply goes missing after the first third of the film even though he is a major villain. Edited out of the *MST3K* version was his death scene, leading to Servo later commenting that Saxon seemed to be missing in the movie, and while this at least acknowledges the character's disappearance, it is a bit of a cheat, since the joke implies that the filmmakers simply forgot about him when it was *MST3K*'s editing that cause the character to disappear.

- Movies needed to be easily accessible for viewers to follow. This meant the picture and sound quality had to be clear enough to understand, although there were allowances where certain night scenes or "deep hurting" sandstorm scenes created good opportunities for gags to be made at the expense of the film. (A bad splice in the film print of *The Girl in Gold Boots* that makes a character suddenly appear in a restaurant booth is too good of an opportunity to have the character anxious for approval of his ability to teleport, for example.) Far too many "bad" movies simply involved bad camerawork and audio mishaps that might be funny at first but could irritate over the course of a two-hour program. (*Castle of Fu Manchu* is a good example of an exception proving the rule when showing a bad print of a movie with questionable camerawork and lighting. While it helped create a good story line in the host segments by nearly breaking Joel and the bots, it tended to fall near the bottom of fans' favorites because they, too, felt the pain in trying to watch it.)

- One of the most important features was that movies needed to have empty spaces where jokes could be inserted, as it was discovered early on that if dialogue was covered up by a joke—even a great joke—the audience would get frustrated in having missed what was said and would not appreciate the interruption. This was a major element that Joel found separated the show from people simply yelling at the screen. "You have to treat it like the audience is your friend, and the audience doesn't wanna spend time with you if you're an asshole. . . . Heckling is when you're not invited to talk, and riffing is when you are, so it's a different thing," Hodgson told Flavorwire.

As it turned out, even with HBO pulling movies for them to select from, it was not as if it was a free library where anything could be used without cost; if the movie was not in the public domain, licensing fees needed to be paid to the owners of the movies, and that was not always a simple yes-or-no proposition. With HBO behind them, the program sometimes found that film owners expected too much money for a license; for others, the license would be just about to be granted when another group would pop up claiming they owned the movie instead or even the original owners changed their minds at the last minute, raising more headaches. And after all that, there would be situations where the program would eventually lose its license to a movie and not be able to convince the owners to allow the episodes to be repeated on air or released on video. The main thing was, after all the trouble of getting a license for a movie, the writers were stuck with having to riff it. This sometimes was a fresh level of pain, since a film that looked good in the early stages would not play well when it came time to write riffs for it. The *Amazing Colossal Episode Guide* makes mention of *Radar Secret Service* (season 5, episode 20) as a good example of this situation, where Kevin Murphy saw the movie and loved it, but the show could not obtain the licensing for it. Finally in a later season, the license became available, and Murphy was excited to start riffing on it, only to discover that he could not remember what he saw in the movie in the first place, making it a chore to get through for the week.

The most notorious situation with being stuck with a movie occurred with the second film of season 2, *The Side Hackers*. This quasi–motorcycle gang exploitation movie features Michael Pataki (probably best remembered as the Klingon in *Star Trek*'s "The Trouble with Tribbles" who thinks the *Enterprise* should be "hauled away as garbage") and Ross Hagan (your choice when Doug McClure or John Ashley is not available) involved in some oddball racing using gimmicked motorcycles with sidecars that allow the drivers to speed around corners faster if weight of a passenger in the sidecar is placed correctly. Up to that point in seasons 1 and 2 of the Comedy Channel era, the writers chose movies by watching the first ten to fifteen minutes of a movie, asking for the license, and then screening it completely after getting the rights to it. After all, why watch a full movie only to find you couldn't get the license to it? As it turns out, about thirty-five minutes into *The Side Hackers*, the protagonist's girlfriend, Rita, is raped and murdered in a lingering flashback scene, throwing off the entire point of making a comedy show about the movie. After much discussion on whether the episode should just be tossed, it was decided to edit out the six-minute-long sequence (with just enough left to imply something terrible happened) and have Crow inform the audience, "For those of you playing at home, Rita is dead," before moving on. After that, it was decided that at least one writer would be assigned to watch a movie in full if it was likely to be used for the show in order to avoid paying for a movie that was going to be nearly impossible to riff for a family audience.

As to writers themselves, it was still Jim, Kevin, Josh, Joel, and Trace, but they felt they needed an "apprentice writer" in the room to help type up their riffs as they watched the movies and to throw in additional gags when they had some. Jim and Kevin were so busy with behind-the-scenes issues pertaining to staging and filming on the new sets that they could not be counted on to be available to watch the movies like the others could. It was at this point that Josh mentioned a guy he knew from the comedy circuit that he thought was "really funny and a smart guy": Mike Nelson.

Michael J. Nelson (October 11, 1964–) was born in St. Charles, Illinois, and moved to Wisconsin when he was twelve. Inclined to play the piano, Mike became a musician while also getting the acting bug after performing in his high school's production of *Brigadoon*. Financial issues led to an early jump-start into the University of Wisconsin–River Falls at the age of sixteen, and while he was an honor student in high school, the need to start college at such a young age left him unsure of what he really wanted to pursue. He left after three years without a degree. After a brief stint in summer theater and performing with a friend in a musical act, Mike ended up in Minneapolis and began trying his luck at stand-up comedy at the Comedy Cabaret, while working as a waiter at a TGIF. His ability to make people laugh got him touring around the area with fellow comedians, as well as running into several members of the *MST3K* cast, who performed at the same clubs every week. This association led to the job offer in September 1989 with Best Brains after Josh recommended him. Since Mike knew how to type, understood the WordPerfect program on the computer that Best Brains had just bought, was a musician who would be working for a series that was increasingly adding songs to the host segments, and was funny, everyone was agreeable to the addition. Nelson was happy as well, for although the money was minimal, it meant a steady paycheck doing comedy, which was perfect, as he was three weeks away from marrying a fellow stand-up from the area, Bridget Jones (September 24, 1964–).

Bridget had been raised in Sauk Rapids, Minnesota, where her father was the mayor and the owner of a nightclub called The Commodore Club, in which he occasionally did some stand-up comedy. Going to the College of St. Thomas in Saint Paul, she graduated with a degree in communication and theater only to find herself working as a buyer at a department store. Hating the retail life, Bridget decided to become a stand-up comic, which was a struggle at first, but she found that she had one element that helped her get gigs that many others didn't: she had a car. "It was unpleasant, but I could be the opening act if I agreed to drive the headliner around for a week. I'd be the opening act, another comedian would be the middle act, and some older, drunker comedian would be the headliner," as Bridget told the Official *MST3K* Info Club Web Site. She would also, like most other members of the *MST3K* writers, perform at "open mic" events, and it was at one being emceed by Frank Conniff in a club called That Comedy Place where she met Mike Nelson for the first time. He impressed her with jokes no one laughed at about poet Robert Frost, and she intrigued him by using the word "pontificate" onstage (which was no doubt annoying to the audience). They began dating and were getting ready for their wedding when Mike was offered the position with Best Brains.

While Mike would soon be working in the facility of Best Brains, Bridget started on the show sometime later in 1990 as a "home writer," which meant watching the movie at home and trying to come up with jokes. "They'd give me a tape of the movie," as Bridget described the job to the Official *MST3K* Info Club Web Site, "and I'd sit at home and write comments with the time codes. I tried to come up with a lot; about three [jokes] a minute. It was interesting doing it that way. When you're looking at it all by yourself, sometimes you're able to see things you wouldn't see if you were with a group in the writing room, while the movie is slowly choking the life out of you." If it sometimes felt painful to Bridget, it would be even worse for Mike who had already spent hours looking at the same movie in the office and then, as Bridget later told *Wired*, "Mike would come home and the movie was still on the VCR, and he'd be like, 'Oh, God—please!'" While Bridget was brought in as a full-time writer on the program and frequent performer, starting in the third season of the series in 1991, the position of "home writer" remained a regular internship for new people on the program over the coming years.

Meanwhile, back at Best Brains, the writers set up a standard schedule to work their way through each movie, with Mike settling into the core group from the KTMA days easily as he began producing material in the writers' room. The process had changed quite a bit from the later part of the KTMA days of looking at a movie on a Thursday and then trying to write a few things before popping in the next day to film everything within a few hours. Instead, the process began in a room where there was a television set up in a corner and chairs and sofas circling it. This was done so that everyone could see as the movie was played, but also for another reason. "I wanted to avoid ever saying no to anybody in the writers' room," Joel told *Wired*. "I knew that would be really bad. And there was no one sitting at a table and pitching jokes—you said your riffs to the TV. That's what allowed us to do them so quickly; it freed up everybody's id." The process did take quite some time, with movies being paused every few seconds for people to throw out gags, and with those pauses to gather all the jokes made and work through taking as long as fifteen minutes each. Ninety minutes' worth of film to get through could take up to a day in the writers' room at Best Brains.

One negative aspect that came with rewatching movies multiple times was familiarity breeding the tendency to want to write gags that referenced things occurring later in the movie. This was spotted by Dan O'Shannon, a writer well-known for his work on shows like *Cheers*, *Frasier*, and later *Modern Family*, after seeing the last episode of the first season, *The Black Scorpion*. O'Shannon contacted the writers to remind them that the characters in the show were supposed to be watching the movie for the first time. Having the characters comment on things to come was a cheat and could be confusing to viewers who didn't know what the jokes were referencing. The writers agreed and after the first season tried to avoid the tendency. The writers also soon begged off from doing jokes where the film would be manipulated for a laugh, such as in *The Robot vs. the Aztec Mummy*, where Joel blocks the mouth of a character and the movie's soundtrack becomes muffled. Mike Nelson in *The Amazing Colossal Episode Guide* pointed out that the gag "broke the rules of the show" and apologized to readers for it happening.

This drawn-out process of riffing the movies minute by minute could be rough for the writers, especially once it got to midafternoon. For one movie, *Untamed Youth*, the writers were so depressed over having to continue the process with the movie that midway through they decided to add a bar to the room with tequila and Mickey's Big Mouth malt liquor. Although it loosened everyone up, they found that it did nothing to add to the productivity and mainly left everyone with hangovers, and a quick decision was made to never do it again.

After this process (the writing, not the drinking), the best jokes from the writers' room and from the "home writers" were typed into the computer with a timecode to keep track of where the jokes would possibly go in the script. The next day, the writers created the host segments for the show. The day after they went through the movie again while looking at jokes already created to pick out the best, refined them, and maybe come up with a few more along the way. Once the lines were pretty much set, they watched the movie again to assign lines to each of the characters, concentrating on giving lines to the characters that best suited them instead of worrying about if everyone had equal amounts of things to say.

The biggest headache in scripting all the riffs came with trying to figure out how to get the material from the mouths of the writers to the pages of the typed script. Professional typists and stenographers were tried, but they had issues keeping track of timecodes and all the references yelled at them by the writers in the room. Over time, and reluctantly, as it was certainly less fun than shouting out lines while sitting on a couch, they found that having one of the writers do the typing worked the best. Even with this system, things would be misunderstood and typed into the script that made little sense to those later reviewing it. Ironically, politeness and unwillingness to look like the clueless kid in class kept people from speaking out when they saw lines that didn't make sense until the last possible moment. "There would be comments in there that would actually end up in the final script," Mike told IGN. "And it would come to a read-through, and finally somebody would speak out and say, 'I don't even know what this means—does anyone know what this means?' You'd ask around the room, and everyone would go, 'No,

Untamed Youth (1957) may have had Mamie Van Doren, but it was a rough movie for the writers at *MST3K*, leading to the first and last open bar while riffing. WARNER BROS. PICTURES / PHOTOFEST ©
WARNER BROS. PICTURES

I don't know what that means. What is it? How did that get there?' and it would be the most bizarre comment, and it had made it all the way through to the script."

A final script was then completed and given to the cast and sent off to HBO, while set, props, and costumes were made for the host segments. The actual filming would sometimes be shuffled around, but typically the movie riffing was done in one block and all the host segments in another. Josh commented in an interview with Ken Plume that during the first season for the Comedy Channel, it was not uncommon for him and Trace to be filming their Deep 13 material last, with the clear understanding that everyone would be itching to get out the door for the weekend. This soon reversed, with the host segments filmed first in a day, where lighting, effects, and whatnots would take more time to do, and then the movie riffing on a second day, where filming was typically much simpler. Early reports stated that the show was usually running on an eight-day schedule to do an episode, which then turned to nine and eventually around season 7, when the look of the show became a touch more sophisticated with its move to the Sci-Fi Channel, it took ten working days to complete an episode. Everything was done by the cast and crew, which was simply part of the mentality of the people living in the area, as Jim Mallon told the *Star Tribune* right before the series was to premiere on the Comedy Channel: "The way we make television here, we make our own props, we clean the carpets, we do everything. In New York City, you get on the phone and raise enough money to pay people to make the props and clean the carpets. That's the difference—we don't talk about it, we just do it."

Filming of the first episode, *The Crawling Eye* (also known as *The Trollenberg Terror)*, and the second, *The Robot vs. the Aztec Mummy*, were completed in the first half of November and sent on to the Comedy Channel. The channel itself began on November 15, with as much fanfare as one could expect for a channel that was seen in a small percentage of the country, since many cable providers were waiting to see how the channel would do before jumping onboard. Because of this, the first sparkling, brand-new episode of *MST3K* to ever be aired nationally was not seen internally in Minneapolis. Instead, the closest area showing the channel was in Bloomington, Minnesota. So that Saturday morning, the cast and crew met at Zack's Bar in Bloomington and watched the show on its large television screen while drinking beer and eating chips and salsa.

Immediate reactions to the channel were mixed, leaning toward negative. Since the focus was on movie clips and those clips were for films HBO was currently showing, the critics naturally dismissed the channel as being nothing more than advertising for HBO broken up by ads. Even the early original programming on the channel got ripped apart, but eventually the mood softened as viewers began to grow comfortable with the hosts. Response around the country about *MST3K* was very slight at first. Bob Langford at the *News and Observer* in Raleigh, North Carolina, was an early defender, speaking out for the show on November 15, 1989, before the first episode even aired, although he could back it up: "Sure it sounds dumb, but I saw this in Minneapolis where [Joel] started it and it's hilarious." Some reviewers were confused as to what the show was to be about when first discussing the channel, referring to the program as being about robots acting like movie critics Gene Siskel and Roger Ebert in reviewing recent science fiction movies. Many, like Susan Wloszczyna for the Gannett News Service, gave it faint praise, calling *MST3K*, "Not exactly cutting edge, but at least it's different. Which is a lot more than you can say about most of the Comedy Channel."

The Comedy Channel was set at a low bar and seemed to just be staying above water in the confusing days of multiple new cable channels popping up. The one thing it did have in its corner was a growing fan base for this little program called *Mystery Science Theater 3000*, and although there would be only thirteen episodes that first season, the Comedy Channel would air the episodes frequently (it also ran the other show Hodgson brought to them, *The Higgins Boys and Gruber*, often, including selected "best of" spots from the week on the weekends, proving Hodgson to be a huge early asset to the channel). *MST3K* was running Saturday mornings and repeated at midnight, with additional airings during the week to help fill out the schedule. The base and the amount of fan mail at Best Brains and Comedy Channel continued to grow, and the people at Best Brains knew it. "We totally believed that we were incredibly hot shit who'd beat the system and knew how to do show business better than anyone else," Weinstein reflected to *Wired*. "They like to aw-shucks-it, language-wise, but I mean, Christ—the company was called Best Brains!"

But the season would be over in mid-February 1990, and the Comedy Channel was struggling. The anticipation of the new HA! Channel had many people in the country thinking the two channels were one and the same. Even *The Amazing Colossal Episode Guide* mentions that the trip to Bloomington to see the first episode at Zack's ended with someone asking them where to find the show, only to assume that the cast was mistaken in thinking there was a channel called the Comedy Channel, since HA! was the comedy channel, right?

In fact, HA! wasn't to start until April 1, 1990, but even so it was clear that the Comedy Channel knew it had competition just around the corner in an environment that hadn't seen cable providers stampeding to add the Comedy Channel to their line-up. The reviews for the channel were mixed at best, and while the network had an option to pick up *MST3K*, the problem was that they weren't sure if they would even make it long enough to tell Best Brains to do a second season. "Measuring success on our channel is complicated," John Newton told *Corporate Report Minnesota*. "We operate on the basis of subscribers, not individual show ratings. But I can tell you,

[*MST3K* has] gotten more attention than anything on our channel, or the competition." While it was looking good for a renewal, all they could do at Best Brains was sit tight and wait it out. Fortunately, by June, the word had come that the Comedy Channel had agreed to a new season. Unfortunately for Best Brains, they would be one man short.

6

The Circus of Dr. Lao

The Joel—Trace—Frank Years

Dr. Erhardt! So that's what happened to him!

—Joel pointing out an ill-fated character who
looks like Dr. Erhardt a year and a half after his
disappearance and who is about to be eaten by a giant
spider in *Earth vs. the Spider* (season 3, episode 13)

It was not all smooth sailing in the first year of the show at the newly created Best Brains. Establishing the production company, building sets, writing, and filming episodes—all these elements were hard enough for a small group, even with the additional help of people like Alex Carr, Clayton James, and Faye Burkholder moving over from KTMA to continue to work on the show. Nearly everyone had two jobs and sometimes three, especially the men writing the show. Kevin was doing the lighting and editing on the show; Trace, who also had duties as art director, and Joel were involved with set designs; while Jim was responsible for the business end of the company.

At the top of that work chain were Mallon and Hodgson, and the stress of being the ones who made the final decisions only added to the workload. "We worked seven days a week, 12 hours a day to build sets, design robots, write the shows in the beginning," Hodgson told *Corporate Report Minnesota*. "We went six weeks at the start without a paycheck." Mallon agreed that the stress was digging at those working there: "Everyone was working their butts off, but somebody would leave to go to do their laundry or something perfectly understandable, and the rest of us would look at him like it was a betrayal." It began to reach a point where meetings descended into Mallon and Hodgson having confrontations over decisions and duties, leading to things not getting done. Eventually the two started joint therapy to try to work out their issues, where it was decided that the company really needed structure, with designated job descriptions and regular nine-to-five hours instead of the manic pace they set for everyone that was quickly becoming a major source for burnout among the cast and crew. Weekly lunches with just Joel and Jim alone to discuss things helped as well, and eventually the edge started to taper off between them. "Ultimately," Hodgson went on to explain in the article, "our notions of where the company should go were exactly the same."

Not that they were the only ones dealing with tension at Best Brains. Josh had entered the first season at the Comedy Channel, knowing quite well that the show had been started with five members—Jim, Joel, Kevin, Trace, and himself—but he had been left without a share in Best Brains. There were rumors that the others felt that Josh, at seventeen, was too young to be a partner, but even if that was the case, there could have been allowances made to keep him involved with the business side or to at least partake of some type of profit sharing. Instead, the other four would meet to discuss the course of the production company without him and to Josh. "It became hostile," he told Ken Plume years later, "and I don't think I handled the hostility particularly well." In later years, Weinstein has reflected that some of the issue may have been due to him being at least ten years younger than the others and not feeling the weight of *MST3K* as a make-or-break point like the others did for their careers in that first year with the Comedy Channel. Yet having earned his stripes previously as a confident stand-up comedian and a writer-performer for over a year with the program, to be pushed aside as nothing more than an intern who "should be happy to be here"—which is how Josh said Mallon referred to him when arguing over how he was being treated—was demeaning.

In reaction to this, Josh because combative on the set and in the writers' room at Best Brains, feeling he needed to act in such a manner to get his point of view across but only further shutting down communication with the others. The moment that sealed the deal, however, was an incident where Mallon had gone to Weinstein and Nelson's office at Best Brains to use their Mac computer. According to Weinstein in his Plume interview, Mallon completed his work and then left, only to accidentally leave behind a list on Josh's desk showing everyone's salaries. Although not his business, Josh couldn't help but look at it to see that he—a writer-performer on the show who had been there since day one—was getting paid less than the secretary they had recently hired. Confronting Mallon, the two squared off, and Mallon essentially told Weinstein that if he wanted to quit, he could. Committed to finish up his contract and for the sake of the show, Weinstein stayed on to finish the season, but the situation burned bridges for Weinstein at the production company. When the thirteen episodes were done, he left Best Brains and went back to doing stand-up full time for several months in the Minneapolis area before finally moving on to Los Angeles to seek work as a writer and stand-up. This turned out to be a positive move, as he soon found success out in Hollywood, but more about that in chapter 9.

Josh's departure was agreed by everyone at Best Brains to be handled as delicately as possible to not worry fans or the higher-ups at the Comedy Channel. In hindsight, this was handled perhaps too delicately. Weinstein's exit from the program was only indirectly mentioned in the spring 1990 issue of the official newsletter, *MST3K Satellite News*, where it was stated the Comedy Channel had finished negotiations with Best Brains in June 1990 (and yes, that means, the "spring" 1990 issue of the newsletter was late, but that wasn't unusual) for a new season of thirteen episodes that would start filming in "late August or early September." Further news in the article also mentioned Jeff Maynard joining the staff as "shop foreman and building guy," while "our technical/comedic wizard Kevin Murphy will handle the part of Tom Servo," and "comedian Frank Conniff will be writing for the show as well as playing the part of Dr. Laurence Erhardt, the evil mad scientist from Gizmonic Institute." Nowhere was a mention that Josh Weinstein had left the show, although it was clear his characters were being handed to other people.

The surprising idea of Conniff coming in to replace Weinstein in the same role of Erhardt may be seen as a misprint in the newsletter, but the subsequent newsletter, for summer 1990, had an article on its front page that advertised the second season by mentioning that "Clayton Forester and Lawrence Earhardt [sic]" will soon be perpetuating more evil experiments on Joel, Crow, Tom Servo, and Gypsy. If such plans were seriously considered, they were gone by the beginning of September, when the Comedy Channel began preparing for the new season by announcing a "*Mystery Science Theater 3000* Marathon," on September 2 (the Sunday before Labor Day). As reporter Chris Cornell from the *Philadelphia Inquirer* stated from a press release about the marathon, "A new actor, Frank Conniff, has been hired to play a different mad scientist (Weinstein's character will be written out of the show), and one of the writers, Kevin Murphy, will provide the newly altered voice of Servo." This was all fine and good, but then Cornell goes on to state that "Josh Weinstein, who played one of the evil scientists and supplied the voice of Tom Servo, has left. The producers won't give any details, but it appears to be a case of 'creative differences.'"

And it was this tendency to write off his exit as "creative differences" that obtained a continuing assumption that Weinstein left because he only wanted to improvise and not have to follow a script on the program. Admittedly,

Weinstein did enjoy the early improvised atmosphere of the KTMA season, as he told the *Mystery Science Theater 3000* Review site in 2007, although he saw the downside as well: "It was definitely more fun to improvise—primarily because it meant watching a really crappy movie once instead of six or seven times. Less work, more fun. However, just like all improv, it's more fun to be the one doing it than it is to watch it." Looking at the history of the program, it was clear that everyone including Weinstein knew the show was better with prepared material. Nevertheless, the legend of his departure being solely about Weinstein as somehow being lazy and not wanting to work from a script has prevailed to this day, even though "it was total bullshit," as Weinstein said to Plume. It also seemed ironic such a notion would exist, considering his long career as a scriptwriter after leaving the show. But since everyone at Best Brains had agreed that they would treat his departure from the show as agreeable by all, Weinstein felt he shouldn't rock the boat any further and for the time let it go.

With Weinstein leaving, it was decided to bring in another writer, and it wasn't long before Mike Nelson mentioned Frank Conniff as a possibility. No one objected, as everyone knew of Frank, and most of them had worked with him. Frank Conniff Jr. (August 30, 1956–) was born in New York City and grew up in Manhattan, the son of Pulitzer Prize–winning journalist Frank Conniff (1914–1971). With his father being an author, Frank naturally found himself leaning toward a career in writing himself, although his preference was to work in television. Quitting high school, Frank attempted to begin a career as a stand-up comedian, which went well enough to show he had strong potential, but a dependency on alcohol and drugs stymied his plans in New York. After a family intervention, Frank agreed to go to Minneapolis and enter a drug rehab treatment program there, since Minnesota was well-known at the time for their rehab community. ("Come for treatment, meet the Vikings," was Frank's slogan for the city in his stand-up act, where he talked about his reasons for being in the city.)

The decision was positive for both his health and career, as he came to Minneapolis in 1985 just as the big comedy splurge was beginning in the clubs around the city. After a time, Frank felt confident enough in his treatment to begin working the clubs, first at the Ha Ha Club due to its non-alcoholic policy, but eventually he moved on to other clubs. His performance history soon found him in a niche as either an emcee (which led to him doing open mic nights, where he was introduced to both Mike and Bridget) or as a middle act between an opener and header. Both spots were beneficial as they usually provided enough time, typically a half hour, to work through a proper set without rushing, and the crowd was neither too drunk nor worn-out to appreciate the act.

Over several years, Conniff worked onstage with practically everyone from *MST3K*. He had also become friends with Bridget and Mike to the point that the pair had made sure to put in jokes in *MST3K* that they knew only Frank and a couple of other friends would get. With his reputation in town, it was easy for the others to sign on to the idea of bringing Frank in as a writer for the series. After a stand-up show out in North Dakota, Frank got a call in his hotel room from Mike, asking if he would like to join the program for its second season on the Comedy Channel. "That was a moment of just being on the road doing stand-up comedy and then being told on the phone that I was getting this great opportunity," Frank told Plume in an interview from 2007. "I've had only two or three moments like that since then."

Frank was brought in but found that the first month of work on the show involved doing no writing at all. Instead, it was building sets for the second season, for which Frank had no prior experience, and even an attempt to help by buying wood resulted with Mike and Frank delivering the wrong kind. "I remember Joel looking at me and going, 'We sent a boy to do a man's job.'" For a time, he worried he would be fired for not being able to use a hammer, but things soon settled down once the building was completed and the writers—mainly Joel, Mike, Trace, and Frank, as "Jim and Kevin were always really busy with all the other stuff they had to do [that season]"—moved back into the writers' room to work on movies for the second season.

From learning quickly that everyone involved typically ended up acting on the show at some point, Frank knew that he would probably be performing in the new season, but he was not quite sure how he would be incorporated into the program. It was only as they got closer to recording the first episode that there was a natural assumption Frank would be playing the new mad scientist alongside Dr. Forrester on camera, although there was never much talk beforehand about him agreeing to it. Even though it was pretty much a done deal, Frank still had to test for the role and found himself being jammed into Weinstein's scientist suit from the first season, as Frank remembered in the Museum of Broadcasting interview, a costume that could not be washed due to how it was made for the show. After the tryout, his dark costume, based much on that of Josh's outfit, became the norm for his tenure in the series. Frank also volunteered to take on the role of watching the movies selected in full after *The Side Hackers* incident mentioned in chapter 5, since nearly everyone else on the show had multiple duties while he stuck with writing and performing and had more free time. As he would commonly point out in interviews about the assignment, it amused him that he had grown up being told that he wouldn't be able to make money sitting around watching television, only to end up in a job where he got to do exactly that.

As to Kevin Murphy taking on Tom Servo's voice, it was a simple case of him asking Joel and Jim if he could do it. With a good voice, an established track record of being on camera with KTMA, and already being paid to be on staff, there was no reason not to give him the additional role. Thus the stage was set for the new season of the program, with some slight adjustments to the opening credits in order to showcase Frank, along with some snippets from the new season (such as Joel's invention exchange from the first episode of the new season). There was even a whimsical reminder to "keep in mind it's just a show," by having Dr. Forrester and Frank pop up at the bottom of the screen to sing backing vocals after the Satellite of Love floats by in space.

The new season began airing on September 22, 1990, with *Rocketship X-M*. Tom Servo's new voice is explained as an upgrade in an opening skit very reminiscent of the upgrade he received back in the KTMA season to allow Josh to adjust the character's voice. In the opening skit, Frank appears for the first time, and it seems he is working in Deep 13 as a fast-food worker, ready to take Joel's and the bots' orders. It turns out that Dr. Forrester had hired Frank from an Arby's.

As for Erhardt? It is only reported that he is "missing," and a milk carton with his picture is shown on camera. As the quote at the beginning of this chapter points out, in the episode for *Earth vs. the Spider*, a character is trapped and killed by the giant spider who looks remarkably like Josh Weinstein in character as Erhardt; thus, making it appear that perhaps he got tragically caught in an experiment himself. Yet the newer *MST3K* seasons that began over on Netflix in 2017 established that Dr. Erhardt is still alive, and the *Earth vs. the Spider* gag was simply that—a gag and nothing more sinister (. . . unless that Dr. Erhardt is from Earth-KTMA and. . . . What? Okay, I'll get on with it). While Erhardt has some impulsive, kidlike moments, Frank seems somewhat scatterbrained and slow on the uptake, even nearly bringing Joel and the bots back down to Earth in his first episode before Dr. Forrester stops him. His next achievement in the same episode of completely ripping off Joel's invention in the invention exchange led to a punishment from Dr. Forrester, and their "loving" relationship was pretty much set into place for the next few years. As for the references to "TV's Frank" that developed over time, it had no meaning beyond being a joke based on how certain television celebrities would always be referred to as "TV's so-and-so."

The first season on the Comedy Channel went well enough for the network to continue the program, but it was the second season where all the elements began to really come together to make for a strong two hours of comedy. Some early fan favorites also came out of the second Comedy Channel year, starting with *Rocketship X-M* and continuing with others like *Catalina Caper* and *Lost Continent*, and even the grungy depths of three biker movies, including the notorious *The Side Hackers*, couldn't spoil the fun. The difference between the two seasons was felt to be so vast that, as mentioned on the Official *MST3K* Info Club Web Site, later in 1991 Best Brains requested that the network no longer repeat episodes from the first Comedy Channel season, due to "poorer quality," different look, and "different performers." Jim Mallon's rationale for doing so was that showing the first season Comedy Channel episodes diminished the newer ones: "It's like if someone wanted to judge you based on the work you did in kindergarten."

They never could get *Mars Needs Women*, but they did get the Tommy Kirk–starring *Catalina Caper* (1967), with Lyle Waggoner (and, no, he's not showing off the implant). CROWN INTERNATIONAL PICTURES / PHOTOFEST © CROWN INTERNATIONAL PICTURES

There was also a strong injection of music added to the series, and while the earlier seasons had some musical moments, such as Joel pulling out a guitar to sing part of the theme song in episode 18 at KTMA, it was clear that between Kevin Murphy's fine singing voice and Mike Nelson's strong musical background (as well as contributions from everyone else), music would become an integral part of the show. Many episodes were known for having at least one musical interlude, and season 2 has several songs well remembered by fans, including "Only Love Pads the Film" (*The Side Hackers*), "My Creepy Girl" (*Catalina Caper*), and "If Chauffeurs Ruled the World" (*Ring of Terror*). The sheer volume of songs created for the show led to two volumes of music being released on CD and vinyl: *Clowns in the Sky: The Musical History of Mystery Science Theater 3000* in 1996 and *Clowns in the Sky II* in 1998. The two volumes were reissued as one two-disc CD or vinyl set called *the Complete Clowns in the Sky* in 2019, and a look at the credits shows that after the various versions of the theme song (credited to Joel and Charlie Erikson), Mike Nelson's name is credited for nearly every song, typically with help from another member of the cast and crew.

As the second season began to play out on national television, critics were beginning to point to the program (along with standouts like *Night after Night with Allan Havey*) as worth actively seeking out. Keith Olbermann, in his regular column for the *Los Angeles Times* on December 17, 1990—an article explaining why the Comedy Channel was much more worth checking out than the tepid reruns on HA!—told readers, "Wrapped in the guise of a kids' show, *MST3000* contains some of the hippest, deepest satire of the generation." Recognition of the show was beginning to appear in magazines as fan mail increased, showing clear signs to HBO that the show was one of the biggest and perhaps only success from the channel in the first two years. Other shows had their followers and a certain cult status, but *MST3K* was beginning to cross over into the general public's radar. It was even listed in *Time* magazine's "Top Ten Best Television Shows" of 1990 (alongside *Twin Peaks*, *In Living Color*, and *Maniac Mansion*) and as "Best of Tube" in *People* magazine the same year. "We all went to the mall for lunch," Trace Beaulieu told *Wired*, "so we went and bought a copy of the magazine and read it as we were eating our pink gravy from the Chinese restaurant. We went, 'Oh, that's really cool. Other people are watching it. I guess we'll go back to work now.'"

During the show's rise in popularity came the news that the fight between the Comedy Channel and HA! had come to a rather limp end, with both companies finding that they could pool their programming and at least lose money together rather than separately. After close to a year and a half, the Comedy Channel would be renamed, on April 1, 1991 (a year after HA! was started), as CTV: The Comedy Network. This lasted for two months before it was required to change its name due to there already being a CTV, a Canadian network. To avoid confusion and possible legal hassle, the network changed the name a final time to Comedy Central on June 1, 1991, which coincided with the premiere of the third season of *MST3K*, starting with the classic riff of *Cave Dwellers*.

With that changeover came negotiations of what would stay and what would go for the various programs airing on the merged network. This wasn't that hard, as old sitcoms still made up most of the HA! schedule, and while a number of these would pop up for a time on the new Comedy Central, especially the more cult-remembered ones like *Quark*, *Captain Nice*, and even *Camp Runamuck*, Comedy Channel's schedule dominated the new network, with *MST3K* surviving the cull. As it turns out, it ended up even being part of the negotiation between Viacom and Time Warner, the owner of HBO, as Time Warner was looking to sign Best Brains to produce the show for HBO rather than for the new channel, but such negotiations were dropped when it was deemed to not be in the spirit of the merger.

Cave Dwellers (1984) was an early example of a star letting Best Brains know that he liked the riffed movie, with Miles O'Keefe inviting the cast to come to his house if ever in the area. NEW LINE CINEMA / PHOTOFEST © NEW LINE CINEMA

Comedy Central opened with the combined viewership of both the Comedy Channel and HA!—a total of 12.5 million subscribers in the spring of 1991—and was happy to have *MST3K* as its cornerstone. Comedy Central struck a new deal with Best Brains: the show would produce twenty-four episodes for the next season, at a projected license fee of $50,000 (some sources say $40,000) per episode. The network was so keen on keeping the series that the order for *MST3K* was for three seasons of twenty-four episodes each. It was a huge weight off everyone's shoulders at the production company. "That was sweet," Mike Nelson reported to IGN, "there's no doubt about it. Nobody gets that long a contract. I mean, that era is over completely—unless you're *Friends*, or something. It was cable, and I think the show was cheap and filled a lot of time." With the news of *MST3K* expanding to more episodes came excitement as to what could next be produced by the production company. "If you talk to me a year from now, I hope we have another show in production," Mallon told *Corporate Report Minnesota* in April 1991, after the announcement of the contract with Comedy Central had been made public. "We want to give people like Trace Beaulieu a chance to do their own projects. Now we've got the experience and the track record to make it happen." There was also talk of a spin-off Joel was putting together called *Robotropolis*, which would feature Crow, Servo, and other robot puppets created by Joel interviewing famous people "about what it's like to be a human being," and "exploring the relationship between man and robot and the level of sophistication that robots will achieve in this decade," as Hodgson told Dave Matheny in 1990.

For the moment, however, the concern was getting the next season under way. With the additional funds, more could be done on the program, including hiring new writers. As mentioned, Bridget Jones Nelson would eventually emerge from home to start partaking of the writers' room with everyone. With more technical people added behind the camera, Kevin Murphy was able to join back in on the writing, while fellow stand-up comic Paul Schersten, who went by the stage name of Paul Chaplin, was also hired. Chaplin was born in 1955 and raised around the Chicago area, eventually getting his master's from the Humphrey Institute of Public Affairs. Working as a community organizer in Saint Paul, Minnesota, he began doing stand-up during open-mic nights at the Comedy Gallery. According to Paul, in an interview with the Official *MST3K* Info Club Web Site, "Joel once told me that he and Mike were intrigued by me because they saw me host an open stage that was horrendous from start to finish. Joel said he admired how I never gave up." Having gotten to know Mike Nelson a bit, he was surprised when one day Mike came up and asked him about working at Best Brains, "using the same tone of voice as someone saying, 'I'd like to talk to you about your insurance needs.'"

By this time, Michael had been made head writer, so he was directly involved with hiring new writers. According to Nelson, when talking to IGN back in 2003, his duties as head writer pertained mainly to coordinating the others as they moved through the movie and "being the final arbiter of 'if half of the room likes this joke, half of the room likes the other one'" when there were differences about using a riff. Nelson found that the biggest arguments usually pertained to questions as to how dark or adult they wanted to get with the gags, since they knew families watched with their kids.

When Chaplin joined, he became one of the first recipients of the proper tryout process for new writers after the immediate hiring of Frank Conniff. It was quite similar to what Bridget had gone through as a "home writer," only the person would have to go home with a tape and write material or the first ten minutes of a movie (in Chaplin's case, it was for *Daddy-O*, which was the seventh episode in season 3). At one point, Joel wanted each potential writer to fill out a questionnaire that he had prepared, which Mike tried to dissuade him from doing. "He wanted the process to be a little Joel-ish and goofy, and I remember kind of fighting him on that, 'Not everyone has your goofy world view—they just want to get the job. Let's make it straightforward.'"

Once the sample was done, the prepared script was then sent around to all the other writers to "sign off," making it rough for all involved, but Chaplin was quickly accepted. Naturally, part of the reason was that his material was funny, but he also found out they needed another writer because they planned to branch out, as he remembered to the Official *MST3K* Info Club Web Site: "When I was first hired in 1991, I was told it was because they were soon to be working on a movie and they needed writers to work on the TV show. So then the movie happened almost right away, four years later, and we all worked on it."

Will he be so sleepy he can barely keep his eyes open? You'll gasp as Hercules naps in *Hercules* (1958), the first of several Hercules movies to play on *MST3K*. EMBASSY / PHOTOFEST © EMBASSY

Besides Chaplin, other writers came in that would contribute for various periods of time on the program, such as John Carney, a magician who was a friend of Joel's, who worked on two movies early in the fourth season, *City Limits* and *The Giant Gila Monster*, before moving on (he would later pop up on Joel's post-*MST3K* 1995 pilot, *The TV Wheel*). Colleen Henjum-Williams, a comedian and musician who was a friend of Frank's, would be a longtime contributor between seasons 3 and 5, starting on the second episode of the third season, *Gamera*. David Sussman also worked on a few episodes, mainly in season 5. The other main success story of this period besides Chaplin came in season 4, when Mary Jo Pehl was added as a writer, although she, too, worked for a time as a "home writer" before becoming part of the team.

Mary Jo Pehl (February 27, 1960–) was born and raised in Circle Pines, Minnesota, where her father was mayor for a time. Pehl grew up leaning toward a career in nursing and pursued it into her twenties, when she realized it was not the job she really wanted. Instead, she decided to become a stand-up and began working at various open mics in 1987, leading to her falling into the same circle of comics that included Frank, Bridget, Mike, Trace, Josh, and Paul. In Mary Jo's case, she was not sought out by anyone from the cast; instead, she heard that *MST3K* was hiring writers and called up Mike, asking if she could apply even though she did not own a television set and knew nothing about the program. "I was intrigued because I'd been doing standup comedy on the road for several years and I was really quite ready to not be doing road gigs," Pehl told Austin.com in 2013.

Given the "home writer" test, she was invited to write a portion for the program at the beginning of the fourth season. As mentioned in *The Amazing Colossal Episode Guide*, her first riff occurred in *Teenagers from Outer Space* (season 4, episode 4), where "they invited me in on a trial basis, and honestly, I think they forgot that I was there on a trial basis." Thinking she had failed after two weeks and with no mention of a job offer, she walked through the offices thanking everyone before heading for the door. "I clearly remember each of them in turn—Mike, Joel, Kevin, and Trace—looking at me blankly as if they'd forgotten it was just a trial period," Mary Jo told the *Mystery Science Theater 3000* Review website in 2007. "There was a quick meeting and they let me stay for another two weeks." Mary Jo, Paul, and Bridget all found their way into the show in character roles soon after starting as well. "We were always very much 'in house,' and pretty laid back and it was usually the path of least resistance," Pehl told Austin.com. "So we'd write a part in the host segments, and it'd always be someone already on staff or maybe a friend of ours." While Bridget and Paul ended up playing minor roles through various series, Pehl ended up getting the most exposure in front of the camera.

As newer writers on the program, and not needed in front of or behind the camera, Mary Jo and Paul usually found themselves paired off to review the lines scripted for the movie-riffing portion of the show to make sure they ran well, while Paul also helped rehearse with Joel for the host segments. Yet there was always the talk that the "junior writers" would be needed to do more on the television show, since the writers who had been there longer would soon be busy with a bigger project now that the show was in a safe period of a three-year contract with the network.

And Comedy Central was definitely feeling the love for its flagship series *MST3K*, with multiple airings in the regular weekly schedule and even a thirty-hour-long Thanksgiving marathon in November 1991. Fans (who recognized that Thanksgiving was also the anniversary of the show starting at KTMA) lovingly refer to such annual marathons as "Turkey Day," with the first such marathon featuring intros for each episode that contained a wraparound story line, where Dr. Forrester looked to dominate the world by way of the marathon while Frank attempted to set up a holiday feast. The marathon also gave way to a tradition of bringing back minor characters that had popped up in Deep 13 over the previous season, such as Plant-Guy (from *The Amazing Colossal Man* episode), played by Kevin, and Mike as Jack Perkins (from *Fugitive Alien*; Perkins was a reporter who became best known as the host of *Biography*, a series on the A&E channel). The first marathon would be followed up with a similar thirty-hour marathon in November 1992 and a short documentary, *This Is* MST3K, narrated by Penn Jillette, and offering comments from various fans, such as Dan O'Shannon and Neil Patrick Harris.

As the fourth season started in June 1992, the group was busy getting ready for a different type of venture when it set up a live show at the Uptown Theatre in Minneapolis the weekend of July 10. The live show featured Joel, the bots, Forrester, and Frank, with a live riff of the movie *World without End* (1956), costarring Rod Taylor in an early role. The movie would never be used in the series itself, although elements of its story line—present-day people being rocketed into a dangerous future—would be used in several other films, including *The Time Travelers* (1964, and riffed in season 11; and it didn't hurt that such a plot point was used by the astronauts in *The Planet of the Apes*, but let's get back to *MST3K* here). The show included breaks in the movie, with the cast singing various songs from the show and a cover of Lou Reed's "Satellite of Love." The production was an experiment by Best Brains to see if the show could be put on live, and while the two shows did well at the theater, the concept of a tour would have to wait a few more years. (For those curious, Joel explained, in character, for the *Star Tribune* that Dr. Forrester allowed them to come to Earth to do the show but only if they wore "stun collars" so they couldn't escape.)

It also played toward the idea of expansion that led to the idea of trying to make a theatrical version of the series, like how *Star Trek* and a handful of other television shows were able to branch off into the theaters. To some it seemed like the natural next step for the program. "The more people we had in the room, the funnier it got," Mallon told the *Star Tribune* in 1995. "So, where can you find a lot of people in a room? Hmmm. A movie theater!" Even so, there was still a lot of work in front of them to get such a project off the ground; Best Brains may have had the copyright free and clear from Comedy Central, but it also meant that there was no studio automatically behind such a movie either.

Hodgson initially went to Casey Silver, who had helped get movies like *Beverly Hills Cop* and *Top Gun* made at Paramount, with the aim of using the movie *When Worlds Collide* (which, Trace Beaulieu admitted to Adam Carston in a 2021 article, "would have been terrific but almost too good"). Joel, who was as interested in pursuing the idea as everyone else at the time, explained the initial concept of the movie in an A.V. Club article from 2021, which had Forrester and Frank at a mad scientist convention in Las Vegas trying to get people to come to their booth to see their experiment about a guy "up in space and we make him watch bad movies," to the disinterest of everyone attending. The movie would end with an exciting segment where the SOL is about to crash into Vegas, only to be saved by a giant monster who catches the SOL "like a Hail Mary pass in football," saving everyone on the SOL before throwing it back out into orbit with Joel and the bots still aboard (thus keeping the concept of the show intact). The first take on the project was to be more about the characters and less about the movie riffing, but that soon changed. As Frank Conniff told Adam Carston, "I think it was a mutual decision of the studio and Best Brains [to say], 'It's going to be mostly the movie riffing but with host segments, just like the TV show.'" At one point in discussion with Paramount, there were even talks of turning the movie into an "origins" story about how Joel ended up in space and created the robots (essentially a ninety-minute version of the theme song), but talks finally broke off after the studio reps insisted that they could replace cast members if they felt it wasn't going well.

The project followed an ongoing pattern with Paramount: some interest from the studio, a buildup of support leading to work on the plot and scripting, and then everything falling apart over a detail here or there. There was even talk of going directly to the fans to raise money for an independent movie, but Mallon decided the risk of being able to concentrate on a fundraiser when they needed to worry about another season of the show made little sense. With the shifting placement of the project inside Best Brains, along with the show barreling onward toward a fifth season, the tension between Jim Mallon and Joel Hodgson increased. With Mallon's suggestion that he direct the movie, which seemed like a logical progression for someone within the team who had already directed a feature film, even if it was *Blood Hook*, things blew up. As Hodgson told *Wired* after discussing the making of a movie, "Jim said, 'OK, well, I'm the producer and I'm the director.' And I just felt like that didn't acknowledge my position. I'm like, I created this. Where's my acknowledgment?" Feeling it was a power grab by Mallon, Hodgson told him, "If you direct this, I'm leaving."

"I wasn't saying I should direct the movie," Joel would tell Ain't It Cool News several years later, "because I didn't want to do that, but it really wasn't Jim's thing. That became a fight that . . . if it was to run its course, it would wreck the show. I didn't think Jim and I were going to resolve that, so that's why I left." The idea of Joel moving on in some capacity was not unexpected for the people at Best Brains, who could tell Joel was itching to start new projects, but seeing him abruptly announcing his departure was surprising. "He and Jim just had their differences, and you'd get inklings of it," Mike told IGN. "He had talked about wanting to create other shows, and there really wasn't any time to do it while you're doing *Mystery Science*, you know? It was kind of assumed, 'Well, he'll probably be moving on at some point.'" Mallon explained his position to the Official *MST3K* Info Club Web Site: "My memory is that Joel got frustrated with aspects of the evolution [of the show], and he decided to preserve what he termed his 'creative ecology' by leaving the series."

Joel's departure also sidetracked a possible outside project for Best Brains offered to them by musician Frank Zappa. In late 1992/early 1993, Kevin Murphy received a call from Wallis Nicita, a producer and casting director at Warner Brothers (*Mermaids, The Butcher's Wife, Six Days Seven Nights*), who told him that "Frank Zappa has this script, and he has watched you guys and he thinks you're out of your gourds, and he'd like you to consider developing it into a movie." Murphy's response was to blow her off with the request that Zappa himself call if he wanted to do something with Best Brains. A half hour later, Zappa did exactly that, leading to a mutual-admiration conversation between Murphy and Zappa (Murphy mentioning hearing *Freak Out!* as a kid and thinking it was "so fucking weird," while Frank had turned on *Fire Maidens from Outer Space* just as Timmy turned Joel into a clown roasting

Servo over a fire and thought, "You guys were too fucking weird for words"). Zappa's idea went back to an earlier project he had put together in 1972, which was a two-act play called *Hunchentoot* that, as was described by Murphy to Plume, "was going to sort of be *The Queen of Outer Space*—you know, the spider lives in a cave on the moon—except told from the spider's point of view." Zappa thought they could do a soundtrack for the music and dialogue and then have the created characters lip-synch. Murphy told him that they would like to consider it, but things occurring within the company made it "nothing that we can move on right away." While Nicita tried to push Best Brains to consider it, "We, sadly, had to sort of walk away from it because at the time, we didn't know where we were going, much less trying to develop a script for Frank Zappa." Zappa would be dead within a year, and the following January would see *MST3K* pay tribute to the musician with an end card dedicated to him at the end of the *Village of the Giants* episode (season 5, episode 23), which included the song "The Greatest Frank of All."

Joel's leaving was at first handled under the radar to not upset fans or ruin chances for the series at Comedy Central. As the fifth season was being prepared, it was decided that Joel would do the first x number of episodes to ease things in and then have a new host brought in for the series. To do that, auditions were held. "They were mostly friends of Joel and professional acquaintances," Mike told IGN. "There's a local actor, Kevin Kling, who's very big in the local theater scene—great guy, really funny. He tried out. There was, I think, a few actors from L.A." Meanwhile, the writers were wondering why Mike Nelson wasn't being put up for the role, since he was not only familiar to everyone but had appeared plenty of time on the program, could sing, and had shown he could act. It was also more comfortable to have him rather than a new face. Nelson finally was asked to audition with Trace and Kevin as the bots; soon after he was offered the job, and he immediately agreed. "I think without me even thinking much about it, it

Mitchell (1975) would be the start of a lovefest for Joe Don Baker on *MST3K* and also mark Joel's farewell from the series. ALLIED ARTISTS PICTURES / PHOTOFEST © ALLIED ARTISTS PICTURES

was just like, 'Well, I've always been an actor and a comedian—sure.' I don't even know if I put much thought into it." With Nelson in place to take over, the production company went to work on preparing the fifth season of the show, with Nelson's character to be introduced in Joel's final episode, *Mitchell* (season 5, episode 12).

On May 11, 1993, a little more than two months before season 5 was to begin, Best Brains sent out a press release announcing Joel's departure. The reason given in the press release was that he wanted "to become a behind-the-camera guy. I want to get on to the next weird show. I want to be an idea man." Yet along with those gentle thoughts, Joel did manage to throw in a slight touch of snark as well, saying, "Besides, there's an old show business adage I once heard Adam West say: 'Stay in the same costume and before you know it, you end up signing pictures at an RV show.'" *Mystery Science Theater 3000* was announced in April that year as having won the prestigious Peabody Award, awarded for excellent and enlightened American programming, but Joel did not attend the ceremonies in May. Instead, the award was picked up by Mallon, Murphy, Beaulieu, and Nelson, with Mallon introducing Nelson as the new host of the show, and Tom Servo got the last word by thanking the committee for making the award out of chocolate.

On October 23, 1993, Comedy Central aired Joel's final episode of the original series. In it, Dr. Forrester and Frank have hired a temp named Mike Nelson—using his real name like the old Joel Hodgson character of the KTMA season—whom they decide to eliminate after he finishes his work. On the SOL, and in a parody of HAL listening in on others in *2001*, Gypsy accidentally overhears their plans and assumes they mean to kill Joel. Without Joel's knowledge, Gypsy and Mike transport Joel to an escape pod that had been hidden onboard in a box of Hamdingers (a food product out of Cudahy, Wisconsin, in the 1970s that was sliced pieces of ham fitted to a round can, which could be cooked and eaten like hamburgers). Unable to get back to the ship after being ejected, Joel sends a final goodbye to everyone and leaves the bots with a plaque that spells out the simple moral of the movie *The Seven Faces of Dr. Lao*, which no doubt was not much further from Joel's true philosophy all along: "Every time you watch a rainbow and feel wonder in your heart. Every time you pick up a handful of dust, and see not the dust, but a mystery, a marvel, there in your hand. Every time you stop and think, 'I'm alive, and being alive is fantastic.' Every time such a thing happens, you're part of the Circus of Dr. Lao."

Appreciative stuff for those watching, but not so much for the bots, who freak out over the idea of being without someone like Joel looking over them. Back in Deep 13, Forrester is upset that his test subject for the past several years has managed to safely land in the Australian outback. But before he can punish Frank for unwittingly helping in Joel's escape, Mike asks for his timecard to be signed, and the scientists—well, at least Dr. Forrester—realizes who will be the next test subject for the experiment.

In the episode that aired the following weekend, they used a new version of the theme song, new clips in the opening credits, and, of course, a new host for the bots to annoy. Joel was now gone from his own creation, and he would strive to move past the program that had kept him busy for the past five years, although he found the show hanging over him as he tried to create a new one. As for *MST3K*, the calm of the three-year contract with Comedy Central was coming to an end, and with growing requests for changes in the show as Comedy Central morphed from its "G-rated but with an edge" beginning, as well as promises of a theatrical movie for the show, *MST3K* was about to hit turbulent waters.

7

I'm the God!

The Mike—Trace—Frank Years and MST3K: The Movie

You know, guys, the whole situation of being stuck up here in space, forced to watch cheesy movies, interacting with other life-forms . . . it kinda bites.

—MIKE, IN HIS PREMIERE EPISODE, *THE BRAIN THAT WOULDN'T DIE* (SEASON 5, EPISODE 13)

Mike Nelson slid into the role of host in the next episode of the fifth season, *The Brain That Wouldn't Die*, a nasty little horror film about a doctor who hangs around the strip clubs in search of an "appropriate" body to stick his fiancée's still-living head on. Naturally, with a new host, there were many immediate changes made to the opening credits. The first was the deletion of the Gizmonic Institute that had been at the beginning of the show for many years, as well as any mention of the Institute in the show (to be fair, Deep 13 had gotten much more mention over the previous seasons than Gizmonic did, so it didn't affect the flow of the show). The reason for the Gizmonic change was that Joel had used the term for quite some time before *MST3K* even began, and he viewed the term as closely associated with his work. With his departure, he asked that the show no longer use it. Instead, the focus shifted solely to Deep 13, and the opening credits reflected that switch from

Michael J. Nelson and the bots, ready to take on the world in the final season of *MST3K* on Comedy Central. COMEDY CENTRAL / PHOTOFEST © COMEDY CENTRAL

the previously common sight of the convertible *Thunderheads*-like Gizmonic Institute into a globe "in space" that is turned around to show Deep 13 at the center of the planet's core. In fact, everything about the opening credits is new as Mike takes over, such as showing Forrester and Frank going over the "evil plan," conking Mike on the noggin as he looks at a steampunk hot dog, shooting him into space, as well as new footage showing Mike trying to figure out how to fix Servo, and the bots being unwilling to let Mike loose after he is tied up.

The theme song also reflects these changes, from Mike to Deep 13 to slightly different intros for the robots. Even Forrester and Frank's "la-la-la" after the Satellite of Love floats by is revised to put them into a different position. Cambot is also given a makeover, looking more like a floating ball. The tunnel is changed after a few years as well, with new methods for the doors to open, although it still leads to the same theater as before and with

Servo to the left and Crow to the right of the human host. Meanwhile, the invention exchange, which had been a major part of the show when Joel was there, simply stopped after a time. This mainly happened because Joel was the main inventor in the group and, while the others would occasionally have some ideas, the stress of trying to keep up with two per episode just wasn't worth the trouble.

The emotional dynamics of the characters changed as well. Joel, who was the creator of the robots, had always come off as a parental figure for the bots, showing them how to do things, explaining elements of humanity, and making them go to their room or to a corner as punishment for being naughty. Mike, on the other hand, was quickly shown not to be very knowledgeable about the ship or the bots and to demonstrate why being a temp was probably a career goal. With that in mind, Crow and Servo tended to look upon Mike as an idiot, but more often as a sibling than as a parent. As the series continued, this change in relationship began to affect the tone of the riffs as well, with the jokes sounding more like three guys living in a college dorm than reflecting the gentler style that prevailed during Joel's run on the show. In other words, it got a tad ruder the further it moved away from the Joel years.

The movies also seemed to become more adult in nature. *The Brain That Wouldn't Die* not only focuses on a doctor "looking for something sleazy" (as Crow puts it during the movie) but features a gore scene commonly cut from the movie where a character has an arm ripped off and smears blood from the wound along a wall as he tries to climb the stairs. The movies after this point leaned toward leering at the female body—such as in *The Atomic Brain*, with an old woman (and the audience) ogling young women; *Alien from L.A.* setting up supermodel Kathy Ireland to climb a ladder so we can see up her skirt—and into season 6, where Crow finally gives up during *Angels Revenge* and announces he's "just going to look at the boobs."

It's Jan in a Pan! *The Brain That Wouldn't Die* (1962) would be Mike's first film at the SOL. AMERI-
CAN INTERNATIONAL PICTURES / PHOTOFEST © AMERICAN INTERNATIONAL PICTURES

But perhaps the biggest difference and the most controversial thing for
some fans was that there was someone named Mike standing where a guy
named Joel used to be. By this point in 1993, computers, and more specifically the internet, began to enter homes of the public, and with it the opportunity to interact with other people via online communities. The program
jumped right in by creating an official website that was run by those doing the
Mystery Science Theater 3000 Information Club called MST3Kinfo.com (and
the basis of some of the Official *MST3K* Info Club Web Site quotes listed
here), which still exists today, although some areas of the site have not been
updated since before the return of the program in the 2010s. At the time,
the fan club, the online interactions via emails, and those with the *MST3K*
communities online were done through Julie Walker, a former executive at
Microsoft and fan who became the head of marketing for Best Brains and

helped set up a lot of the items the company would sell in its catalog, which fans would get upon joining the fan club.

As expected in any situation where people could talk without having to say it face-to-punchable-face, rudeness led the way when it came to the internet, and it was not uncommon for various extended arguments that do not serve any purpose, or "flame wars," to erupt in many such communities online. And one such "flame war" for *MST3K* was the argument over who was better, Mike or Joel. The situation escalated, and members of the cast were innocent enough to read what was going on, to their bewilderment. "Not long after Joel Hodgson left *Mystery Science Theater*," Mike told A.V. Club, "someone printed a transcript of me screaming at him and throwing him out of the building, because they said they were there, and they over-heard it. It was a word-for-word transcription, and of course it was utter fiction and made up. But I thought it was so funny that someone would go to such lengths." Mike tried to ignore the hostilities, but Joel's take after being told about the fighting and reading some of the heated exchanges was to egg it on a little, as reported to the Official *MST3K* Info Club Web Site: "Well the moderator came in to break it all up and say something like, 'They're both good in their own ways, and I thought we agreed not to fight about this any-more.' Everyone had calmed down and was smoothing out their feathers and saying they were sorry and then my friend and I wrote, 'Yeah, but when you think about it, Joel's better!' And then we took off."

Mike had more immediate concerns, anyway, as he tried to settle into the role while concentrating on his duties as being head writer, as he told IGN. "I remember also feeling like, 'Wow, I think I really stink,' because nobody's saying anything to me. Mary Jo Pehl, I remember, came, and I said, 'Mary Jo, do I really, really suck?'" She assured him that everyone was feeling so good about his job that they didn't feel the need to tell him anything. Besides, the ratings were staying steady with the changeover, so whatever debates were being played out by some fans online didn't appear to affect the value of the program to the network. It did lead to a little bit of a ribbing within the show itself in the first episode from season 10, *Soultaker*, when Joel, wearing a Gizmonic Institute jumpsuit, returned for a special guest appearance on the show. Showing up in the story line to help fix the ship after Mike finds he can't do much of anything to save its malfunctioning systems, Joel describes his life after the SOL (working for the band Man or Astroman, and then running a "hot fish" shop in Osseo, Minnesota) before heading off to do repairs. After he leaves, Mike starts talking about how Joel's life is so much better than his and how Joel is simply a better person when Tom jumps in to say, "Hey, don't compare yourself, Mike, it ain't healthy." Mike agrees as they go to commercial, and they move on from the topic.

Comedy Central was still strongly committed to the show at this point, even with the announced change in hosts. One growing concern Comedy Central did have was that the network was growing, getting more attention, and had more opportunities to put on new programs that viewers wanted to see. Yet *MST3K* was two to four times the running time of many of its other shows, leading to the program not being a good choice for primetime during the week when it was still considered a flagship program (and that leading to it mainly appearing in the mornings or late at night during the week when repeated, when the prime advertising dollars were less). It was also noted that, since the first Comedy Channel episodes were no longer being repeated, the series was left with a limited number that could be repeated, with the possibility that viewership would diminish due to the constant re-airing of episodes. Something was needed to reclaim that audience during a primetime hour where advertising dollars meant more.

The matter led to the creation of *The Mystery Science Theater Hour*, premiering in November 1993, which broke up thirty episodes from seasons 3, 4, and 5 into sixty hour-long two-parters, with the first half of the film in one

Soultaker (1990) with Robert Z-Dar and Joe Estevez will be remembered by *MST3K* fans for the return of Joel and Frank for a final farewell in the original series. PACIFIC WEST ENTERTAINMENT GROUP / PHOTOFEST © PACIFIC WEST ENTERTAINMENT GROUP

episode and the rest in another. To help with the breakup of the movies, new wraparound segments were created with Mike Nelson reprising his Jack Perkins character (although never referred to by that name in *The Mystery Science Theater Hour* episodes) to introduce or summarize the action of each movie, in the character's long-winded, bizarre tangents manner. This also helped give the episodes a fresh dose of new material that could bring back viewers who had seen the episodes in their original form. Oddly, after all the talk of wanting to make the show an hour long because two hours was too much, Comedy Central scheduled the hour-long program for Monday through Friday in the evening hours while continuing to air the two-hour-long episodes in repeats Monday through Friday after primetime.

The abundance of episodes running on the channel began to erode the viewership. There was no need to get people together to watch an episode as they were no longer special events, since you could watch them twice a day and new episodes on the weekend. Recording episodes on videotape, a resource that the show encouraged at one point in the closing credits to spread the news about the show, also meant fans could rewatch their favorites whenever they liked. Therefore, the next Turkey Day marathon during the fifth season had poor viewership, although there were more reasons than a hearty overdose of repeats. Comedy Central offered Best Brains the opportunity to do new material for the Thanksgiving special as they had in the past, but the money offered was so low that Best Brains decided to pass. Instead, Comedy Central used segments featuring fans at a Halloween party put together by fan Debbie Tobin, which was amusing in a geeky manner but hardly the stuff to keep fans watching, leading to lower ratings and a shifting idea at the network that perhaps *MST3K* had outlived its usefulness.

While Comedy Central was beginning to grow a bit cold to throwing money at the program as it had for the past three seasons, such concerns didn't stop more than two thousand fans from attending the first full-fledged convention for the program between September 16 and 18, 1994, at the Radisson Hotel in Bloomington, Minnesota. Called ConventioCon ExpoFest-A-Rama, the convention included a Q&A with the cast, along with appearances by some of the actors who had appeared in the movies being riffed, such as Beverly Garland (*It Conquered the World*, *Swamp Diamond*, and *Gunslinger*, and praised by Paul Chaplin in *The Amazing Colossal Episode Guide* book, and rightly so), David Worth (director of *Warrior of the Lost World*), and John Humphries (who played Mikey in *Teen-Age Strangler*). While the convention was going on, the *MST3K* team would also be at the Historic State Theater to perform another live *MST3K* riffing of a movie on September 15 and 16, with a convention-goers-only show on the seventeenth. It was a chance to give back to the fans by doing another live performance, and an opportunity to show executives who had flown in from Universal Studios to see how an audience would react to the group performing a riff on *This Island Earth* (1955), a movie being considered for the possible theatrical movie. "They're going to see that enthusiasm," Mallon told the *Star Tribune* before the event. "Half the people there are going to be in costume. This is going to be one of the most colorful events since the Jesus people owned that theater in the Seventies."

And the performances did help with getting the film pushed at Universal, although there were delays in getting it green-lit. Fans who had organized letter campaigns earlier in 1994 to help convince Comedy Central to renew the show for a sixth season then sent another five thousand letters to Universal when, in the summer of 1994, Universal announced it was backing out of the movie. By the time of the convention, Universal was back on board and the writers were sent to Universal's film library to pick a movie because, as Mallon mentioned to A.V. Club, "[Universal] said to us, 'It would be a heck of a lot easier if you took a film that we already owned.'" The writers then went to the screening room on the Universal lot to watch an assortment of films, with the emphasis that they wanted to stick with something that was in color, along with the usual requirements of riffable movies. This presented an issue, as Universal may have been the home of classic horror films (*MST3K* would later even do one of those, *Revenge of the Creature*, featuring the Creature from the Black Lagoon), but nearly all of these were black-and-white. The number of science fiction films Universal had done was quite limited as well (science fiction tended to fall more to Paramount), so for a time, the group began looking for anything that might work as an alternative, including episodes of television shows like *Kolchak: The Night Stalker* and *Night Gallery*.

But they always came back to *This Island Earth*. *This Island Earth* was a 1955 movie that took over two years to develop and produce for the studio. It was considered a prestigious movie, based on a popular science fiction novel by Raymond F. Jones, who would later do a children's book adaptation of the Richard Basehart series, *Voyage to the Bottom of the Sea*, in 1965. The story is about a scientist, Dr. Cal Meacham, who is enticed to join a group of futurists who proclaim to be doing things to benefit Earth but turn out to be aliens using the Earthlings to try to save their home planet Metaluna (snicker, hey, I remember the joke from chapter 1). An extended segment of the movie shows off special effects as the heroes travel to another planet but is really about everyone essentially getting into the car and driving to Grandma's, only to be told that their brains are going to be scrambled as the planet is destroyed. Meacham, old swimming buddy Ruth, and mighty high-head alien Exeter make it back to Earth, only for Exeter to die when his flaming hat of a ship explodes over a lake or ocean or some such.

The description above is to be taken lightly, but back in 1955, the movie was highly praised by reviewers for its special effects and serious adult tone for the times when it came to a "outer space" movie, and it is still considered a classic science fiction movie. On the other hand, there is something to be said about the *MST3K* writers feeling that the dialogue was a bit too earnest, the pace was slower than needed, the trip to Metaluna really added nothing to the story, the reluctance of everyone to note the weird foreheads of the aliens was laughably weird . . . and why keep the slack-wearing mutants around as pets when they will kill you? Thus, after much review and time-wasting in the screening room at Universal, *This Island Earth* was the one, and work began on a movie script.

At first, the riffing part was the easiest to do, as the group got together and began putting together riffs as they commonly would for any other movie they did. The real concern came down to the "host segments," because without commercial breaks, there didn't seem to be any reason for the movie to depart from the film to do story line material with Mike and the bots. To fix this, they created moments where the film breaks, and Tom mentions he has an interocitor (the communication device Cal builds to show his worthiness to join the staff). What was to be a third and climatic moment in the movie was interrupted when a meteor shower threatened the ship, which was cut from the movie, but more about that in a moment.

At one point the script was going to be like a regular episode, with various songs created for Crow, Tom, Gypsy, and Dr. Forrester to sing. Kevin Murphy, in his interview with FRED, also recalled that at one point Crow would have a dream sequence where he rescued Kim Cattrall in a parody of Steve McQueen's motorcycle jump from *The Great Escape*. Then the studio had a focus group watching the movie *Billy Madison*, which they tore apart because of a musical segment in it. With that in mind, Universal's executives told *MST3K*, "The one thing we don't want to do is to have any music whatsoever. We just screened a film that had music in it and the audiences hated it so much," as Mike remembered it to A.V. Club. "We're quietly tucking that draft behind our back: 'Oh, yeah. No, of course. Music? What? We hate it.'" Interference from the studio executives over the script slowed things down and frustrated the writers. For example, referring to the mutant as famous guitarist Bootsy Collins, a joke they thought was solid, was changed to long-forgotten heiress and tax-evader Leona Helmsley. In March 1995, it appeared that the studio was once again going to pass, and Best Brains began looking into producing the movie independently with a different movie to riff, but then things were back on, and the filming began in April 1995 at Energy Park Studio in Saint Paul with a budget of $2 million.

Meanwhile, Comedy Central was airing the sixth season and was still feeling confident enough in the show to have the cast put together a half-hour special for March 1995 where Mike and the bots reviewed the movies that were nominated that year for the Oscars in *The MST3K Little Gold Statue Preview Special*. Things seemed to be moving along, but the 1994 Turkey Day marathon had once again sidestepped Best Brains for filler between episodes aired and instead hired former Batman and *Zombie Nightmare* villain Adam West to make some jokes in between the movies for the marathon. Viewership had once again dropped from the previous year, and Comedy Central was beginning to get hesitant about continuing with the series, leading to repeats that had traditionally filled morning and late-night schedules to finally stop.

Then came the news that Frank Conniff was leaving the show. Unlike Josh and Joel before him, Frank's reasoning was not due to any issues with the program or the production company but rather his feeling that it was simply time to move on. In a statement to fans that was later posted on the Official *MST3K* Info Club Web Site: "I've discovered that after five seasons and 109 episodes, I have a need to change, even if change means losing the best job I've ever had and most likely will ever have. I have a need to grow and evolve and to find new challenges and adventures in my life." The cast and crew accepted his reasoning and, in the final episode of season 6, *Samson vs. the Vampire Women*, a story line was created where Frank is visited by Torgo, a character from the very popular *MST3K*-riffed movie *Manos: The Hands of Fate*. Torgo, once again played by Mike Nelson, who played him

The Master (Tom Neyman) from *"Manos" the Hands of Fate*. His assistant Torgo became a recurring character on *MST3K* as played by Mike Nelson, and would emerge as Torgo the White in season 6 to take TV's Frank to Second Banana Heaven.

in a couple of earlier episodes, is now Torgo the White, a specter who offers to take Frank to Second Banana Heaven. Frank accepts and ascends, only to return briefly at the end of the episode to push the button one final time for Dr. Forrester.

The final episode with Frank aired on March 25, 1995. A month later, the *Star Tribune* had photos of the cast and crew moving ahead and working on the theatrical movie. New, bigger sets were created for the movie, and Trace redesigned the SOL to make it more presentable for the big screen. The expansion of the SOL allowed fans to see more of the ship and the daily lives of the characters, such as Mike's exercise routine on a treadmill that parodied a portion of *2001*, while a look in Servo's room shows that he has an unhealthy fascination with underwear, and Crow gets to spend time trying to dig his way back to Earth in the bowels of the SOL. Dr. Forrester, in an expanded set as well, is given the intro to the movie, talking directly to the audience and without Frank or any other assistant around (although we see a figurehead in the tunnel that is a callback to Frank). Yet even with these updates, much of the movie plays out like an episode of the show, with Mike and the bots watching a movie, interspersed with some scenes outside of the theater, and then everything wrapping up in the finale with Forrester defeated and Mike and the bots triumphant although still stuck in the SOL. Upon finishing the host segments, the cast then moved to Paisley Park Studios, the home studio of performing artist Prince, to record the lines for the film. While all that was going on, back at Best Brains, Inc., Mary Jo Pehl and Paul Chaplin pieced together *The Amazing Colossal Episode Guide* that would be released by Bantam Books in March 1996 to help tie in with the movie.

Although the movie was finished in May 1995, it would not be released until April 1996. The executives at the studio decided the movie wasn't funny enough—with jokes that were too confusing for some test audiences—and needed to be shortened. Ironically, the writers had taken *This Island Earth* and edited it by a few scenes due to everyone feeling the movie was too long. Then the Universal executives kept going back to the movie and asking them to cut even more from the film. Jokes, such as the Bootsy Collins one, were ripped out and replaced with other jokes that would supposedly be less confusing to audiences, although now read as dated material that was nowhere as hip as the original lines. The entire segment that was one of the selling points of the initial signed-off script—a meteor shower that puts Mike in crisis and leads to the robots having to save him—was cut because it didn't move the movie along fast enough. The ending, which had a mutant invading Dr. Forrester's lair and beating him up while Crow attempted to use the chainsaw he found at Servo's to try to cut his way to Earth, was tossed aside for a new, "less scary" ending where Forrester ended up being transported to the Metalunans' shower (to be fair, while the new ending doesn't end with the callback to Crow trying to escape or his mid-movie discovery of the chainsaw, the party/shower ending is actually an improvement). Even the ending credits, a comical and completely metatheatrical moment where the trio get to make fun of the people who made *MST3K: The Movie*, was initially tampered with, as one executive in particular said that the movie needed to end with a "Where are they now?" segment, showing what happened to Tom, Crow, and Mike after the movie, as it would be "much funnier." A call to the head of production put a stop to that nonsense, and the proper ending credit segments stayed. The entire ridiculousness of the movie process led to the writers parodying it in the season 7 episode, *The Incredible Melting Man*, where Forrester and his mother, Pearl, put up the money to produce Crow's long-in-progress script, *Earth vs. Soup*. By the end of the episode, Crows ends up entirely out of the process, all the money goes to the executives, and the movie is released as a trailer after the "focus group" decides they don't like what was filmed.

After all the back and forth, Universal decided to move the finished movie to a dead spot in the year, April, and push the movie on to their smaller subsidiary studio, Gramercy. "We go to our PR person in Manhattan," Mike told A.V. Club, "and she's like 'There's going to be a big push on this. Big push.' But she's also promoting [the Pamela Anderson action movie] *Barb Wire*. So her promotion budget was all focused on *Barb Wire*, because they knew that it was going to only do one week." Best Brains did what they could to help promote their movie, premiering it at the Uptown Theater on April 18, 1996, after going on the road to do various television interviews to drum up interest in the film and the book that was now finally coming up from Bantam. Trace, who had sprained his back just before the press tour, spent hours in awkward positions for such interviews while manipulating Crow, while he and the others did their best with questions that confused the line between their puppets and themselves ("Are you asking me or the puppet?," was a common internal question Trace and Kevin had during the interviews). Beyond the premiere and getting to see the movie on a big screen, though, there wasn't much for the Best Brains people to do. Although critical reviews were positive beyond pointing out the short running time (seventy-four minutes for the movie, which made it about eighteen minutes shorter than a normal episode of the series), prints were only released to a couple dozen theaters around the country. Mallon told the *Star Tribune* that he expected the movie to lead to annual sequels over the next ten years. Instead, the movie did poorly at the box office, although it would do better on video when released in October 1996. The movie, with all its deleted scenes as extras, was finally released on Blu-ray in 2013 by Shout! Factory.

April 1996 was still way in the future when the movie was completed (besides reshoots and redubs) in May 1995. At that point, the cast was

Publicity still for the release of *Mystery Science Theater 3000: The Movie* (1996), with Mike and the bots pointing out a scene that doesn't happen anywhere in the movie. PHOTO BY MICHAEL KIENITZ, © GRAMERCY PICTURES

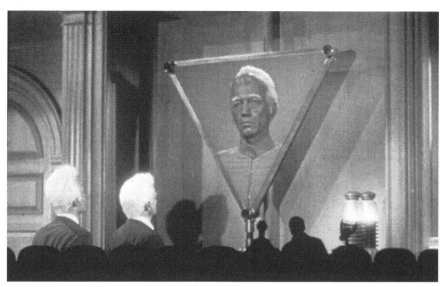

You watching Mike and the bots watching Exeter and Brack watching some boring old Metaluna show. From *Mystery Science Theater 3000: The Movie* (1996). GRAMERCY PICTURES / PHOTOFEST © GRAMERCY PICTURES

waiting to hear about a new season with Comedy Central, which still had an option with Best Brains. The network was slowly going through changes, looking to become less the "G-rated with an edge" channel it had started out as in 1989 and more "adult" and politically oriented. This included doing programs like *Politically Incorrect with Bill Maher* in 1993 and slowly moving toward programs like *The Daily Show* (which started in 1996) and *South Park* (1997). Meanwhile the little apolitical family show that ate up two hours of the schedule every time it was on was looking like something from another era. At one point, there was an attempt by Comedy Central to have the cast do a live riffing of the State of the Union as a means to pull the show more into the direction where the executives at the network wanted to head, but it was decided against after some discussion.

Without the financial backing of Comedy Central, the employees of Best Brains knew that they were in for a barren few months as they waited things out. Mike Nelson, as head writer and face of the show, was given the best break by being kept on salary for a time, but the others had to head down to fill out paperwork at the unemployment office. Trace Beaulieu realized it was time to move on, as he found himself in his later thirties filling out the application and having to say, as Mike told IGN, "I'll travel 35 miles for a puppet show that pays this much." There was also the solid knowledge that the additional television work and new series coming out of Best Brains that had been promised to Trace back in 1991 was not going to happen. Whether by design or not, Best Brains had been set up with a business model that could sustain one show, *MST3K*, and *MST3K* was the only show produced that could finance the company. There were no directions to go beyond that. Staring at an unemployment form with not much to show for the time gone by hardly looked like the fulfillment of a career at that point, and Trace decided he needed to move on, as had Josh, Joel, and Frank before him. By the summer, Comedy Central had agreed to renew the series for another season but only for six episodes instead of the typical twenty-four or even the first two seasons of thirteen each, with hints that this was going to probably be it. It seemed perfect timing, and Trace announced to the press in July 1996 that he would film the next season but then leave the series. "It's kind of bittersweet," he told the *Star Tribune*, "but it was time for me to go."

The first episode of the new season, *Night of the Blood Beast*, aired as part of the traditional Turkey Day festivities on November 23, 1995. That year, Comedy Central did pay for the cast and crew to do new material for the marathon, although the number of episodes aired were cut down to just seven, and Comedy Central insisted that the episodes from the first Comedy Channel season be aired, no doubt hoping that its reemergence after its long absence would get more fans to watch. Also included in the marathon was a new half-hour special called *Poopie Parade of Values*, which featured Kevin, Mike, and Trace intentionally doing a bad infomercial to sell two videocassettes full of bloopers from Best Brains. The story line of the wraparound segments done for the last Comedy Central marathon focused on Forrester once again trying to destroy the minds of the public with the movies, only this time he comes to realize that Frank had sent out invitations to various people for a Thanksgiving dinner before he shuffled off to Second Banana Heaven. This allows for a final visit from many characters played by the writers over the years, including Bridget as Mr. B Natural, Mike as Jack Perkins (who begins hitting on Mr. B, the drunker he gets), Kevin as the kitten from *Kitten with a Whip*, and Paul as Pitch, the devil from the Mexican *Santa Claus* movie. It also saw the return of Forrester's mother, who is . . . uh . . . Mother Forrester, played by Mary Jo Pehl.

Mother Forrester, also known as Mrs. Forrester, also known as Pearl, first appeared in the sixth season episode *Bloodlust!* when she came to visit her son and instead became fast teatime friends with Frank. With her return for Thanksgiving, Pearl became a regular fixture in Deep 13, moving in and spending much of her time berating Clayton and showing us why he might be the mess that he was.

Although the first episode of the season aired in November, the full season was pushed back to February 1996. "Our contract with Comedy Central provided us to make six shows this year, and they have technically till the end of January [1996] to tell us about next year," Jim Mallon told the *Washington Post*, "but before Thanksgiving, they said they wouldn't be renewing us beyond the current season." Around this time, Comedy Central had brought in a new president, Doug Herzog, who changed programming at MTV to move away from music videos to reality programs and game shows in the early to mid-1990s. "As we begin to evolve, it's time to kind of look for different ideas," Herzog also told *The Washington Post* in the same article announcing the end of the series. "*MST* has been on the air for seven years, which is a good run for any show anywhere."

It was a determination that the people at Best Brains hadn't worried about before, as Trace told Jon Bream: "We were as surprised as everyone else. We've not been held up to ratings before." Mallon would try to put the best spin on it he could, saying they were already looking to move it elsewhere, possibly the Sci-Fi Channel. As he also told Bream, in early December 1995, "We don't feel our mission is completed yet." Hopes were high after all, what with the movie that was due to come out and the book that was being published and even a CD-ROM being discussed. There was also talk of another convention to be held Labor Day weekend in 1996, which just showed that interest was still there. Some network was bound to pick them up. Just wait and see.

For the moment though, the series ended its seven-season run on Comedy Central with a finale to wrap up some loose ends in the last episode, *Laserblast.* Finding his funds have been cut off (maybe the Institute finally figured out he was down there in Deep 13), Forrester cuts the SOL loose as he begins packing up all the equipment with the help of his mother. Mike and the bots are sent adrift and momentarily play out some final *Star Trek*–driven scenarios (a menacing robot is laughed off the ship; and approaching a black hole, Mike turns into Captain Janeway from *Star Trek: Voyager* and then, it seems, into Tina Turner), before finally reaching the end of the universe. Okay, in a moment they do. There.

Reaching the end, Mike and the bots discover that they can become beings of pure energy, so they decide to go outside the SOL and play. Back at Deep 13, Dr. Clayton Forrester discovers himself in a reenactment of the ending to *2001*, flying through the years until he's on his deathbed, whereupon he sees a black monolith standing before him: the worst movie ever made on a giant videocassette. Reaching out to the movie, he is transformed into a space baby like the one in *2001*, only for Pearl to grab him and tell him that she plans to raise him right this time, as Forrester says, "Oh, Poopie."

With that, the series continued in repeats for a time on Comedy Central. April saw the quick release and dismissal of the theatrical movie. The CD-ROM planned by the Voyager Company, with two new shorts and heavy involvement by Trace, was never completed. The book, featuring input from all the current writers, was released and did only modestly. Things were looking like the end of a good run. But as Mike Nelson told the *Star Tribune* at the end of 1995, when things were looking bleak, "Nobody ever really dies in sci-fi. We can always land on a Genesis Planet or something."

8

I'll Get You!

The Sci-Fi Channel Years

You did it! You finally did it!

Damn us all to hell, yes, yes.

It's a madhouse! A ma—

A madhouse, yes, I know!

—MIKE AND DR. BOBO, WHEN MIKE REALIZES THAT HE HAS ARRIVED
BACK TO EARTH, WHERE IT IS THE FUTURE AND BEING RUN BY APES IN
THE FIRST EPISODE ON THE SCI-FI CHANNEL, *REVENGE OF THE CREATURE*

There were some upsides that came in April 1996: Comedy Central continued to rerun episodes and would do so until February 1997; that at least kept
the product name out there for people to see and could be a promotional
tool if Best Brains found interest at another network. Unfortunately for fans,
several episodes could no longer air due to the rights to certain films having
expired, including those for the Gamera movies, which were always fan favorites. Further, thanks to their connections with HBO, which was owned by
Warner, the series was being reissued on videotape through Warner's branch
company Rhino Home Video starting at the end of April (the first three

episodes released, according to a *Time* magazine article, were *Cave Dwellers*, *The Amazing Colossal Man*, and *Mitchell*—all Joel episodes). Or at least that was the idea; as it turned out, Rhino had problems getting licensing rights to many of the movies planned, and it took a while before the videos could actively be released (more success would come a few years later when they began releasing the movies in DVD box set form, which was then carried on by Shout! Factory).

Also, no matter how the theatrical movie would play out in theaters, which it would for a time that spring, thanks to the extended art-house release of the movie to theaters (limited number of prints that were moved around the country to a couple dozen theaters at a time, thus lessening the need to blanket the country with advertising in areas where it was not being seen and also cutting down on film prints), the company had gotten a little bit of cash that helped them winter the period of uncertainty. There was also the good fortune that the Sci-Fi Channel had a natural inclination to consider the show once Comedy Central had passed it up.

The Sci-Fi Channel (known since 2009 as SyFy) was conceived in 1989 by Mitchell Rubenstein and Laurie Silvers and eventually picked up by the USA Cable Network (the home of *Night Flight*) in 1992. The concept of the channel was to have programming that featured mainly science fiction movies and television shows, along with documentary programming discussing space travel and other issues of scientific interest. Its initial output of original programming even included segments with author Harlan Ellison, a man known for doing what he wanted, and gave the channel the air of wanting to be taken seriously. The channel thus had a reputation as being slightly smarter than some of the other cable networks out there, although it did occasionally drift into pseudoscience material, such as with *Sightings* in 1996.

It was also known for showing a lot of old television series and movies that were in the library of USA Network, which had affiliations with Paramount and Universal at the time. This can't be emphasized enough: Sci-Fi ran a lot of old material and even had a daily hour in its programming where series that had lasted only one season or less (such as *The Immortal*, from 1970) aired. For a lot of fans who had vague memories of this programming, it was a fantastic channel to be able to see these older shows. There was also a drifting emphasis toward showing horror material as well, such as the old *Dark Shadows* soap opera and a few classic horror films, although at first it was more of a rarity. Mainly, it was a land of repeats, with little in the way of fresh programming.

Older movies made up the bulk of the schedule for the channel, especially on the weekends, making the idea of *MST3K* a natural. It could feature the lesser-quality movies the channel had access to, was a cheap show to make, and had an established history. "*Mystery Science Theater* transcends the category of a good cable program," Sci-Fi's vice president in charge of programming, Barry Schulman, said when the channel picked up the program in June 1996. "It won a Peabody Award, and it became a major motion picture. Very few programs do either." Negotiations took a couple of months between the network and Best Brains, but once the dust settled, Best Brains was guaranteed a first season of twenty-two episodes. The only issue was that the channel wanted to wait to start the show until after Comedy Central's contract had run out in February 1997.

There was general relief at Best Brains when the news was announced. "It's been a struggle," Mike told the *Star Tribune* at the time. "I celebrated by calling credit card companies and telling them it won't be long now." It also made the prospects of the gang getting together to attend the upcoming second convention that Labor Day weekend a bit more relaxing. "Had this not come through," Mike continued, "they would have woken me up in the gutter, given me a quick talc bath, and propped me up in front of all the people. We'd all have been there with hanging heads talking about how we used to have that show." Yet there were still some lingering concerns from the Sci-Fi Channel and a segment of fans once the news was released in July 1996 that Trace was leaving and would not appear at all in season 8. Schulman at Sci-Fi assured fans that the loss of Trace as Forrester and Crow was not a "deal-breaker," while Mike would tell Colin Covert at the *Star Tribune*, "We've had lots of cast changes before. Whenever we worried that it would ruin the chemistry, we just reminded ourselves that all we're doing here is making fun of movies." The big question fans had as they waited for the season was what would change on the show once it returned.

It was a question on the mind of those who attended the second official *MST3K* convention that Labor Day weekend. The con, called ConventioCon ExpoFest-A-Rama 2: Electric Boogaloo, was held at the Minneapolis Convention Center, had a similar attendance as the 1994 convention. This was a disappointment from the four thousand hoped for, but some assumptions were that the smaller number came about when it was clear there would not be a live riffing event like at the previous convention, especially considering Beaulieu's departure from the show. Trace did appear for the Q&A portions of the program, which were somewhat awkward with Sci-Fi's own Barry Schulman there to introduce the cast, especially after he gamely tried to convince Beaulieu to stay on for another season to no avail.

Among the guests were Kim Cattrall (star of *City Limits* and a constant callback on the program as being the apple of Crow's painted eyes; she was initially listed to appear at the 1994 convention but had to back out that time), Russell Johnson (from *This Island Earth* and, of course, remembered mainly for his role as an irritated customer in an episode of *Bosom Buddies . . .* okay, and as the Professor in *Gilligan's Island*), and Rex Reason (Cal from *This Island Earth*), who had a Q&A with fans at the show. Among those brought up onstage to talk about writing on the show was a new face, Bill Corbett. He and a few other writers had been brought in to help with shows in the sixth season as work was being completed on the movie. While there were some suspicions at the convention as to whether Corbett would become a bigger part of the team, the Best Brains people kept it quiet for the moment.

Bill Corbett (March 30, 1960–) was born and raised in Brooklyn, New York, and attended Yale College, receiving a BA, before moving to earn an MFA in playwriting and screenwriting at the Yale School of Drama. Corbett performed and taught acting and writing for a time, particularly at the Playwrights' Center (where he was given a seven-year term as a core member back in 1991) and the Guthrie Theater in Minneapolis, finding it easy to make the city his home after arriving in 1989. His one-act play *Motorcade* was first produced professionally at the Playwrights' Center in January 1993, where he also did periodic readings. His subsequent plays, *This Ridiculous Dreaming* and *The Big Slam*, were produced in Minneapolis between 1993 and 1995, while his parody of A. R. Gurney's *Love Letters*, which he titled *Hate Mail*, cowritten with Kira Obolensky, was first performed in 1996 (Michael and Bridget Nelson would later do a performance of this play).

Because of his connections with local theater and comedy, Bill had gotten to know some of the *MST3K* crew, although—like Mary Jo before him—he was not overly familiar with the show. When the word went out that the program was looking for additional writers in 1994 to help with scripting season 6, Corbett sent Mike some samples of his work, and he was asked to contribute to some of the later episodes of the season. With his background as a writer and performer, when the time came to add a new writer and have someone perform as a new robot puppet after Trace's departure, it was natural to look to Bill.

And that was the initial thought: since Trace was so associated with the role of Crow, it was decided to pursue the idea of not bringing back Crow and instead create a new puppet. That was quickly discarded, however, as the show had been locked into the dynamics for Tom Servo, Gypsy, and Crow for so long it would have been like dismissing another actor from the program. Instead, Crow stayed, and auditions were held to see who would work best (Mike in his IGN interview mentioned he had even given it a try during rehearsals, finding the voice difficult to maintain). Bill recalled to the *Mystery Science Theater* Review website that his audition did not go smoothly: "I auditioned for the part, complete with spazzy puppetry, and my voice totally out of sync with Crow's mouth movement. . . . The effect was like a live version of a badly dubbed Japanese film. I thought there was no way they would ask me to do it after that." Nevertheless, Corbett was offered the role, which took him a few early episodes to find his comfort zone. "At first, I think I tried to imitate Trace's voice a little too much," Bill told the *Mystery Science Theater 3000* Review site. "But my colleagues were great in letting me off the hook about that. They encouraged me to find my own way into Crow and put more of myself into it, for better or worse." Having never worked with a puppet before, Bill also joked that it first appeared that Crow was recovering from a stroke, with uneasy mouth and arm movements that took a while to get used to.

Just as it took Corbett some time to adjust to the character, so, too, did it take some fans to get used to the character's new voice and slightly different personality that came with the change in performer under the felt—or plastic and steel, as it were. A bigger adjustment for fans was the new antagonist in the program, Pearl Forrester, once again played by Mary Jo Pehl. For the return of the series, it was decided to establish a story line that involved more than simply Mike and the bots returning to Earth to be part of an experiment again in modern times. Instead, the first episode showed Gypsy, Mike, and Tom reappearing on a slightly redesigned Satellite of Love in their physical forms after having been elements of light for several hundred years. There they find Crow, who returned to the ship a short time after being turned into an essence of the universe because, he says, "I got bored." The difference in time allowed the change in Crow's voice and attitude within the story line, although Mike would go on to spend a couple of episodes noticing a change in Crow. Regaining control of the ship, the crew quickly jump from the edge of the universe back to Earth (well, "keep in mind" and all that). Upon arrival, they discover that it is the future and apes now rule the earth. A discussion with Dr. Bobo (Kevin Murphy) and Peanuts (Paul Chaplin) leads to a discovery that Mike and the bots will go back to watching bad movies in the theater as per the demands of a mysterious "lawgiver." It is then revealed that the lawgiver is none other than Pearl Forrester. Pearl explains that she tried to raise the space-child version of Clayton, only to realize he was going to end up as messed up as the previous version of him, and so she smothered him and moved on (or, at least, that's Pearl's story in the episode; season 11's reveal that Clayton had a daughter named Kinga and that his ashes were later stored with Frank's—who had become an disembodied entity with no body to cremate in season 6—suggests that there are more stories to tell about Clayton and Frank that we have never seen). Pearl announces that she plans to continue the experiment with Mike and the bots.

In retrospect, it is hard to see what the big deal was about Pearl being the villain of the show, especially after the years of Kinga in the later series, but for a time there was nearly as much of a heated argument in the internet communities over Pearl as a character on the show as they had been with the whole "Mike versus Joel" clash from a few years prior. Certainly, in revisiting the episodes from seasons 8 through 10, one sees the gradual adjustment of the character to become the equivalent of Clayton before her; having to put up with associates who are inept while also showing clear signs that being a mad scientist means having to fall back on the whole mad thing a lot. Perhaps part of the issue was that Pearl had been played up in the earlier season as being so hard on Clayton, she could come off as simply unlikable rather than "evil," and it took time for fans to build up a tolerance toward her, which really came around by the nineth season. For whatever reason, the response on the internet was unnecessarily cruel at times, and comments were often directed at Mary Jo Pehl instead of the character. This for a person who once refused to accept payment for a stand-up gig because she thought she hadn't been good enough to receive the money. "This was happening around the beginning of the ascendency of the internet, and on chatrooms—whatever they were back then—people were very vocal, disparaging my personal appearance, hating that a woman was taking Trace's role, and so on," Pehl told Loryn Stone in 2018. "It got pretty personal; someone called me the Yoko Ono of *MST3K*." Dealing with impostor syndrome (the feeling that you are not up to the task given you and will fail) on top of that, Pehl felt herself "buying into" the abuse. "Then I kind of turned around, like, whoa, I have this job that I love and I get to do, why should I let people take that away from me? I feel like it made me grow up a little bit."

In the whirlwind of changes in front of the camera, the channel also made two stipulations for Best Brains. The first was that the movies picked had to be science fiction and not the random assortment of movies that had made up the run with Comedy Central. The argument Best Brains made in return was that since they were on a spaceship with robots watching the movies, any film would automatically be considered science fiction, but the Sci-Fi Channel made the good point that there would no doubt be people who turn on the show midway through, see a biker movie playing, and assume they were not watching the Sci-Fi Channel. Thus the movies would remain geared toward science fiction, with a few horror films added in here and there, although they were able to stretch a bit in the final season with movies such as *Girl in Good Boots* and a black-and-white German television version of *Hamlet*.

The other request by the Sci-Fi Channel was that the show begin to have a recurring story line in the host segments, instead of each episode standing on its own without any attachment to the episodes around it. Although the writers were annoyed with the request, such story lines did amount to the series adding two new regular characters that gave both Muphy and Corbett more to do, while allowing Pearl to have assistants she could beat on, as Forrester had with Frank. It also gave Mike and the bots the sudden ability to do things with the SOL that had never been available to anyone in previous seasons, thanks to the Nanites.

The appeal by Sci-Fi for a story line began in the first episode with Dr. Bobo and the various mountain apes who appeared in the first four episodes of the eighth season. The first episode of the season also introduced the Nanites, macromolecular machines that can perform tasks on a level invisible to the human eye. This allows for magical creation of devices and changes around the SOL, from creating steering systems for the SOL out of the blue, to an impossible hairdo for Mike in one episode. (Oddly enough, the science fiction comedy series *Red Dwarf* would introduce the same type of nanotechnology, called nanobots on the show, in the episode "Nanarchy," which aired a month later on BBC2 and resulted in similar gags. Great minds thinking alike, as it were.) The Nanites were blocky puppets that we are shown through a microscope device Mike uses to communicate with them. They can do powerful, magical things around and outside the ship but have a strong union and seem very involved with proper paperwork, thus making them not the easiest resource on the ship. The voices for them were performed by Murphy, Chaplin, Pehl, Jones, and Patrick Brantseg.

In the fourth episode of the season, *Deadly Mantis*, the apes help mutants that have a malfunctioning doomsday device as their god (much like the plot of *Beneath the Planet of the Apes*). Mike innocently helps the mutants activate the device, leading to a quick countdown for the destruction of Earth in the year 2525 (yeah, you're thinking of that song again too; I know). The Nanites are talked into creating the steering system so that Mike can drive the SOL out of orbit just in time, but instead of it being the end of Pearl, it turns out that she is chasing after him in her van, the Widowmaker, with a stowaway on board, Dr. Bobo.

The following episode finds the SOL orbiting a planet where there are aliens called the Observers, who have vast mental powers that allow them to control lesser beings, such as Pearl and Bobo, and can create things out of thin air. They capture Pearl and Bobo to experiment on them while also letting the bad movie experiment continue on the ship. Trying to escape from the Observers' planet was a story line that filtered through several episodes until episode 8, *The She-Creature*, when Mike asks the Nanites to stop the Observers from messing with the SOL navigational system. Unfortunately, they comply by destroying the planet (thus leading to Mike being named the "destroyer of worlds" by Tom). Once again, Pearl escapes, only this time with Brain Guy (Bill Corbett) along with Bobo for the ride. (It should be mentioned that as the season continues, Dr. Bobo gets gradually dumber, while Brain Guy becomes less a brainiac and more of a snob.) Everyone then goes to a camping planet and meets up with Space Children, but that planet is also destroyed a few episodes later by Mike, leading to a galactic trial in the next episode where Mike is found guilty and sentenced to community service. After that, the SOL and the Widowmaker travel through a wormhole and end up orbiting Earth in ancient Roman times for several episodes.

While having to work with the episodic story lines was irritating for the writers, what bugged them even more was that the channel began airing the episodes out of order, thus making nonsense of the entire process. By the end of the season, everyone seemed to be in agreement that it wasn't working, and the story lines went back to being more singular in nature.

A more serious moment for Best Brains came midway through production of the season when the eighteen-month-old daughter of Jim Mallon passed away in February 1997. Jim, who had played the part of Gypsy since the show's first year on the Comedy Channel decided to break away from the part and slow down his daily involvement with the show to focus on his family. In his place, Brantseg was drafted to take over for Gypsy and would remain in the role for the rest of the original series. The distancing, although no way intended to be anything prolonged, would no doubt affect how Mallon felt about his involvement with the show.

Thanksgiving 1997 saw a minor return of the Turkey Day Marathon, with the Sci-Fi Channel airing seven episodes during the day while also airing two additional specials during the year: *The 1st Annual Summer Blockbuster Review*, a half-hour special with Mike and the bots reviewing trailers for movies being released to theaters (*The Fifth Element*, *Men in Black*, *Batman & Robin*, *The Lost World*, and *Contact*) and a short documentary on the series, called *The Making of MST3K*. There was also news that Sci-Fi had picked up the show for another season, albeit an abbreviated one of thirteen episodes with a possible nine to follow if ratings looked good.

In the story line, the SOL and the Widowmaker had made it back out of the wormhole and to modern-day Earth. Pearl then takes up residence at Castle Forrester, where she stays with Bobo and Brain Guy until the end of the series (and the final version of the opening credits, featuring the castle setting). The season went along without many concerns, although the gang did have a struggle with one movie title that had been sent their way, as Mike recalled to IGN: "I remember Barry Schulman had a film that he picked for a showing on the air uncut, or un-*MST*-ized. Somehow that got sent to us, and we thought it was a screener, and we said, 'Oh, yeah, we have to do this thing,' and it got back to him. He said, 'I am never going to let them do a movie that we showed straight. That would be counter to the mission here.'" The Best Brain writers kept after Schulman, however, and he finally relented to have them use the movie *The Quest of the Delta Knights* for the end of the ninth season. As was common in such cases where the writers fight for a film, the experience of finally riffing it turned out not to be as much fun as anticipated, although fans now consider it to be one of the better episodes in the Sci-Fi years.

The season ended on September 26, 1998, with Sci-Fi deciding not to follow through on the nine-episode pickup, leaving the season at just thirteen episodes. As it turns out, Barry Schulman was also set to move on from Sci-Fi and was leaving the channel in the hands of Bonnie Hammer, who moved over from the parent network USA. Schulman did agree to renew *MST3K* for thirteen more episodes in a tenth season as one of his final acts for the channel. While Best Brains appreciated the effort, Hammer, as it turns out, was not happy with Schulman's order, as the series was showing little sign of rising ratings and ate up two hours in the schedule that could be used for other programming. She also initiated more oversight on the program, with insistence that the show make changes to scripts or other aspects that were more than Best Brains had experienced in any other capacity, even when doing the theatrical movie. As Kevin put it to Ken Plume, "The folks at Sci-Fi—wonderful people. Salt of the earth. Loved the show. The folks at USA—they really just dropped their pants and emptied their bowels on us as much as possible."

The tenth season went much like the ninth, with Sci-Fi showing no interest in adding additional episodes to the ordered thirteen for the season. Best Brains did offer fans the opportunity to see Joel Hodgson return (as mentioned previously in chapter 7) as part of a ploy for better ratings. That episode also had the return of TV's Frank for a brief follow-up, showing that he had been kicked out of Second Banana Heaven and was now working as a "soultaker," eventually playing with Bobo's soul as the episode came to an end. Fans were disappointed to see that the show had gone through the trouble of bringing back Joel but then not having him appear in the theater to do any riffing. When fans questioned Joel about this, he admitted that he did not participate in writing the riffs and therefore didn't feel right being in the theater to do someone else's jokes. Joel went on to say he liked the experience

but felt odd working face-to-face with another human being after all the years
of working with puppets.

With the manner that USA was treating the show as a misfit of science
(fiction . . . yeah, that was a reach, wasn't it?), it came as no surprise for everyone at Best Brains when Sci-Fi in February 1999 said that it was considering
not picking up the show for another season. Best Brains went public with
the news that same month, leading to Sci-Fi to publicly reply that the option
was still on the table, but by April it admitted the rumor was now fact and
MST3K would not be returning with new episodes.

Jim Mallon tried to put a positive face on the news, telling the *Star Tribune* that they had been there before and hoped to find another home, but
Murphy was more resigned, telling the newspaper, "I really have no regrets.
How many TV shows, except *Gunsmoke*, get to stay on that long?" To be fair
to Jim's optimism, there were two outlets looking into continuing the show,
the first being Rhino, who suggested continuing *MST3K* as a direct-to-video
series, which would be sold on videocassette on a periodic basis, but it soon
became clear that the expenses would be too great, and the idea was abandoned. According to Jim Mallon in his audio interview with Joshua Murphy,
there was also a brief discussion of continuing the program over on AMC,
back when it was still American Movie Classics and had not gone into producing other programs like *The Walking Dead*, as it soon would. Mallon told
the *Star Tribune* that Best Brains would be taking a brief break "to get some
perspective" before moving on to new projects, but after ten years of working
on the program that dominated his life and could be seen as having stagnated
his career, Jim Mallon felt the show and the production company had come
to a natural end. At first, some of the other cast members were upset that
there wasn't more of a push to carry on, with both Mike and Bill feeling the
show still had a few more years left in it, but Kevin and Jim—who had been
there since the beginning—were feeling the time was right, and Mary Jo Pehl

agreed, as she told *Wired* in 2014: "It had been coming down the pike, and I was not surprised. And I don't want to speak for everyone else, but I also remember being pretty pragmatic about it. I had worked there seven years, which was the longest I'd ever had a job in my whole life, and that is a great life for a television show."

By June 1999, Best Brains had closed up shop at the studio built in the warehouse in Eden Prairie, while an eBay auction sprang up in April 1999 by Jim Mallon to sell off pieces of the sets, props, and other bits and pieces around the offices, which did not sit well with Mike Nelson when he went back into the office to pick up a jacket he had left there along with a few other things from his desk. He told Something Awful in 2006, "I went back in to work to get some personal items and a few of them were already on the auction block and I had to actually physically rescue my own property." The auction, along with some items that were still available by way of the catalog sent to fans, took over a year to complete but had raised more than $50,000 by late 1999, with items like the two-foot model of the SOL selling for $1,294, and the planet logo for $5,500. Although it was a bonanza for fans to get pieces of the show, it was a resounding closure to the idea of the program coming back anytime soon, now that pieces of the program were going away. While there were some initial protests about the cancellation, Mallon and Murphy were most probably right; the show had run for over ten years, had seen success unimagined at the start, and had earned itself its own theatrical movie. It had survived multiple cast changes, channel jumps, and taste in movies—not a bad run at all, and work to be proud of for all involved, especially for Jim Mallon who had seen it all from before day one.

In the final episode of the original series, for the movie *Diabolik*, Pearl accidentally starts landing procedures for the SOL that cannot be undone, allowing Mike and the bots to escape while Pearl, Brain Guy, and Bobo pack up to head off to start life anew elsewhere. In the final scene of the last

Danger: Diabolik (1968) will be the last movie seen by Mike and the bots on the SOL before crashing to Earth and ending the original series. PARAMOUNT PICTURES / PHOTOFEST ©PARAMOUNT PICTURES

episode, Tom, Crow, and Mike now share an apartment and settle down to watch an old movie on television. As they watch the opening credits to *The Crawling Eye*, the first movie *MST3K* did when it moved to the Comedy Channel, they all begin riffing on the film, just like we all used to do on the couch with movies before we had ever even heard of *MST3K*. Crow remarks to Servo that the movie looks familiar, though they can't quite seem to place it. It's as if the whole process would never really end.

As it turns out, that would be true. It just took on other forms in the process, as time would tell.

9

Insert into the Time Tube

RiffTrax, The Film Crew, and Cinematic Titanic

We have got a gem of a Christmas movie. It is called Santa Claus Conquers the Martians.

Whaa? A-ho-ho, no, no, no, no, nooooooo, waaaaaaahhhhh!

—TRACE BEAULIEU SCREAMING AND RUNNING AWAY IN TERROR
AFTER BEING TOLD THE MOVIE HE WILL BE FORCED TO WATCH AS
PART OF *CINEMATIC TITANIC* IS ONE THAT HE HAD ALREADY BEEN
SUBJECTED TO WHEN DOING *MYSTERY SCIENCE THEATER 3000*

Mystery Science Theater 3000 may have shared its finale with fans on the Sci-Fi Channel on August 8, 1999, but that didn't mean the series itself immediately disappeared. As a matter of fact, there was still an episode to run on the Sci-Fi Channel: the rather tepid *Merlin's Shop of Mystical Wonder*, which had been missed in the confusion but finally aired on September 12, 1999.

Rhino continued to release videocassettes of episodes through January 2001, though it had switched over to individual DVD releases of movies in March 2000, several of which included the original uncut and unriffed version of each movie as an extra. In November 2002, Rhino began releasing DVD box sets of the program, with three to four movies in each set, along

Four of the seven or eight Musketeers—from left to right, Jim Mallon, Kevin Murphy, Trace Beaulieu, and Michael J. Nelson, on the set for *Mystery Science Theater 3000: The Movie*. PHOTO BY
MICHAEL KIENITZ, © GRAMERCY PICTURES

with various extras, such as introductions by cast members, interviews with
people connected to the movies, various shorts, and even bonus discs for
those who ordered through the Rhino website. As mentioned in chapter 5,
the tenth box set, which was released in August 2006, had to be pulled from
sale as it was released without having proper clearance for *Godzilla vs. Megalon*. This led to a short sketch as a bonus feature with the replacement disc
of *The Giant Gila Monster* that featured Joel, Frank, and Trace reprising their
roles to tell fans how to "trash" the disc (there is even a sly wink in the sketch
to show that everyone knew fans weren't going to dispose of the disc that
should not have been released, although they should) and replace it in the
box set with the new disc of *The Giant Gila Monster*. Even with that mishap,
Rhino released two more sets, ending with volume 12 in February 2008.

In the case of *Godzilla vs. Megalon*, as with *Godzilla vs. the Sea Monster*,
it came down to the dreaded issue of film rights. What was available to the

Comedy Channel and *MST3K* in season 2 and subsequent reruns for a few years was gone by the time Rhino put out the DVD box set, and those representing Toho Studio were not particularly running to have their Godzilla films ridiculed—certainly not when releasing the films unriffed could net them a bigger profit. The same thing occurred with the Gamera movies, and for a time it was assumed that those five films shown on *MST3K* would never be released. But eventually the rights were renegotiated and the films turned up in a box set by Shout! Factory as well as on the streaming services. That didn't stop fans from assuming for years that Sandy Franks had an issue with the way he was mocked on the program, even though other movies from Sandy Franks, such as *Time of the Apes* and the *Fugitive Alien* films never seemed to have any issues. It was more a matter of money than anything suggesting pride.

Jet Jaguar is having a rest as Megalon and Friend decide if they're going to stick his hand in a bowl of warm water in *Godzilla vs. Megalon* (1973). TOHO COMPANY / PHOTOFEST © TOHO COMPANY

Other films from the run began disappearing as well, with one of the best-remembered examples being *Rocketship X-M*, which was the first episode of season 2 and had the first appearance of TV's Frank and the introduction of Kevin Murphy doing the voice of Tom Servo. Certain rights to that movie were and still are connected to Wade Williams, who was mentioned in an earlier chapter for his agreement to allow *The Hideous Sun Demon* to be redubbed as *What's Up, Hideous Sun Demon*. When attempts were made to have the *MST3K* version of *Rocketship X-M* released on video, however, Williams said no. This led to speculation that Williams was holding back the rights because of issues he had with the concept of *MST3K* "ruining" movies that he owned the rights to, but Joshua Miller's interview with Williams from 2017 refutes that assumption. "I appreciate what they did," Williams told Miller in the interview when *MST3K* came up as a topic. "I thought that some of the comments were very funny." He also recognized that the program invested money—and paid well—for films that many other cable channels had little interest in or wanted to buy straight out to make part of their permanent library rather than use them for a specific period of time. "I think they keep a lot of these films alive that no one would have ever heard of. You're not going to get syndicators to buy a lot of the stuff they put on there."

Rather, his issue was that, unlike some other films like *Robot Monster* that probably "deserve" such riffing, *Rocketship X-M* was a classic science fiction movie that should not have been picked for the treatment given to it (corresponding with the protest that came with *This Island Earth* being used in the theatrical *MST3K* film). More importantly, when the movie had been picked up by the program for season 2, Williams did not own the television rights, and he had nothing to do with the movie rights being granted to the show. That didn't stop fellow fans of the movie from aggressively complaining to Williams for allowing the movie to be used by *MST3K* for many years. Thus his attitude on the film was strictly one of having "been there, done that" and not wanting to deal with the headaches that would come his way if he allowed it to be released on video.

Another reason for episodes missing from the show's run can be seen with Susan Hart, the widow of American International Pictures cofounder James H. Nicholson. Hart owns the rights to several AIP films, such as *It Conquered the World, Attack of the The Eye Creatures, I Was a Teenage Werewolf, The Amazing Colossal Man, and Terror from the Year 5000.* All of these movies were favorites among *MST3K* fans, and except for the short-time release on VHS of *The Amazing Colossal Man*, none of them has been released, as the cost of licensing them is so high that it makes the chance of any profits from a release difficult. This pertains not only to their release as *MST3K* riffs but in formats as simply straight presentations, and several of these films, remembered so well by so many from the days of various *Shock Theater* programs, have simply vanished. Wade Williams, in his interview with Miller, worried that Hart was diminishing the value of the movies by not letting others see them and allowing them to be forgotten, but that is the way it goes sometimes with licensing: people and studios place values so high that video companies pass them up, which has led to other films outside of those controlled by Hart, such films as *Soultaker* and *Final Sacrifice*, to disappear from availability after a time as well.

In some cases, the films have continued to be released, although a backlash sometimes remains from those connected to or who are celebrity fans of specific movies. *The Amazing Colossal Episode Guide* has anecdotes about lectures the writers have gotten from people like comedian Dennis Miller and writer Kurt Vonnegut about riffing movies, and those connected have even joked about avoiding Hollywood because they would be uncomfortable with meeting someone they had made fun of on the program. In an April 2014 interview at Indiana University Cinema, Roger Corman, a director and producer with many films that popped up on *MST3K*, was asked his opinion of the program; he quipped, "If you don't have any ability yourself, maybe you can make money by making fun of those who do." Jeff Lieberman, the director of the rather good movie *Squirm*, was livid about the film being used in the tenth season. It wasn't so much because of the riffing, as he told Devin Faraci for the website Birth, Movies, Death in 2013: "I don't give a shit what anybody says. It's a movie about worms." His dissatisfaction was that "some jerk at MGM sold it to them. They pay so little. I own 12% of *Squirm* and it's going to cheapen the value of the movie from then on." Lieberman felt that the movie was selling well, so why reduce it to be part of a package that makes it so "you can't sell it to stations at the same time"? On the other hand, while Rick Sloane was surprised at some of the harsh comments made about him at the end of the *MST3K* episode featuring his movie *Hobgoblins*, he appreciated the attention the show gave his movie, much as David Giancola did when the show did his film *Time Chasers*, and the cast and crew for the film had a party to watch the *MST3K* version.

As previously noted, at least many of the actors involved see and appreciate the humor in the show and have participated in some of the conventions done for the program over the years. David Warner, in a 2017 interview with A.V. Club, looked back fondly on making *Quest of the Delta Knights*, while admitting that it was such a low-budget affair that it naturally ended up on *MST3K*, and this was a common reaction when members of the *MST3K* cast and crew met actors from these films. Hodgson, in an interview with Brian Truitt of *USA Today* in 2013 stated that to those in the movies, it was a gig and okay to look back on it and laugh: "At the end of the day, all the people making them kinda go, 'Yeah, you know, a friend of ours was doing a movie and he wanted us to be in it and we made $600 that week.' They have a clear impression of what that means." As for the notorious supposed feud the show had with Joe Don Baker (who starred in *Mitchell* and *Final Justice* on the program), it's hard to say. Baker has never made much public comment about the show, and while in *The Amazing Colossal Episode Guide,* the writers make it clear there is a feud, they've also made contradictory comments, saying it was mostly just a joke. Even so, the rumors continue to the point where some say Baker actively hates the show simply because interviewers always ask about the feud, while it was suggested as well that his issue wasn't so much that the show made fun of his movies but that it went too heavy with personal comments about his weight and appearance. If this was the case, however, one would think there'd be more proof of it in the press, and there simply isn't. Maybe Baker simply doesn't care enough to worry about the jokes, which seems to be how many others involved with the movies used have reacted over the years.

Back in 2002, Bob Emmer, Garson Foos, and Richard Foos of Rhino sold off their interests in the company to Warner and then moved on to create a new company very similar to their original vision of Rhino, which was always about releasing obscure audio and video that may not be quite the most popular of tastes. The new company was named Shout! Factory, and among its early releases was a box set for the series *Freaks and Geeks* in 2004 as well as selected episodes of *SCTV.* There was also a more fan-based drive to get legal rights to material that other companies were passing up because it was too mired in legal red tape or—as referenced above—cost too much (such as finally achieving a release of the entire *WKRP* series on DVD after years of being pushed off because of music rights entanglement). In 2008, Mallon moved *MST3K* from Rhino to Shout! Factory, which began a vigorous schedule of more box sets of the show, starting in October 2008 with a "20th Anniversary" edition that continued with the volume numbers Rhino had used while also releasing some of the earlier single-volume DVDs that had gone out of print from Rhino when licensing had dried up. It would take nine more years, but in November 2017, the final full release of movies came out with volume XXXIX. These and other related content released from Shout! Factory helped keep *MST3K* fresh in the mind of fans, while streaming channels also picked up the show, with Netflix, Vudu, and Amazon offering episodes for free or for rent. More recent years have seen channels devoted to the earlier episodes on commercial-based streaming channels like Pluto and Tubi and even Shout! Factory's own streaming channel, allowing old and new fans a chance to catch up on the program.

As the brand continued to simmer, the various cast members moved on to other jobs. Josh Weinstein had lingered around Minneapolis for a year or so before moving out to Los Angeles, where he continued to work as a stand-up while trying to get work in the television industry. Having worked as a writer and performer on *MST3K*, even during the year when it was on national television, turned out to not exactly open doors. "[*MST3K*] was a help in the sense that it was a credit," Josh told the Official *MST3K* Info Club Web Site. "I wasn't starting totally from scratch. Many people didn't know what it was, or kinda knew but they had flipped by it." He found work with the NBC late-night program, *Later*, which had moved on from its original one-on-one talk show format with Bob Costa to a more traditional comedy show with interviews interspersed, after Greg Kinnear, whom Josh briefly worked for on his E! channel program *Talk Soup*, became the host in 1994. When Josh began writing in LA, he discovered the Writers Guild had an issue with his name, as there was already a Josh Weinstein working as a writer-producer in Hollywood (known mainly for his work on *The Simpsons*). It even caused some minor confusion for *MST3K* fans to see Josh's name appear in the credits of the animated show, only to later realize it was not the same guy they knew from the Minneapolis program. Josh decided to go with the stage name of J. Elvis Weinstein, for reasons he gave CNN in 2010: "I gave myself the Elvis because I loved that it gave me the initials J.E.W. and also somewhat inspired by being a fan of Elvis Costello, but mostly it's about J.E.W."

Weinstein stayed with *Later* for two years, becoming the head writer in his second year on the show. He then moved on to work as a writer-producer for the sitcom *Malcom & Eddie* in 1996. In 1999, Josh helped create a short-lived FX series called *Fast Food Films* with Trace Beaulieu, which took assorted theatrical and television movies and reedited them into parodies. His next credit was as writer-producer on the cult series *Freaks and Geeks,* remembered by *MST3K* fans for Weinstein's involvement and appearances by Trace Beaulieu in six episodes and Joel in two (with Dave Allen and Steve Higgins from *Higgins Boys and Gruber* appearing as well). Besides these and working on a couple of other series, *Dead Last* and *My Guide to Becoming a Rock Star,* Josh became a writer on the revised *America's Funniest Home Videos* in 1998 and worked with the show for many years. For those not familiar with the program, the show features various videos that everyday people made and thought were amusing. Typically, the videos involved children, pets, or home-bound accidents, with at least one "nut-shot," so it wasn't rocket science when it came to the level of humor, but it was mildly amusing and made for family-oriented television that anyone could watch. The show centered around wise-cracks made by the host(s) during the videos or in their introductions. As it turns out, the writers on the show used a style in the writers' room very much like that used at Best Brains for *MST3K.* The videos were played as the writers sat around the television set, made selections, and worked through gags that best fit the material. "I think the fact that I had been on *MST3K* interested the *AFV* people," Weinstein admitted to *Wired,* which along with his other work by that point helped him land the job. Always working on new material after leaving *America's Funniest Home Videos,* Josh has more recently produced documentaries, such as *Andy Kindler: I Wish I Was Bitter* (2014), *Michael Des Barres: Who Do You Want Me to Be?* (2015), and *I Need You to Kill* (2017).

Joel Hodgson was the next to leave the show, and he jumped into creating with his brother Jim as part of a production company called Visual Story

Tools. One of the first projects was a pilot for HBO called *The TV Wheel*, which was a comedy sketch show that had the premise of being filmed in real time on a television stage Joel invented called the X-Box. The stage was set up with a stationary camera in the center with all the sets built around it on a turntable, so when one sketch was over, the table would move to show the next sketch in another section of the stage. The pilot also deployed other in-camera tricks that created illusions of depth and objects not really there that would later be played off in *Cinematic Titanic*, plus an assortment of puppets to help Joel explain the process. HBO decided not to air the pilot on its channel and instead went with broadcasting it after the last episode of *MST3K* on Comedy Central. While it had naturally inventive moments and some funny segments, it also featured artists like Doug Benson, Paul Feig, David Cross, and Judd Apatow. Comedy Central allowed the pilot to air without commercials and with the ten-minute introduction by Joel to explain the process, but it was not picked up for a series.

There was also *Statical Planets*, which was a fifteen-minute "trailer" for a possible movie starring Morwenna Banks, who had appeared in *The TV Wheel*, and Frank Conniff. It was another project where the idea was to do most of the effects work in-camera while also setting up the film so that there would be a form of audience participation, as in the films of William Castle. While the trailer circulated to raise money, it never was completed, as the production would require so much work at the theaters to get the audience participation portion across that it would be cost prohibitive. There was also a project called "Pet Cassette," which Joel referred to in his A.V. Club interview from 1999 as being like the Tamagotchi game, where you had to care for and feed a video pet, only the pet would be on a videocassette; you'd watch the pet do things until you "reversed the process," and the pet would go back into the cassette as you pop the tape out. There was also a project with UPN that was mentioned in the A.V. Club interview that did not get past discussion. It was like Joel was throwing every idea he had up in the air, and nothing was leading to anything, and he soon realized he was panicking.

"After *Mystery Science Theater* ended," Joel said in reflection to *Wired*, "I felt like people were expecting me to break open a rock and find a new color of the rainbow, you know. So that's what I kind of thought I had to do." Feeling uptight in trying to create the next "big thing," Joel went to see Clint Holmes in Vegas who had only one big hit, "Playground in My Mind." In his show, Holmes mentioned that having the one hit for a time made him anxious to create another until he realized that he still had one more hit than most people. "Once he said that," Joel continued with *Wired*, "I went, oh shit, what am I trying to do? What are the chances of having another hit like *Mystery Science Theater?*"

Noting that such projects may have been great creatively but not great at getting something out that people could enjoy watching, Joel went back to work on more traditional projects, such as being a script doctor on *George of the Jungle* (1997) and cowriting *Honey, We Shrunk Ourselves!* the same year. He also worked on the game show *You Don't Know Jack* and on *Jimmy Kimmel Live!*, while helping as a "magic consultant" on the first season of the comedy series *Sabrina the Teenage Witch* in 1996. As an actor, he popped up doing the voice of the mayor in *Steven Universe*, while appearing on-camera as the hippie-like crewmember Zalian in the science fiction comedy series *Other Space*, which was created by Paul Feig (*Freaks and Geeks*) and featured Trace Beaulieu as the voice of a robot named Art (which was sometimes given as Crow's first name on *MST3K*).

Frank took off next, ended up in LA as well, and soon hooked up with Joel as he was starting on the *Sabrina* series for ABC. Frank worked on the show as a writer-producer while even popping up a handful of times as an actor. Frank would also do work on *Invader ZIM* and *The Drew Carey Show*, along with other television writing and the occasional acting gig, such as in the *Darkstar* game (which featured the cast of *Cinematic Titanic*—see further on in this chapter for more on that venture—in other roles) and in the movie *God Bless America*. In 2007, Conniff began working on a monthly live show with Jerry Beck at the Steve Allen Theater in LA called *Cartoon Dump*, which was performed as a very bad children's show set in a garbage dump where old, very odd, cartoons were shown. Besides creating *Cartoon Dump*, Frank played a secondary character called Moodsy Owl (who looks pretty much like a guy with no mask dressed in a bad owl costume). More recently, the show has moved to the QED Astoria in Astoria, New York, where it still continues. Another interesting side project involving Frank was that of *The Frank* (2014) a ten-minute short film, written and produced by and costarring Trace Beaulieu, with guest appearances by Dave Allen, Bill Corbett, Mary Jo Pehl, and J. Elvis Weinstein, along with vague glimpses of a certain two robots and possibly Joel in a jumpsuit. The film is a musical comedy about a mad scientist (Trace) who decides to bring his old friend Frank (Frank Conniff as a Frankenstein monster) back to life.

Beyond all of the above, Frank has also been quite prolific as an author, having published seven books of novellas and short stories out of Podhouse 90 Press, which appears to be his own publishing company. Podhouse 90 is also the name of a series of radio plays that Frank has written and made available through his website, https://frankconniff.com, such as *Dracula Has Risen in the Polls*, *South by South Satan*, and *The Steve the Talking Car Show*. His books include one on about twenty-five movies he had to watch at *MST3K*, called *Twenty Five Mystery Science Theater 3000 Films That Changed My Life in No Way Whatsoever,* along with *How to Write Cheesy Movies*, *Action Packed Apartments!*, and *You're Ruining the Dystopia for Everyone!*

As can be gauged by the way his name keeps popping up so far in this chapter, Trace certainly wasn't quiet after leaving the show, what with his connections to projects that Josh and Frank were involved in. Trace moved out to Los Angeles after leaving *MST3K* without any plans and only his savings to get him by. Soon after arriving, his agent landed him an audition with the *Star Wars* franchise. He received the script for *The Phantom Menace* and was told that he would be trying out for the part of Jar Jar Binks. Trace was hesitant about the part, "I got like three pages," Beaulieu told Ken Plume in 2007, "and there's this creature speaking to a Jedi master. And I didn't know. I thought, 'Boy, this is really awful! Oh, well, must be good, though!'" To do the voice audition, Trace needed recording equipment and knew Josh had some with a band he played in, so Trace contacted him. Although the audition failed, the reconnection with Josh led to a job offer that had opened on *America's Funniest Home Video*, which Beaulieu accepted and stayed with for many years.

As with Josh, Trace found that *MST3K* did little to open doors to get jobs in Hollywood, but it did get him noticed on the alternative comedy scene, which allowed him to perform in clubs when other work wasn't available. Trace appeared in a number of series performing either in small roles like that of his six appearances on *Freaks and Geeks* or in voice roles for animated shows, including an appearance as Crow in an episode of the puppet comedy series, *Transylvania Television* (2017). This was a series created out of WUCW, the old KTMA TV-23. (In a cutaway gag where Joel, Tom, and Crow are in silhouette in the theater after being forced to watch three thousand straight hours of bad movies, Crow is glad that they made it through the ordeal, only for Joel's head to explode afterward, leading to Crow to quip, "Huh, guess the theme song was wrong.") Trace also wrote for a variety of other formats, such as the excellent 1997 one-off comic book by Trace from Event Comics called *Here Come the Big People*, which was drawn by Amanda Conner. The comic deals with an alien invasion of thirty-foot-tall women who look and act like stereotypical mothers from 1950s sitcoms. A lone Earthling woman tries to determine what the aliens' motives are as men around the planet begin to become childlike in the presence of the aliens, but will she find the answer in time? It's a very funny and sweet one-off that hasn't really gotten its due. Trace also wrote another book with an illustrator, this time the 2010 book by Amorphous Productions, *Silly Rhymes for Belligerent Children*, with artist Len Peralta. The book is a series of poems about oddball children and (mostly) their demises, which shows off Beaulieu's dark sense of humor well. There was also an attempt in 2016 to crowdfund a comedy series called *Renfest* that was to star Trace, Mary Jo, Frank, and Dave Allen, but the funding was not met, and the project has since gone on the back burner.

Paul Chaplin spent some time writing about sports and investigating the economics of baseball, along with writing for NPR and *Elysian Fields Quarterly*. He has been the quietest of the writer/performers of the show, although he did turn up as one of the observers at Kinga and Jonah's wedding in the finale of season 11 of the series. There was also one more *MST3K*-related event with a Paul connection, as will be seen.

Mary Jo Pehl traveled after leaving the series and worked for National Public Radio (NPR) on *All Things Considered*, as well as writing for various publications. She wrote her first book, *I Lived with My Parents and Other Tales of Terror* in 2004, published by Plan 9, which she would look back on as a disaster. "I had such mortification, such shame about being in over my head and being delusional about what it entailed," Mary Jo told *Twin Cities Daily Planet* in 2011. "I'm so embarrassed to admit this: I thought 10,000 words would be like history of civilization, but it's barely a pamphlet." Spelling errors ran rampant, including her own name being misspelled, which was written off as being correct because it was "fact-checked." An attempt to have Pehl promote the book with an author's tour ended up traveling from city to city via Greyhound bus. After a stint writing a regular column for the *Minnesota Monthly*, Pehl came back with her second book, *Employee of the Month and Other Big Deals*, in 2011; it was a collection of essays about the good and bad that she experienced before and after *MST3K.* She followed that book up in 2022 with *Dumb, Dumb, Dumb* (Redhawk Publications), which is a personal story of Mary Jo digging through a box of reviews her mother had written over the years for books she had read and reflecting on her relationship with her mother, who had passed. In 2007, she moved to Austin, Texas, and began writing for periodicals in the city and state.

Upon moving to Austin, Pehl also became involved with a group called Master Pancake Theater, which performed at the Alamo Drafthouse Cinema located in the city. Headed by John Erler, Master Pancake Theater performs live mockery of movies playing on the big screen in a marriage of both *Mad Movies with the L.A. Connection* and *MST3K.* The group typically performs over more recent hit movies, bypassing licensing issues since people are paying to see the movie with just this "extra" on top of it, and with no claims of ownership in the process. Pehl had been asked to work with them and passed the word on to Joel, who liked the show, although he had reservations when they asked if he wanted to participate in riffing *The Hobbit.* He passed, seeing the movie as being "alive," while he preferred to do work on movies from the past or that were hard to find. "What I love most about movie riffing is, it takes things that are kind of forgotten and makes them fun again, it revives them and shows people," Joel told the MacGuffin. "I think that's one of the things people really like about *Mystery Science Theater 3000* is it shows people all these movies they would never see." But besides the reluctance to do newer films, the group showed Joel that there was still interest in the concept of movie riffing.

Bill Corbett began working with Mike Nelson, Kevin Murphy, Patrick Brantseg, and Paul Chaplin on a website called Timmy Big Hands, which was a collection of oddball humor items, including web games like "Kill-a-Guy," where you kill a man shown in the frame of the game by clicking on him, and articles and artwork that were nonsensical in many ways but always funny.

The website lasted a year and was finally pulled when it was realized that the money being paid from the site did not equal the amount of work there was to do. As Mike Nelson told Paul Czarnowski in an interview for CRC radio, "We thought about perhaps turning it into a book, or doing this or that, but it was just too complicated by that time, so we just folded it down." The year 2001 saw Corbett working on an animated series (actually more like zooming in on artwork that fades to other artwork than proper animation, as the adventure is told in storybook fashion) for the Sci-Fi Channel website called *The Adventures of Edward the Less*, which was created and written by Mike, Bill, Kevin, Patrick, and Paul Schersten and featuring all for the voices, along with Mary Jo Pehl. The series is thirteen episodes ranging from three to five minutes in length, with music by Mike Nelson, and is essentially a parody of *Lord of the Rings*.

With his work for Sci-Fi, Bill submitted an idea for a web series about a spaceship that looks like a human being but is full of tiny humanoid aliens. After Sci-Fi passed on the idea, Bill revived it with cowriter Rob Greenberg (*Frasier, Cloudy with a Chance of Meatballs*), and they developed it into a script called *Starship Dave*. The project was eventually tied to Eddie Murphy and green-lit at 20th Century Fox, where it was given the new title *Meet Dave*. As typical with Hollywood productions, the movie was completely out of the scriptwriters' hands, and additional rewrites and improvs on set changed the intentions of the script. The results, released in 2008, faced heavy backlash from critics and fans and a disaster at the box office at a time when Eddie Murphy—once a prime star in Hollywood—was struggling to regain his status in movies. Corbett stated to *Wired* about the experience, "It turned out to be kind of a shitty movie, but it was a really interesting experience, because I saw how bad movies can be made. I actually liked a lot of the people I was working with—they were not stereotypically creepy Hollywood producers. But when you are creating something so huge—and something that involves so many people with high stakes, often working at cross purposes—the odds of any movie being genuinely good are pretty low."

Kevin Murphy moved into writing a column, "The Bottom Shelf," for *Total Movie & Entertainment* magazine, only for the magazine to fold soon after (although not because of his articles). One of the bigger projects he worked on was that of a book called *A Year at the Movies*. The book details Kevin's odyssey of going to the theater in various ways, each day, for a full year. This included traveling to other countries and continents, seeing the same film with different people, trying to eat a full Thanksgiving dinner in a darkened theater, and—perhaps most interesting—going to the movies after the World Trade Center was destroyed on September 11, 2001. The book is not as humorous as one would expect, nor was it intended to be, yet thanks to the observational nature of the text, it is probably the best-written book released by the *MST3K* writers.

Not that Michael J. Nelson didn't give him a run for his money. Almost immediately after leaving *MST3K,* Nelson produced the book, *Mike Nelson's Movie Megacheese* (HarperCollins, 2000), which was a series of essays about movie and television, including some material he had already seen published in *Home Theater and Entertainment.* The success of that book led to a sequel in 2002 that covered more common-day events and Mike's thoughts about various topics, called *Mike Nelson's Mind over Matters*. A third book appeared in 2003, *Mike Nelson's Death Rat!,* his first novel. While the title suggests it was a parody of a "giant killer animal" movie, it instead is a comical look at the publishing world and how a little white lie (or a few) to help push sales of a book can escalate into something much bigger.

Since that time, Mike has held off on writing more books. When asked on Reddit back in 2010 about any plans for more, Nelson replied, "I'm a little sour on the experience because the editor who brought me on left and the guy that took over hated my writing and didn't get what was funny about it.

Now that's a completely legitimate point of view, but probably not from the editor of my book!" Instead, he wrote the occasional "Watch Dog" column for *TV Guide* in addition to writing for the previously mentioned Timmy Big Hands website.

Mike soon after ventured back into television and video, including as a story editor for *VeggieTales in the House* in 2014. A major focus to his work occurred when he was contacted by Legend Films, a video company that was releasing DVDs of movies that were either public domain or cost-effective to get the licensing. Legend did a fairly nice job cleaning up the films, although it tended to believe that colorization was the way to go when releasing the movies on DVD, which was a deal-breaker for some viewers. While doing these new releases, Legend wanted to add commentary to some of the movies, and Mike Nelson was asked to do solo commentaries, which could be turned on or off on the DVD player, for the releases. The first release was *Reefer Madness* in April 2004, followed by *Night of the Living Dead* in the fall of 2004. Two releases followed each year with his commentaries: *Carnival of Souls* and *House on Haunted Hill* in 2005, *Plan 9 from Outer Space* and *Little Shop of Horrors* in 2006, and finally *Swing Parade* in 2007.

While doing these commentaries, Nelson teamed up with Bill Corbett and Kevin Murphy to create a new series of video and DVD releases for Rhino that would be called *The Film Crew*, and the three would sometimes host introductions to movies under that name on various movie channels, such as AMC, Sundance, and the Starz/Encore channel. *The Film Crew* was set up as being the three men working in a basement at the video company. Commentaries on movies were all the rage at the time, but there were a good number of movies that didn't have commentaries for their DVD releases. So the premise of *The Film Crew* was that they were hired by the video company to do commentaries whether they knew anything about the movies or not. The four films done for *The Film Crew* were *Hollywood after Dark* (also known as *Walk the Angry Beach* and *The Unholy Choice*) from the early 1960s and starring Rue McClanahan as a stripper, *Wild Women of Wongo* (1958), *Killers from Space* (1954 and starring Peter Graves), and *The Giant of Marathon* (1959). The show was set up with the three talking at the beginning to the head of the company, Bob Rhino, who would be off on some hugely expensive adventure and called in to dictate what new movie the Crew was to watch. The three then gathered around the television set and did their riffing until midway through the film, when a "lunch break" occurred that allowed for a short skit that usually involved Kevin Murphy never getting to eat his lunch. The commentary then began again, while a final short sketch at the end tied everything together.

Once production was done on the four films, Rhino decided not to release the video. Fans heard of this and initially thought that because the show was similar in tone to *MST3K*, which was being released through Rhino on video, Jim Mallon had threatened to pull the rights to the show unless Rhino refused to release the *Film Crew* videos. There has never been any proof of this rumor however, and Kevin, in an interview with Plume in 2007, stated that Rhino "didn't think it would be as complimentary as we did." Shout! Factory, on the other hand, was happy to pick up the show (redubbing Bob Rhino's name to Bob Honcho) and released the four episodes in 2007. Although there were some minor discussions on doing more, when Shout! Factory did not request any and the sets were destroyed, it was decided to move on.

What occurred instead was a chance with Legend Films to continue with more commentaries on movies and Mike Nelson suggested doing something a little different. The idea was one that had been around for a little while in science fiction fandom, where fans created alternative commentary—sometimes even with actors or crew members from the productions under discussion—and traded or sold these to other fans on CD and other formats. Nelson's initial concept was to do riffing as was done with *MST3K* but for bigger movies instead of the bad and public domain ones that filtered through in the show and with *The Film Crew*. In other words, what if there was a chance to do more movies that were like *This Island Earth* or even bigger?

Nelson took the idea to a lawyer to see if a legit movie could be released with his own commentary and labeled as satire. After being informed he'd be sued out of existence, he decided to go with another tack: release a CD commentary, much like the fan-generated commentaries mentioned already, and sell those so that people could play them along with the movie when watching it. This would avoid any copyright issues since a person would have to already own a copy of the movie to play the CD. By the mid-2000s, it became easier to move past the idea of CDs and instead go with MP3 and other audio sources that could be purchased over the internet. Thus *RiffTrax* was born in 2006.

RiffTrax began with the previous audios for *Plan 9 from Outer Space* and *Night of the Living Dead*, but in July 2006 the product went wild by releasing a commentary for the Patrick Swayze 1989 movie, *Road House*, followed by *The Fifth Element* and *Star Trek V: The Final Frontier*. As the work continued, Kevin Murphy and Bill Corbett began helping with commentaries as well, and while Mike sometimes would have others contribute, the common practice was to stick with Kevin and Bill. The riffing commentaries became so successful that the company branched out, and in 2015, both Bridget and Mary Jo began working as a duo on several features and shorts as well.

In 2012, Legend Films decided to head off in another direction with the company and sold its interest in *RiffTrax* to Nelson, Murphy, Corbett, and David G. Martin, who was the CEO of *RiffTrax*. From there, the gateway was open for more releases, including films where licensing was available or in the public domain. The online site began expanding to cover both the DVDs (and eventually Blu-rays) of selected titles, while a streaming service was created for several of the films and shorts available for subscribers to be

Flyer for *RiffTrax* live show of *Jack the Giant Killer*.

able to watch and even download. Since 2006, *RiffTrax* has featured close to five hundred movies and over four hundred shorts with humorous riff commentaries, as well as one or two live events each year with the resulting riffs appearing in various theaters across the country in a simulcast.

RiffTrax and the continued sale of older *MST3K* episodes (which the *RiffTrax* site eventually began to sell as well) showed that there was still an ongoing interest in using the riffing formula of the show. Other outlets also sprang up via the internet, with various people trying to do homage to the show, such as *Project Popcorn*, which was a Russian homage (and not a rip-off, as some have said) created by fans Anton Neumark and Timofey Chernov in 2002. *Incognito Cinema Warriors XP* was another homage series; this one, by Rikk Wolf, falls back (perhaps unintentionally) on the idea of a guy stuck in a theater during a zombie apocalypse with two robots and forced to watch bad movies and shorts. Other programming played off the concept as well, such as ESPN's *Cheap Seats* (2004–2006), where Randy and Jason Sklar watched various old sporting events from the ESPN libraries and made fun of them. *Cheap Seats* even went one step further in an episode from 2005 by having Mike, Bill, and Kevin appear in silhouette as their characters at the bottom of the screen to make fun of the brothers hosting the show. The characters also turned up in shows such as *Futurama*, *Arrested Development*, and *The Simpsons*. And while it was fun to get back together, it was while doing a commentary with Joel and Josh for a documentary about *Star Wars* fans that Trace realized he didn't feel much of a connection to the riffing anymore, as he told Plume in 2007: "I realized that without [Crow], I really didn't have a reason to mock anything. I actually kinda like stuff. People have talked about, 'Oh, you know you should do that again,' It's like, 'Well, we did it.' I mean, that's kind of why I left, was like, 'I got it; I did that thing already.'"

It was clear that there was love for *MST3K* out there, even years after the show had ended. With that in mind, Joel Hodgson approached Jim Mallon in

2007 about doing a new season of the show with the old cast. Mallon told the Official *MST3K* Info Club Web Site, "The more we talked the more it became clear that there were many hurdles to overcome . . . we only got so far in our back-and-forth before I told Joel I had to focus on the pending launch of mst3k.com." Which Mallon did; it was an updated version of the older official site and included new material and a series of animated web episodes featuring Tom, Crow, and Gypsy. The episodes, also known as "The 'Bots Are Back!," were written by Paul Chaplin and featured Paul as Crow, James Moore as Tom, and Jim as Gypsy. Four short episodes were completed before the series was abandoned. "I had high hopes for the Flash animation, but it turned out they were four times as expensive as I was led to believe. We really could not afford to do them, and when that became clear I pulled the plug and we shifted the web site [*sic*] direction." Response to the shorts was negative as well, with fans feeling that the writing and voices didn't really match the characters and the quality of the animation was not up to par. Mallon kept the website going for a while before it eventually reverted to the original format.

With a reunion season out of the question, since Mallon owned the rights to the program and Hodgson could not move ahead otherwise, Joel instead decided to reunite with several of the members of the *MST3K* cast in a new venture called *Cinematic Titanic*. Drawing together Trace, Frank, Mary Jo, and Josh, the group wrote riffs for the movie *Brain of Blood*, which had its title changed for the riffing to *The Oozing Skull*. The visual look of the show was like *MST3K*—in fact, one could say that the look and sound of the show was even much more similar to *MST3K* than *The Film Crew* was—with silhouettes of the five members standing or sitting on various platforms and framing the movie as it played and they riffed it.

The show even had a story line to explain the concept, with the five members having been possibly kidnapped by a scientific/paramilitary group who knew of their work before riffing movies. They were asked to take part in an

Santa Claus Conquers the Martians (1964) was such a traditional favorite of *MST3K* that both *Cinematic Titanic* and *RiffTrax* would revisit the movie to riff it again. EMBASSY PICTURES CORPORATION / PHOTOFEST © EMBASSY PICTURES CORPORATION

experiment where they watched films, and then their responses were recorded and put into the Time Tube (which lowered at the end of each episode for Joel to return onscreen with a disc to drop into the tube). Thus, when Trace makes a run for it after hearing they are about to watch *Santa Claus Conquers the Martians*, he is seen being dragged back by force to participate—still trapped, as it were, into watching bad movies.

Each of the story line-related episodes featured a break in the middle of the program to allow one of the cast members to do something that usually involved the illusion of the silhouettes on the screen, such as being able to bring down a chandelier or bring in a famous artist to play for the group. This is even mocked in the *Santa Claus Conquers the Martians* episode when Joel announces he has gifts for everyone that are said to be extraordinary. The black images that appear look promising, but when the others attempt to leave their platform to get the item, Joel makes them back off, thus leading to everyone dismissing it all as just him using cutouts and effects and not really giving them anything.

Besides the version of the show shot in this manner, there were several live performances by the group, starting with a private show for Industrial Light & Magic in San Francisco in December 2007. Some of these live shows, which featured other performers or even some of the members themselves doing material as opening acts, were recorded and later released on video. The live shows were not presented as part of a story line; instead, Joel would simply introduce the cast and then everyone sat to the side of the film to read their scripts as the movie played. These shows would continue every year from 2008 up through 2013, with a final, double-feature performance on December 30, 2013: *The Wasp Woman* and *The Doll Squad.*

Evidently, although Trace in 2007 was off on riffing movies, the bug must have bitten him again, for when *Cinematic Titanic* ended, he and Frank Conniff, who had done some podcasts together besides the work with Joel and the others over the past few years, decided to continue working together. Developing new material as a duo, the two began touring as The Mads Are Back and riffed over movies to audiences across the country. After COVID-19 hit in 2020 and traveling was restricted for health reasons, the pair began doing monthly live events online and have continued with this process ever since, with fans being able to purchase "tickets" to the online events and be able to download their riffed version of various movies In October 2022, the pair even went full "Halloween" and dressed for their monthly online riffing dressed as Dr. Forrester and TV's Frank.

After years of developing the idea of an *MST3K* live tour, *Cinematic Titanic,* The Mads Are Back, and *RiffTrax* all proved that it was feasible and profitable if properly handled. The biggest issue for *Cinematic Titanic* was that the group of five were in various parts of the country, and everyone had projects of their own, so a lot of coordination was required to get everyone together to write and perform. Yet it could be accomplished, and obviously there was a love for movie riffing that Joel and the others had created through *Cinematic Titanic* and that was being carried on by Mike, Kevin, and Bill over at *RiffTrax*. It could work, and it was wanted. *Cinematic Titanic* may have had its run, but Joel was already looking ahead to heading back home for more.

10

All Hail the White Dot

MST3K in the Next Millennium

Forresters never give up!

Well, officially, off the record, they never see anything through to completion.

So, they always keep a useful moron around to pin the blame on. Speaking of which, Max, I'd like to welcome you into the Second Bananas Club with some traditional social grooming.

—Pearl, Brain Guy, and Bobo, when meeting up with Kinga and Max during *Cry Wilderness* (season 11, episode 2)

The deal with Shout! Factory had worked out well for Jim Mallon. There was money to be made with *MST3K*, and the DVD sales had proved that. But that train was nearly at its end in 2015, as the releases had taken care of many of the available episodes and there were only five or six more possible box sets to be released. Of course, there were eventual rereleases to come and other mixes that could be made, but the end was clearly in sight. The attempt to restart *MST3K* as animated web episodes had been a bust back in 2007, and while the writers and actors involved with the old show were coming up with new projects that played off the program, there simply wasn't much for Jim Mallon to do on his own. Besides, he was working his way toward becoming a licensed therapist, with an MA and nearing completion of being evaluated to get his LPCC (Licensed Professional Clinical Counselor licensure). It was looking like the right time to move on.

So when Joel and Shout! Factory came forward with a proposal to buy out his stakes in *MST3K*, he was ready to listen. On November 10, 2015, *Variety* announced that the deal had been made, with Shout! Factory owning all the proprietary rights of the brand, including assets and global intellectual property. Mallon, after having lain low for a few years, even made a public statement mentioned in the *Variety* article, saying, "Fans of *MST3K* can celebrate as Shout! Factory begins a new *MST3K* adventure with Crow, Tom Servo, and Gypsy reuniting with Joel Hodgson. Shout! Factory is perfectly placed for this next chapter as they have been our partner and excellent stewards of *MST3K* for the past seven years."

On the same day that the news dropped, Joel Hodgson wasted no time in announcing a Kickstarter campaign to create new episodes of the series. The initial goal was for $2 million in order to make three new episodes of the show, while the top goal was $5.5 million so that twelve episodes could be made. When the campaign was over, the total was over $6.3 million, allowing for two additional episodes to be made for a total of fourteen for season 11; also known as "The Return."

On November 16, less than a week after starting, it was announced that the new host would be Jonah Ray. Ray (August 3, 1982–) is a musician-comedian from Hawaii who worked with the Upright Citizens Brigade and in such shows as *The Sarah Silverman Program* and *Jimmy Kimmel Live!* He is also known for his work on genre podcast programming and seemed to be a good fit as the new host. Jonah had also grown up on the show and had memorized *Mystery Science Theater 3000: The Movie* (a film he got to see in the theaters when visiting relatives in Nevada) so intensely that when he released albums later in his career, he titled them after dialogue from the film: *This Is*

Crazy Mixed-Up Plumbing and *Hello, Mr. Magic Plane Person, Hello.* He was also the cohost of *The Meltdown with Jonah and Kumail* on Comedy Central between 2014 and 2016, as well as *Hidden America with Jonah Ray* on Seeso from 2016 through 2017.

In 2010, Ray had joined a weekly podcast called *Nerdist*, alongside Matt Mira and Chris Hardwick, that became *ID10T with Chris Hardwick* in 2017. The podcast, an interview show, was where Ray met Joel Hodgson, when Hodgson was interviewed on the program in 2012. The two ran into each other several times over the next few days (so often that Ray felt the need to tell Hodgson that he wasn't stalking him) and began a friendship that would lead to some writing together. When the time came to begin looking for actors for the new version of *MST3K*, Hodgson asked Ray if he wanted the role of host on the new show, and Ray immediately took him up on the offer.

This was followed on November 23, 2015, with the announcement that Hampton Yount (June 14, 1984–) and Baron Vaughn (December 18, 1980–) had been added as Crow and Tom, respectively (Vaughn would later appear on camera as Dr. Kabal, "mysterious financier from the future," in season 13). Felicia Day (June 28, 1979–) was also announced as Kinga Forrester. Day, born in Huntsville, Alabama, majored in mathematics and music performance before moving to LA to work as an actor. She appeared in *Buffy the Vampire Slayer* and had an excellent smaller role in the movie *Warm Springs*, starring Kenneth Branagh as Franklin D. Roosevelt, where she got to sing "I Won't Dance." She also created the web series *The Guild*, a comedy about a group of gamers, which was very popular and award-winning and appeared in *Dr. Horrible's Sing-Along Blog*. Hodgson met Day at the 2015 Salt Lake Comic Con, was impressed with her work, knew after talking to her that she was a fan of the show, and decided that she would be perfect for the part.

Soon after, comedian-actor-writer Patton Oswalt (January 27, 1969–) was added to play Max, TV's Son of TV's Frank. (An announcement that surprised Frank Conniff, as he had not been made aware of the development and wasn't sure how he felt about it. Oswalt admitted surprise as well that Conniff had not been involved in the decision to create a son for his character, but Frank brushed off any anxiousness Oswalt had, knowing that any miscommunications were certainly not Oswalt's fault.) Oswalt had been in a number of projects over the years and was known for comedic work that dove into the world of geekdom at times, so he was a good fit as well. Rebecca Hanson, an alumna from Second City, was added to play two roles: the first woman to play the role of Gypsy/GPC, and Synthia, an awkward clone of Pearl Forrester who at times appears to be possibly the smartest person in the room. Hanson is the wife of Tim Ryder, who wrote and directed on the new show and eventually played Tom Servo on a couple of the live tours to come. Several writers were added, headed by Elliott Kalan, who had worked on *The Daily Show with Jon Stewart*. Other famous faces were added to make guest appearances as well, like Joel McHale, Jerry Seinfeld, Neil Patrick Harris, and Mark Hamill.

Initially, there was talk that the series would involve Trace, Frank, and Mary Jo in their respective earlier roles as a means to introduce the newer characters, with Dr. Clayton Forrester mentoring Kinga, who was to be a more innocent newcomer to the world of mad scientists. However, as things got closer to the Kickstarter, all discussions that had previously been made between Joel and Trace changed. Joel's statement at the time was that the show "is built to be refreshed with new people and new ideas," as he told *Wired*. He went on to say to the *Los Angeles Times*, "We're in our 50s, why not let somebody in their 30s do it like when we started? Most of the narrative out there was, 'Just re-create it exactly as we remember it.' I felt like that that's not the real spirit of it." Trace said little, other than to make clear he was not involved with the new show, as was the statement made by many others of the old cast. Many cited having creative control over their own work, with no need to go back to *MST3K*, while Mike said that he had been pretty much a "hired hand" and was perfectly happy continuing his work with *RiffTrax*.

To some fans, this made sense: everyone had moved on. But to others, there was a sense of loss in not seeing the "band get back together," and rumors spread of all type of reasons as to why the former members of the cast were not back. Perhaps the same midwestern tendency to downplay emotional moments was a factor as well. After all, fans later learned of Josh's reason for leaving and Joel's arguments with Mallon, which were downplayed at the time, so fans tended to wonder if all this "lack of noise" from the other former *MST3K* members wasn't loudly saying they disagreed with the direction Joel was taking the new show. Meanwhile, people like Frank and Trace were finding themselves stuck in a perpetual loop of questions as to when they would be involved with the new show, which would lead to their occasionally somewhat heated responses while saying variations of "no" over and over. It was as if any work done by the individuals after *MST3K* didn't matter, only the old show, and only if the people could somehow transform themselves into how they were in 1989. No wonder there were frustrations. Nevertheless, many original members did have some connections with the new show, such as Paul Chaplin returning to do some writing as well as appear as an Observer in the final episode of season 11. Mary Jo, Bill, and Kevin all returned as Pearl, Brain Guy, and Bob for a couple of episodes that season, while Mary Jo as Pearl is now a regular in season 13 (2022).

To further dispel concerns, on June 28, 2016, Joel and Jonah appeared live with nearly everyone from the old *MST3K* cast to do several shorts for *RiffTrax* for what was called *RiffTrax Live: MST3K Reunion Show*. Joel and Jonah riffed a short and then appeared with everyone else for a couple of quick ones at the end of the show. Fans no doubt enjoyed seeing everyone together and hoped that everyone involved enjoyed being together as well. But that was just a brief moment to share together. Immediately afterward, everyone went back to their own things. Funnily, some probably looked at that situation and felt sad it had to end. But it merely showed how one spark could create so many other things. Joel and Jonah went back to the new *MST3K*, Bridget and Mary Jo went off to do a new *RiffTrax*, while Mike, Kevin, and Bill went to work on their own *RiffTrax* stuff, and Trace and Frank concentrated on the Mads. Four new projects out of one place, and each with multiple plans awaiting them. A further olive branch was delivered to fans during the live *RiffTrax* event on August 18, 2022, which celebrated the team's thirty-second live event and sixteenth anniversary of the group. Before the film were several video congratulations from well-known fans and prominent people connected to *RiffTrax*, such as James Nguyen, who directed *Birdemic* (2010) and *Julie and Jack* (2003), both films well remembered as being riffed by the trio. Included in the congrats were Frank and Trace, together on the screen, to wish the group well, while Joel appeared (sitting next to a presentation of the Gizmoplex from season 13 of *MST3K*) to reminisce about the gang all doing their first live show thirty years before for *World without End* in August 1992 and congratulating the *RiffTrax* team for making live riffing an ongoing reality. Thus, while everyone seems to be quite set on their own projects, they also seem to be satisfied to publicly support the success of the others from those days of the original *MST3K* as well.

Production on the new *MST3K* began in January 2016, with recordings done between September and October of that year in Los Angeles while film clearance was taken care of through Shout! Factory. Movie riffs were recorded at a separate soundstage before filming Jonah, Tom, and Crow in "the theater," thus filming them acting out the dialogue that was already recorded. The sets were updated to speak to a new era, with a large set for Kinga's lab, featuring a band off to one side and a tube on the other side that sends Jonah up to the Satellite of Love. The revised SOL looked similar on the outside, but the inside had developments made to it, including a new tunnel system that finally appears to be livable space (well, as long as you aren't there when each area is closed off and jammed together). The theater area, now fitted to match modern widescreen television sets, had seats farther away from the camera, making Jonah and the bots look smaller than in the previous version of the series.

To set up the story line, Kinga is working on the dark side of the moon in an area called Moon 13. A distress signal was sent out to attract a subject for the movie experiment and Jonah, an expert pilot working for Gizmonic, picks up the call. As with Joel becoming Joel Robinson, Jonah Ray becomes Jonah Heston, having been given the last name of actor Charlton Heston, who played the hero in *The Omega Man*, one of Joel's initial sources for *MST3K* back in 1988. Responding to the call, Heston is captured and transported to a new version of the SOL, along with Crow, Servo, and Gypsy (now given the name of GPC, after concerns that the original name has racial overtones), and forced to continue in the experiment to watch bad movies. As the series moves along, it is clear that Jonah is a creator and seems very intent on building new robots to be pals with Tom and Crow, who are not happy about the idea. After many robots are destroyed, two emerge as regulars on the show (fulfilling an original KTMA idea Joel had of alternating robots with the host on the show, although they have yet [as of 2022] to become normal contributors in the theater segments). The two new ones are M. Waverly, played by Grant Baciocco, and the piano-player Growler, who is supposed to somewhat resemble Rowlf the Dog from the Muppets and is played by Russ Walko.

In July 2016, Netflix announced that it had picked up the series to air on April 14, 2017, with all fourteen episodes and then for another season. The first season ended with a cliffhanger, with Jonah—who appears to be at least eight feet two when standing next to Kinga—about to be forced into marrying Kinga as part of a publicity stunt, only for Max to release a monster who carries Jonah away.

Frank Conniff, Trace Beaulieu, Jonah Ray, Bridget Nelson, Joel Hodgson, Mary Jo Pehl, Bill Corbett, Mike Nelson, and Kevin Murphy—together again, some for the first time, to riff *Superman* at the *RiffTrax Live! MST3K Reunion Show* from 2016.

Jonah, Joel, and others took the show on a live tour in the summer of 2017, riffing on two movies: *Eegah* and *Argoman the Fantastic Superman*. As *Eegah* is famously known among fans for its appearance in the original series and for the line "Watch out for snakes!" the tour became known as the "Watch Out for Snakes! Tour." Prerecorded video was done to include Kinga and Max, while the rest of the regular cast—with Tim Ryder as Tom Servo—appeared in character for the show. A subsequent live tour occurred in 2018; called the "30th Anniversary Tour," it featured *The Brain* and *Deathstalker II*. In 2019 and 2020, "The Great Cheesy Movie Circus Tour," featured *No Retreat, No Surrender* and *Circus of Horrors*. More surprisingly, it would not feature Jonah but instead would have Joel back in the jumpsuit for what he claimed was the last live tour he'd do in character. After COVID-19 finally began to dissipate, the team was back for another tour in late 2021 through early 2022 called "The Time Bubble Tour" and presented new host Emily Marsh (more on her in a moment) as Emily Connor for the movie *Making Contact*.

The return of *MST3K* in 2017 saw the new gang riff on this 1961 Danish movie, *Reptilicus*.
AMERICAN INTERNATIONAL PICTURES (AIP)/ PHOTOFEST © AMERICAN INTERNATIONAL PICTURES

The second season played out with many of the same people and began airing on Netflix on November 22, 2018—Thanksgiving Day. The new season was only six episodes, but it was determined to base the season around the concept of dropping all the episodes at the same time, with Jonah and the bots forced into a "gauntlet" to watch all six new movies one immediately after the other. As for Jonah having been taken away at the end of the previous season and married to Kinga, none of it is really explained other than to suggest that it was over with and time to move on.

The twelfth season also revived Josh Weinstein as Dr. Erhardt, who seemed a lot calmer and had with him TV's Frank's and Dr. Forrester's ashes, which he planned to scatter. Dr. Erhardt returned in the final episode of the season as well. In the ending, Jonah managed to escape and leave Kinga and Max stuck in a mini-theater, where the movies they had forced on him began to replay.

He was a boy, but now he's a man! J. Elvis Weinstein returns to the role of Dr. Erhardt in seasons 12 and 13, proving himself to be the most successful of the Mads. He will bring back Servo's "mighty voice" in Joel's new episodes in season 13.

At that point, things took a nasty turn when Netflix announced it would not be seeking a third season for the show. There were further issues: the 2020 tour ended just as COVID-19 was causing theaters to shut down, and movies and television programming had limited shooting schedules due to concerns of spreading the virus. To no longer be attached to a streaming service like Netflix was going to be rough—for a while, it looked like it might be the end—yet in the spirit of cooperation during the COVID shutdown, the team from the show appeared on streaming channels on May 3, 2020, to show an episode from season 1 of the Comedy Channel, *Moon Zero Two.* The special event was hosted by Emily Marsh, who had appeared in a limited acting role in the previous live tour, as Emily Crenshaw. Emily and the bots then watched and essentially riffed an episode of *MST3K.* The special was followed with a discussion between cast members Felicia Day, Tim Ryder, Rebecca Hanson, and Jonah Ray. As one can expect with such a quickly put together production during a period where there was supposed to be great social distancing, the show had a few hiccups along the way. But it seemed to go over well and was followed up in the summer of 2021 with additional review of earlier episodes of *MST3K* by various cast members and writers.

These special episodes in 2021 also tied in with a new Kickstarter campaign that began on April 6, 2021, called "Let's Make More *MST3K*." The goals were pretty much set up as for the previous Kickstarter, $2 million to help create three episodes and on up, but something new was added: a dedicated streaming channel for all *MST3K* episodes, including the new ones planned for 2022. The new channel would be called the Gizmoplex, would have tiers directing people to various areas of the site to find different items, and would act as a one-stop place for people to buy episodes, talk to other fans, and find some other surprises along the way.

The second Kickstarter was successful, with incentives such as a 3D episode of *The Mask* (1961), with 3D glasses to be sent to subscribers, and episodes hosted by Emily Marsh as Emily Connor. Marsh had been introduced over time through the live tour and on the various one-off reriffs, and she had hosted the tour that took place between 2021 and 2022, so her addition to the cast was not completely surprising. Her being used as an actor rather than a puppeteer was a surprise to her, however. Having trained as a puppeteer with Madcap Puppets in Cincinnati, Ohio, Marsh had embarked on a successful career in puppetry for a few years when she heard that the live *MST3K* tour was looking for puppeteers. Having been a fan of the original show, which she had watched with her dad, she auditioned. She soon received an email offering her a job on the tour, but as an actor instead of working a puppet. "I auditioned, and I got the role, and I got the offer in the email, I was like, 'Wait, this isn't a puppet track. What's happening? Why am I being a human? Oh, I guess I'm being a face actor now,'" she told the *Cincinnati Enquirer* in 2021 while on tour. "Some of my friends came up after a show and said, 'We could see you. It was weird.'"

In the story line, Emily is selected to be a second test subject besides Jonah to help speed the process of the experiment along and is being held in a simulated version of the SOL called the Simulator of Love, along with her own versions of GPC, Crow, and Servo. Marsh's take on the character is a good variation of the traditional role of luckless guy host, with her Emily full of pep and running her side of the show with the energy of a host of . . . well . . . a puppet show, actually, and making for a change of pace from the other episodes with Jonah. The season also returned Joel Robinson for a few episodes as a third test subject when Dr. Erhardt goes through a portal and pulls Joel and his version of the SOL from the year 3000 (with no explanation as to how he got there) to Moon 1, where Kinga and Max work now.

The series was done on a different scale than seen in the Netflix years. It had not quite the budget of the Netflix version and had to be put together during some of the worrisome months of the pandemic. This led to few actual sets in favor of video effects and a form of green screen that was reminiscent of the old *Cinematic Titanic* days, only in bright color rather than in black silhouette. There were floating screens—obviously computer generated—in the background and a tunnel sequence that is clearly a series of miniature cutouts instead of a physical model of a tunnel with workable doors, as seen in previous seasons. The cast was back with additions such as Yvonne Freese, as Mega-Synthia and GPC, who had joined the live show for the *Great Cheesy Movie Circus* tour, and Kelsey Ann Brady as Crow for the Emily episodes, while Josh Weinstein would voice Tom Servo once again for part of the first Joel episode of the season.

Meanwhile, the fans who donated to the Kickstarter were given advance word on the making of the episodes and how things were progressing in the months during and after the Kickstarter was completed in 2021. As time went on, people began to emerge from their homes a little more often, feeling cautiously optimistic of how things were changing for the better as a vaccine

Jonah Ray as Jonah Heston, Emily Marsh as Emily Connor, and Joel Hodgson as Joel Robinson from Season 13 of *MST3K*. Three hosts and their various GPCs, Crows, and Servos, still fighting the onslaught of bad movies in the never-ending experiment named *Mystery Science Theater 3000*!

for COVID came to be handed out. Then came the announcement that a premiere of the first episode of the new season would be given as a live sneak peek on March 4, 2022. The episode, *Santo in the Treasure of Dracula* (1969), was set to start at 8:00 p.m. on the early version of the Gizmoplex. The Gizmoplex has been a new direction for the show, but the effects work done by green screen are reflective of earlier work by Joel Hodgson—the X-Box and the silhouettes in *Cinematic Titanic*. All of that effects work and years of testing and planning have come together in the new Gizmoplex app and the episodes to air in that season.

For many fans, the March 4 premiere was a chance to get parties together with old friends of the show and tune in, while others gathered online to chat as they waited through the countdown of the premiere, all anticipating what new things Joel and the cast and crew would bring to the series under such odd conditions. Finally, the countdown concluded, the screen went to black, and as we held our breath. . . .

A large white dot appeared on the screen.

And it stayed there for quite some time. No audio, no other picture behind it. Just a large white dot.

It was a mistake. And we as fans of *MST3K*, the people who have spent years learning how to poke fun at the miscues, mistakes, and general madness of the movies, did exactly that by poking fun at it. The comments on the online sites began buzzing as we looked upon our new leader, the Large White Dot. As some turned to religious ramifications of the Dot, others contributed conspiracy theories as to what it meant or what it was trying to tell us in secret code. We simply could not get enough of the White Dot and rejoiced in the silliness of such a start for the new channel. And it still is called out every so often in the forums for the show, as it was such a blooper. Eventually the system issues were corrected, and the show started, but we couldn't forget. Even the people at the Gizmoplex would joke about it; the

C'mon, look at those innocent faces! They'd never do anything bad to your movies. Give 'em a chance! COMEDY CENTRAL / PHOTOFEST © COMEDY CENTRAL

next episode began with the same Large White Dot again, but this time, a note followed that said, "Just kidding," and then the real episode began.

In some quarters, such an error could have been embarrassing, yet it was clear that in that moment, riffing had taken hold as a form of life affirming comedy. There we all were, sitting together on a universal couch in front of one highly advanced multimedia theater screen, and instead of anger of the delay or whining over a supposed "lack of care," we knew it was an opportunity to laugh and remember that mistakes happen and we'll survive. Those working on the show joined in the following week with their own take on the gag, because "it's just a show," and we "should really just relax." Which is what *MST3K* and all of its various siblings and children born from it are really all about. After all, we worry about so many things in life—jobs, health, school, finance, family—sometimes we need to remember that laughing at our mistakes can make us feel better. *MST3K* reminds us to let out the faux heckler that has always been there inside of us and to laugh at ourselves . . . and that sometimes the worst we can find are the best memories to remember.

Appendix

Dr. Forrester Sent Us a Great Movie— The Standard, Brief Episode Guide

Did you ever wonder that maybe this spaceship isn't really a spaceship at all, but a television set built for the amusement of the viewing audience, and I'm not really a robot, but a puppet built to look like a robot, who is in reality being controlled by a puppeteer under this very table, and you're not a scientist/inventor trapped in outer space, but just a comedian playing a part on a television show that you wrote?

Nah.

—CROW AND JOEL HAVING A DISCUSSION AT THE
END OF THE KTMA PILOT FOR *MST3K*

Although there are plenty of places to locate information about the episodes that aired on *MST3K* over the years, since the book tosses out a lot of movie titles and references to seasons, I believe it may be best to list all episodes that have aired over the years for the show up through the time of publication, along with some additional details on certain episodes that didn't get previously mentioned.

As for fans looking to see a listing of all the movies that *RiffTrax*, *Cinematic Titanic*, the Mads, and others have done . . . ha, ha! Oh, you kid. Seriously, considering the volume of material put out by these other entities, especially *RiffTrax*, there simply isn't room to add them all. Besides, there are several resources online to locate more details on those movie riffs that fans have available to them. Feel free to partake. I dare you.

Pilot (October 3, 1988)

The Green Slime (1968). Only portions of this movie were used in order to convey a sense of what the series would look like. While there were discussions of doing the movie in the first season, it did not occur. This would be the only appearance of Beeper, who would be transformed into Tom Servo in episode 2 of the KTMA season.

Season KTMA (November 24, 1988–May 28, 1989). The movies with an asterisk would all eventually be redone for later seasons of *MST3K*. In the case of *The Million Eyes of Sumuru*, there will be a thirty-three-year difference between its first appearance on the program and the next. The *MST3K* cast tend to alternate between saying they filmed twenty-one or twenty-two episodes; this confusion no doubt comes from filming twenty-one episodes and a pilot, for a total of twenty-two.

> *Invaders from the Deep* (1981)
> *Revenge of the Mysterons from Mars* (1980)
> *Star Force: Fugitive Alien II* (1987)*
> *Gamera vs. Barugon* (1966)*
> *Gamera* (1965)*
> *Gamera vs. Gaos* (1967)*
> *Gamera vs. Zigra* (1971)*

Gamera vs. Guiron (1969)*

Phase IV (1974)

Cosmic Princess (1982)

Humanoid Woman (1981)

Fugitive Alien (1986)*

SST: Death Flight (1977). This episode was listed in the official newsletter as possibly being reriffed in season 2 of the Comedy Channel run but did not make it for some reason.

Mighty Jack (1986)*

Superdome (1978)

City on Fire (1979)

Time of the Apes (1987)*

The Million Eyes of Sumuru (1967)*

Hangar 18 (1980)

The Last Chase (1981)

The "Legend of Dinosaurs" (1977)

Season 1 (November 18, 1989–February 10, 1990). The first season on the Comedy Channel. The final season with Josh Weinstein as a regular, and the first season with Michael J. Nelson working on the program.

The Crawling Eye (1958). Some sources list this as the second episode aired on the Comedy Channel, with *The Robot vs. the Aztec Mummy* being the first.

The Robot vs. the Aztec Mummy (1958)

The Mad Monster (1942)

The Corpse Vanishes (1942)

The Crawling Hand (1963). This and *Robot Monster* have the silhouettes in the theater looking green rather than black, as the Comedy

Network felt it helped audiences see them clearer against a black-and-white film. The idea was abandoned after the second attempt.

Robot Monster (1953)

The Slime People (1963)

Project Moonbase (1953)

Robot Holocaust (1987). First color film shown.

Moon Zero Two (1969)

Untamed Youth (1957)

The Black Scorpion (1957)

Women of the Prehistoric Planet (1966). Although listed as the fourth episode of the season according to the production schedule, it was the last episode filmed and the last episode aired with Dr. Erhardt as a regular. Mike Nelson makes his first appearance on the show, albeit only as a voice-over when providing the voice of the Isaac Asimov Literary Doomsday Device.

Season 2 (September 22, 1990–February 2, 1991). Continuing on what was still the Comedy Channel, this season saw the introduction of TV's Frank and Kevin Murphy taking over for Servo. The intro and set designs were redone for the new season as the writing began to get tighter.

Rocketship X-M (1950). First episode to become part of a group of episodes that has never been officially released on video or DVD due to rights not being regranted. First on-camera appearance of Mike Nelson, as Valeria, who visits via the viewscreen.

The Sidehackers (1969)

Jungle Goddess (1948). Mmm . . . French-fried potatoes! Jim Mallon makes his first on-camera appearance as one of the idiot fascist hunters on the viewscreen.

Catalina Caper (1967)

Rocket Attack U.S.A. (1958). First episode to have a "stinger" at the tail end of the closing credits, which was a reprise of a dubious moment in the movie just riffed.

Ring of Terror (1961)

Wild Rebels (1967)

Lost Continent (1951)

The Hellcats (1968)

King Dinosaur (1955)

First Spaceship on Venus (1960)

Godzilla vs. Megalon (1973). Not available on video (cough, cough, unless that trashed disc is still around).

Godzilla vs. the Sea Monster (1966). Not available on video.

Season 3 (June 1, 1991–January 25, 1992). The first season with the Comedy Channel rebranded as Comedy Central, after combining with the HA! network. It's also the first season with twenty-four episodes, which will continue for the subsequent three seasons. The films marked with an + were later broken up into hour-long two-parters for *The Mystery Science Theater Hour*, which began airing in November 1993 as a prime-time alternative to watching the series.

Cave Dwellers (1984)+

Gamera (1965)+

Pod People (1983)+

Gamera vs. Barugon (1966)

Stranded in Space (1973)

Time of the Apes (1987)+

Daddy-O (1958)+

Gamera vs. Gaos (1967)

The Amazing Colossal Man (1957)+. Briefly available on VHS, but not
   available otherwise.

Fugitive Alien (1986)+

It Conquered the World (1956)+. Not available on video.

Gamera vs. Guiron (1969)+

Earth vs. the Spider (1958)+

Mighty Jack (1987)

Teenage Cave Man (1958)

Gamera vs. Zigra (1971). First on-camera appearance of Bridget Nelson.

Viking Women and the Sea Serpent (1957)+

Star Force: Fugitive Alien II (1986)

War of the Colossal Beast (1958)+

The Unearthly (1957)+

Santa Claus Conquers the Martians (1964)+. Later done for *Cinematic
   Titanic* and *RiffTrax*.

Master Ninja I (1984)

The Castle of Fu Manchu (1969)

Master Ninja II (1984)

Season 4 (June 6, 1992–January 30, 1993). The Comedy Central run continues with another twenty-four-episode season, the first of a three-year deal
with the network. Those episodes used for *The Mystery Science Theater Hour*
from this season are marked with a +.

Space Travelers (1969)+. Condensed and renamed version of the movie
   Marooned.

The Giant Gila Monster (1959)+

City Limits (1984)

Teenagers from Outer Space (1959)+

Being from Another Planet (1982). Paul Chaplin makes his first on-camera appearance.

Attack of the Giant Leeches (1959)

The Killer Shrews (1959)

Hercules Unchained (1959)+

Indestructible Man (1956)

Hercules against the Moon Men (1964)+

The Magic Sword (1962)+. Later to be reriffed by *RiffTrax*.

Hercules and the Captive Women (1961)

Manhunt in Space (1954)

Tormented (1960)+

The Beatniks (1960)+

Fire Maidens of Outer Space (1956). Not available on video.

Crash of Moons (1954)+

Attack of the The Eye Creatures (1967)+. Not available on video. The made-for-television movie was originally *The Eye Creatures* before someone decided to slap on "Attack of the" in front of the title to make it sound more interesting. That the font style used for the onscreen title is different from the rest as a clear sign of how cheaply this was thrown together, and—as *MST3K* fans know—someone just didn't care that "the" appears twice due to the insert. Because of this, *MST3K* fans know this movie *Attack of the The Eye Creatures*.

The Rebel Set (1959)

The Human Duplicators (1965)+

Monster a Go-Go (1965)

The Day the Earth Froze (1959)+

Bride of the Monster (1955)

Manos: The Hands of Fate (1966)+. Although typically considered by the writers as an average episode, fans view it quite favorably. *Manos*, a creepy and low-budget movie about a family looking for lodging being turned into servants for the "Master" and his weird assistant Torgo, is a perfect example of how *MST3K* could take a movie no one knew about and turn it into something legendary. The film would not be the first to nearly break Joel and the bots emotionally (*Castle of Fu Manchu* beat it to the punch), but it came close.

Season 5 (July 17, 1993–February 5, 1994). The final season with Joel, and the first with Mike as host. With the changeover came a new intro for the show, with new theme song lyrics and filmed opening. A handful of early episodes in the season became part of *The Mystery Science Theater Hour* package and are marked with a +.

Warrior of the Lost World (1984)

Hercules (1958). First on-camera appearance of Mary Jo Pehl.

Swamp Diamonds (1956)

Secret Agent Super Dragon (1966)+

The Magic Voyage of Sinbad (1953)+

Eegah (1962). Later done on the live "Watch Out for Snakes!" tour in the summer of 2017, with all new riffs.

I Accuse My Parents (1944)+

Operation Double 007 (1967). Also known as *Operation Kid Brother* and released on video with that title, the title seen in the film itself is *Operation Double 007*.

The Girl in Lovers Lane (1960)

The Painted Hills (1951)

Gunslinger (1956)

Mitchell (1975). Last episode with Joel, while Mike is introduced as a character named "Mike Nelson," making him the only host of *MST3K* to use his real last name after Joel abandoned the practice with the KTMA season.

The Brain That Wouldn't Die (1962). First episode with Mike as host.

Teen-Age Strangler (1964)

The Wild Wild World of Batwoman (1966)

Alien from L.A. (1988)

Beginning of the End (1957)

The Atomic Brain (1963)

Outlaw (1988)

Radar Secret Service (1950)

Santa Claus (1959)

Teen-Age Crime Wave (1955)

Village of the Giants (1965)

12 to the Moon (1960)

Season 6 (July 16, 1994–March 25, 1995). The last season to feature twenty-four episodes. This was also the last season with TV's Frank, who left in the final episode of the season. Mary Jo Pehl's Pearl Forrester character will mark her first appearance this season.

Girls Town (1959)

Invasion U.S.A. (1952)

The Dead Talk Back (1993)

Zombie Nightmare (1987)

Colossus and the Headhunters (1963)

The Creeping Terror (1964)

Bloodlust! (1961). First appearance of Mary Jo Pehl as Pearl Forrester.

Code Name: Diamond Head (1977)

The Skydivers (1963)

The Violent Years (1956)

Last of the Wild Horses (1948). In a parody of the *Star Trek* episode, "Mirror, Mirror," Mike and the bots control the experiment, while Frank and Forrester are the experiment subjects for one segment of the program.

The Starfighters (1964)

The Sinister Urge (1960)

San Francisco International (1970)

Kitten with a Whip (1964)

Racket Girls (1951)

The Sword and the Dragon (1956)

High School Big Shot (1959)

Red Zone Cuba (1966)

Danger!! Death Ray (1967)

The Beast of Yucca Flats (1961)

Angels Revenge (1979). This film would be later revisited by Bridget and Mary Jo for *RiffTrax*.

The Amazing Transparent Man (1960)

Samson vs. the Vampire Women (1962)

Season 7 (November 23, 1995 for one special episode; February 3, 1996–May 18, 1996). This was the final season on Comedy Central, with only six episodes in the season. Pearl Forrester is a regular in the season, leading to changes in the theme song lyrics and visuals for the open credits. Comedy Central continued to air repeats until February of the following year, where the Sci-Fi Channel picked up.

Night of the Blood Beast (1958). This episode premiered originally as part of the "Turkey Day '95" marathon, with host segments specifically designed for the marathon. These segments would be replaced with other host segments in repeats, although Comedy Central is known to have repeated the "Turkey Day" version at least once by accident.

The Brute Man (1946)

Deathstalker and the Warriors from Hell (1988)

The Incredible Melting Man (1977)

Escape 2000 (1983)

Laserblast (1978). Last episode with Trace Beaulieu as Dr. Forrester and Crow.

Season 8 (February 1, 1997–December 6, 1997). First season on the Sci-Fi Channel and a twenty-two-episode season. The season would see the debut of Bill Corbett as Crow and Brain Guy, while Kevin would take on a second role as Professor Bobo. The program would experiment with story lines for the host segments that ran through several episodes. As expected, a new opening was created with a new variation of the theme song.

Revenge of the Creature (1955). First appearance of Bill Corbett as Crow, first appearance of Kevin Murphy as Professor Bobo, and first appearance of the Nanites.

The Leech Woman (1960)

The Mole People (1956)

The Deadly Mantis (1957)

The Thing That Couldn't Die (1958). First appearance of Bill Corbett as Brain Guy.

The Undead (1957)

Terror from the Year 5000 (1958). Not available on video.

The She-Creature (1956)

I Was a Teenage Werewolf (1957). Not available on video.

The Giant Spider Invasion (1975)

Parts: The Clonus Horror (1979)

The Incredibly Strange Creatures Who Stopped Living and Became Mixed-Up Zombies (1964)

Jack Frost (1965)

Riding with Death (1976)

Agent for H.A.R.M. (1966). First episode with Patrick Brantseg as Gypsy, after Jim Mallon decided to take a break from the role.

Prince of Space (1959)

The Horror of Party Beach (1964)

Devil Doll (1964). Probably the sleaziest movie every shown in the series, although *Blood Waters of Dr. Z* gives it a run for its money.

Invasion of the Neptune Men (1961)

Space Mutiny (1988). This film would later be revisited by *RiffTrax* as a live presentation.

Time Chasers (1994)

Overdrawn at the Memory Bank (1983)

Season 9 (March 14, 1998–September 26, 1998). Second season on the Sci-Fi Channel, for thirteen episodes. The series will settle into the Satellite of Love orbiting present-day Earth with Pearl, Bobo, and Brain Guy operating out of Castle Forrester, leading to a new opening for the show with new theme song lyrics.

The Projected Man (1966)

The Phantom Planet (1961)

The Pumaman (1980)

Werewolf (1997)

The Deadly Bees (1966). Not available on video.

The Space Children (1958). Not available on video.

Hobgoblins (1988)

The Touch of Satan (1971)

Gorgo (1961)

The Final Sacrifice (1990)

Devil Fish (1984)

The Screaming Skull (1958)

Quest of the Delta Knights (1993). Episode features Pearl in the theater for a segment where she tries to understand why the experiments are not getting the results she wants.

Season 10 (April 11, 1999–September 18, 1999). The final season of the original series and the last for the Sci-Fi Channel.

Soultaker (1990). Guest appearances by Joel and Frank.

Girl in Gold Boots (1968)

Merlin's Shop of Mystical Wonders (1996). Although listed as the third episode in the production code, this movie was the last original episode of *MST3K* to air on the Sci-Fi Channel on September 18, 1999, more than a month after the showing of *Diabolik*, which featured a conclusion to the show's story line.

Future War (1994)

Blood Waters of Dr. Z (1971)

Boggy Creek II: And the Legend Continues (1984)

Track of the Moon Beast (1976)

Final Justice (1985)

Hamlet (1961)

It Lives by Night (1974)

Horrors of Spider Island (1960)

Squirm (1976)

Diabolik (1968). Last produced episode of original series, resolving Mike's imprisonment on the SOL.

Season 11 (April 14, 2017). The first season of the revised series, with Jonah Heston (Jonah Ray), Forrester's daughter Kinga (Felicia Day) and TV's Son of TV's Frank, Max (Patton Oswalt). The season will see a large expansion of the villains' lair, a new theme song, and many other additional characters, robots, and guest appearances. Due to the nature of streaming services, all fourteen episodes premiered on the same day.

Reptilicus (1961)

Cry Wilderness (1987)

The Time Travelers (1964)

Avalanche (1978)

The Beast of Hollow Mountain (1956)

Starcrash (1978)

The Land That Time Forgot (1974)

The Loves of Hercules (1960)

Yongary, Monster from the Deep (1967)

Wizards of the Lost Kingdom (1985)

Wizards of the Lost Kingdom II (1989)

Carnival Magic (1983)

The Christmas That Almost Wasn't (1966)

At the Earth's Core (1976)

Season 12 (November 22, 2018). The final season on Netflix would be dropped on Thanksgiving as a theme series called *The Gauntlet*, where viewers were supposed to watch all six episodes in a row, as in the days of "Turkey Day" marathons. The season would see the return of Josh Weinstein as Dr. Erhardt in two episodes and a new recurring character: Dr. St. Phibes, played by Deanna Rooney.

> *Mac and Me* (1988). Features Paul Rudd's favorite clip.
> *Atlantic Rim* (2013)
> *Lords of the Deep* (1989)
> *The Day Time Ended* (1979)
> *Killer Fish* (1979)
> *Ator, the Fighting Eagle* (1982)

Season 13 (March 4, 2022–December 16, 2022). As part of a new Kickstarter campaign in 2021, an online service called the Gizmoplex was created that could be used to watch thirteen new episodes of the series, along with various older episodes. This season also saw the debut of rotating hosts for the movies along with Jonah Ray as Jonah Heston, with the introduction of Emily Marsh as Emily Connor and the return of Joel Hodgson as Joel Robinson. Subsequent episodes and seasons are considered possible as well as episodes eventually airing on other services over time, allowing *MST3K* to possibly continue for years to come.

> *Santo in the Treasure of Dracula* (1969)
> *Robot Wars* (1993)
> *Beyond Atlantis* (1973). First movie with Marsh as a host.
> *Munchie* (1992)
> *Doctor Mordrid* (1992)

Demon Squad (2019). Joel Robinson returns to riff starting with this
    episode.

Gamera vs. Jiger (1970)

The Batwoman (1968)

The Million Eyes of Sumuru (1967)

H. G. Wells' The Shape of Things to Come (1979)

The Mask (1961). First 3D movie shown.

The Bubble (1966)

The Christmas Dragon (2014)

Bibliography

Abel, Lionel. *Metatheatre: A New View of Dramatic Form*. New York: Hill and Wang, 1963.

Amaya, Erik. "Joel Hodgson on That Special *Mystery Science Theater 3000* Season 12 Cameo," Comiccon.com, November 23, 2018, https://www.comicon.com/2018/11/23/joel-hodsgon-on-that-special-mystery-science-theater-3000-season-12-cameo.

Ashford, Barbara. "Film about Young Has Plot That's Well Matured," *Buffalo News,* June 18, 1964.

"Ask Me Anything." Reddit.com, 2010. https://www.reddit.com/r/IAmA/comments/g96eq/iama_writer_and_actor_founder_of_rifftraxcom.

Bailey, Jason. "Flavorwire Interview: Joel Hodgson on 25 Years of *Mystery Science Theater 3000*." Flavorwire, November 22, 2013. https://www.flavorwire.com/426106/flavorwire-interview-joel-hodgson-on-25-years-of-mystery-science-theater-3000.

Barbour, Andrea. "Leon Varjian Papers, 1952–1985." Archives Online at Indiana University. https://webapp1.dlib.indiana.edu/findingaids/view?doc.view=entire_text&docId=InU-Ar-VAD9380.

Baxter, John. *Woody Allen: A Biography*. New York: Carroll & Graf, 1998.

Beaulieu, Trace, Paul Chaplin, Jim Mallon, Kevin Murphy, Michael J. Nelson, and Mary Jo Pehl. *The Mystery Science Theater 3000 Amazing Colossal Episode Guide*. New York: Bantam Books, 1996.

Bell, Art. *Constant Comedy*. Berkeley, CA: Ulysses Press, 2020.

"Best of TV." *Time* 136, no. 28 (December 31, 1990).

Bizzardi, Carol. "'No Big Deal,' It's Just Magic." *Green Bay Press-Gazette*, July 11, 1976.

Boone, Brian, "The Untold Truth of *Mystery Science Theater 3000*," Looper, May 8, 2017, https://www.looper.com/48365/untold-truth-mystery-science-theater-3000/.

Brauer, David. "The Million-Dollar Sight Gag." *Corporate Report Minnesota*, April 1991.

Brauer, David. "*Mystery Science Theater 3000*—The Last Voyage?" *Twin Cities Reader*, May 31, 1989.

Bream, Jon. "Cable Channel Pulls Plug on *MST3K*." *Star Tribune*, December 6, 1995.

Bream, Jon. "3 Area Comedians Think Los Angeles Is the Way to Go." *Star Tribune*, March 18, 1994.

Carroll, Harrison. "Behind the Scenes in Hollywood." *Portage Daily Register*, September 15, 1934.

Carston, Adam. "*Mystery Science Theater 3000: The Movie*: The Oral History." A.V. Club, April 19, 2021. https://www.avclub.com/mystery-science-theater-3000 -the-movie-the-oral-histo-1846694612.

"Comedian Hodgson to Perform Sept. 18." *Marshfield News-Herald*, September 7, 1982.

Coons, Robbin. "Here's New Way to Get into Films—Build Camera." *Columbia Record*, October 2, 1934.

Corliss, Richard. "Cinema: Robocritics Take Flight." *Time*, April 22, 1996.

Cornell, Chris. "TV Today." *Philadelphia Inquirer*, September 1, 1990.

Covert, Colin. "Comic Hodgson Is Back on the Stage." *Star Tribune*, May 22, 1987.

Covert, Colin. "Comic Weinstein and Juggler Bliss Have a Ball Collaborating on New Play." *Star Tribune*, August 1, 1999.

Covert, Colin. "*Mystery Science* Crew's Wit-Filled Wake." *Star Tribune*, December 25, 1995.

Covert, Colin. "*Mystery Science Theater 3000* Renewed." *Star Tribune*, June 25, 1996.

Covert, Colin. "Soon to Be a Minor Motion Picture." *Star Tribune*, April 25, 1995.

Czarnowski, Paul. "Michael J. Nelson." CRC Radio, January 22, 2003. https://web .archive.org/web/20030122222815/http://www.crcradio.net/i13/mikenelson .html.

Dawson, Dylan. "New Yorkers Loving *Cinematic Titanic* with Reunited Satellite of Love Crew." MinnPost, May 17, 2010. https://www.minnpost.com/minn post-asks/2010/05/new-yorkers-loving-cinematic-titanic-reunited-satellite-love -crew.

Ebert, Roger. "Review of *It Came from Hollywood*." RogerEbert.com, January 1, 1982. https://www.rogerebert.com/reviews/it-came-from-hollywood-1982.

Edwards, Philip. *The New Cambridge Shakespeare: Hamlet, Prince of Denmark*. Cambridge: Cambridge University Press, 2018.

Faraci, Devin. "Why the Director of *Squirm* Was Furious about the *MST3K* Version of His Movie." Birth, Movies, Death, August 14, 2013. https://birthmov iesdeath.com/2013/08/14/why-the-director-of-squirm-was-furious-about-the -mst3k-version-of-his-movie.

Forest. "Interview with Mary Jo Pehl." The *Mystery Science Theater 3000* Review, November 2007. https://web.archive.org/web/20070811022604/http://www .mst3kreview.com.

Fuller, Jim. "Ch. 23 Tries to Create an Audience from Scratch." *Star Tribune*, October 6, 1986.

Gerds, Warren. "They're Keeping Ventriloquism Alive." *Green Bay Press-Gazette*, September 24, 1978.

Harris, Will. "David Warner on *Twin Peaks, Tron, Titanic, Time Bandits*, and *Teenage Mutant Ninja Turtles II*." A.V. Club, July 26, 2017. https://www.avclub.com/ david-warner-on-twin-peaks-tron-titanic-time-bandits-1798265384.

Hearle, Andrew. "Hamlet's Advice to the Players." StageMilk, November 25, 2018. https://www.stagemilk.com/hamlets-advice-to-the-players.

Heffernan, Harold. "*Fractured Flickers* Fought with Fury." *Columbia Record*, January 4, 1964.

Hoevel, Ann. "*Cinematic Titanic*'s Struggle with 'Weisenheimer's.'" CNN, September 6, 2010. http://www.cnn.com/2010/SHOWBIZ/09/06/dragoncon.cine matic.titanic/index.html.

Holston, Noel. "The *Mystery Science* Show Touching Down at the Uptown." *Star Tribune*, July 10, 1992.

Homenick, Brett. "Godzilla's Crowning Moment! UPA's Post-Production Supervisor Richard Krown on Americanizing Toho Classics!" Vantage Point Interviews, September 14, 2021. https://vantagepointinterviews.com/2021/09/14/ godzillas-crowning-moment-upas-post-production-supervisor-richard-krown -on-americanizing-toho-classics.

Itzkoff, Dave. "The Show That Turned the Mockery into the Message." *New York Times*, November 9, 2008.

"Jim Mallon Speaks!" Official *MST3K* Info Club Web Site, 2008. http://www.mst3k info.com/satnews/brains/mallon.html.

Justin, Neal. "The Final Frontier." *Star Tribune*, February 25, 1999.

Kerr, Euan. "After 25 Years of *MST3K* Joel Hodgson Explains the Magic of Movie Riffing." MPR News, November 2, 2012. https://www.mprnews.org/ story/2012/11/02/after-25-years-of-mst3k-joel-hodgson-explains-the-magic-of -movie-riffing.

Kyanka, Rich. "Interview: Mike Nelson." Something Awful, November 15, 2006. https://www.somethingawful.com/feature-articles/interview-mike-nelson.

Langford, Bob. "Comedy Channel Kicks Off on Cable." *News and Observer*, November 15, 1989.

Liebenson, Donald. "What's Up? *Tiger Lily* Makes a Return." *Los Angeles Times*, January 16, 1998. https://www.latimes.com/archives/la-xpm-1998-jan-16-ca-8739-story.html.

Matheny, Dave. "Area Artists Say Work Does Not Depend on Decadence." *Star Tribune*, November 7, 1989.

Matheny, Dave. "Great Fun If You Can Get It." *Star Tribune*, April 1, 1990.

Matheny, Dave. "TV Supplies Witty Companions to Help Watch Bad Old Movies." *Star Tribune*, December 19, 1988.

Maza, Michael. "Best of the Worst." *Arizona Republic*, November 4, 1982.

Miller, Joshua. "Wade Williams Interview Part 1 of 2." JM Archives, November 15, 2017. https://www.youtube.com/watch?v=0wQVUfvoDfQ&t=2255s.

Mr. Beaks. "Mr. Beaks Interviews *MST3K* Mastermind Joel Hodgson!" Ain't It Cool News, October 28, 2008. http://legacy.aintitcool.com/node/38901.

Murphy, Joshua. "An Interview with Mystery Science Theater 3000 Producer/Actor/Director/Writer Jim Mallon." JM Archives, May 17, 2018. https://www.youtube.com/watch?v=SWMDzjhSgGc.

Museum of Broadcast Communications. "MBC Presents: Mystery Science Theater 3000 (Part 1 of 2)." MBCTVStudio, November 16, 2013. https://www.youtube.com/watch?v=fe9y9d8Ue8E&t=736.

Mystery Science Theater 3000 Wiki. https://mst3k.fandom.com/wiki/Mystery_Science_Theater_3000_Wiki.

Nason, Benjamin. "Interview—Joel Hodgson—Riffing Myself." The MacGuffin, March 8, 2013. https://macguff.in/macguffin-content/interview-joel-hodgson-riffing-myself.

Olbermann, Keith. "Comedy Channel or Ha!: Which Has the Last Laugh?" *Los Angeles Times*, December 17, 1990.

O'Leary, Devin D. "Play MSTIE for Me." *Alibi* 23, no. 26 (June 26, 2014). https://alibi.com/feature/47188/Play-MSTie-For-Me.html.

Petkovich, Anthony. "Robert Clarke, Part Two." *Psychotronic*, no. 18 (Summer 1994).

Phipps, Keith. "John Hodgson." A.V. Club, April 21, 1999. https://www.avclub.com/joel-hodgson-1798207993.

Plume, Ken. "A Bit of a Chat with Ken Plume & J. Elvis Weinstein." FRED, March 9, 2010. http://asitecalledfred.com/2010/03/09/j-elvis-weinstein-ken-plume-chat.

Plume, Ken. "Interview: Kevin Murphy." FRED, July 18, 2007. http://asitecalled
fred.com/2007/07/18/interview-kevin-murphy.

Plume, Ken. "Interview: Trace Beaulieu." FRED, May 16, 2007. http://asitecalled
fred.com/2007/05/16/interview-trace-beaulieu.

Plume, Ken. "An Interview with Mike Nelson." IGN, March 17, 2003. https://www
.ign.com/articles/2003/03/17/an-interview-with-mike-nelson.

Raftery, Brian. "*Mystery Science Theater 3000*: The Definitive Oral History of a TV
Masterpiece." *Wired*, April 22, 2014. https://www.wired.com/2014/04/mst3k
-oral-history.

Regan, Sheila. "Mary Jo Pehl on Comedy Writing, *MST3K*, and 'Man Saved by Con-
diments' (a True Story)." Twin Cities Daily Planet, December 23, 2011. https://
www.tcdailyplanet.net/mary-jo-pehl-interview.

Rife, Katie. "Michael J. Nelson on Eating Worms, Stealing Pop-Tarts, and Why
the Emmys are Overrated." A.V. Club, July 6, 2016. https://www.avclub.com/
michael-j-nelson-on-eating-worms-stealing-pop-tarts-1798249100.

Smith, Robert Lewis. "Metatheatre in Aeschylus' *Oresteia*." *Athens Journal of Philology*, January 2014. https://www.atiner.gr/journals/philology/2014-1-X-Y-Smith
.pdf.

Steele, Mike. "For Comedy, Come to the Cabaret, My Friend." *Star Tribune*, September 14, 1981.

Stone, Loryn. "Nerdbot Exclusive Interview: Mary Jo Pehl—Actress and Writer
from *Mystery Science Theater 3000*." Nerdbot, August 1, 2018. https://nerdbot
.com/2018/08/01/nerdbot-exclusive-interview-mary-jo-pehl-actress-and-writer
-from-mystery-science-theater-3000.

Strickler, Jeff. "*Blood Hook* Took 12 Years to Hatch." *Star Tribune*, May 15, 1987.

Strickler, Jeff. "Comic Hodgson Quits While He's Ahead." *Star Tribune*, October 25,
1984.

Strickler, Jeff. "Local Comedian Gets Last Laugh in Competition." *Star Tribune*,
October 1, 1982.

Sullivan, Kevin, "Interview with *MST3K's* Mary Jo Pehl," *Austin.com*, October 8,
2013. https://austin.com/interview-mst3ks-mary-jo-pehl.

Truitt, Brian. "Sunday Geekersation: 25 Years of Joel Hodgson's *MST3K*." *USA Today*,
November 24, 2013. https://www.usatoday.com/story/life/movies/2013/11/24/
joel-hodgson-sunday-conversation/3675845.

Turbovsky, Rob. "Interview: *MST3K* Creator Joel Hodgson on *Cinematic Titanic's*
Art of Bad Film." *Boston Phoenix*, October 28, 2010.

Varias, Chris. "How Playing $250 Rent in Norwood Led to a Tour with *Mystery Science Theater*." *Cincinnati Enquirer*, October 31, 2021.

Wagmeister, Elizabeth. "'Mystery Science Theater 3000' Acquired by Shout! Factory, Kickstarter Launched for New Season." *Variety*, November 10, 2015.

Weiner, Robert G., and Shelley E. Barba. *In the Peanut Gallery with* Mystery Science Theater 3000: *Essays on Film, Fandom, Technology and the Culture of Riffing*. Jefferson, NC: McFarland & Company, 2011.

Weintraub, Steve. "*Mystery Science Theater 3000* Exclusive Interview—Trace Beaulieu and Jim Mallon." Collider, August 3, 2008. https://collider.com/mystery -science-theater-3000-exclusive-interview-trace-beaulieu-and-jim-mallon.

Werts, Diane. "*MST3000*: Comedy Central Pulls the Plug." *Washington Post*, January 28, 1996. https://www.washingtonpost.com/archive/lifestyle/tv/1996/01/28/ mst-3000-comedy-central-pulls-the-plug/3145c536-190e-420b-9691-9297ad 7bf02f.

"What Roger Corman Thinks of *Mystery Science Theatre 3000*." furryisthenewedgy, April 19, 2014. https://www.youtube.com/watch?v=WZwyi00xGAU.

White, Mike. *Mad Movies with the L.A. Connection*. Albany, GA: BearManor Media, 2015.

White, Mike. "Say What?" *Cashiers du Cinemart*, no. 18 (2014): 190.

Wloszczyna, Susan. "Comedy Channel Comes Up Short on Laughs." *Argus-Leader*, January 19, 1990.

Woerner, Meredith. "The New Crew of *Mystery Science Theater 3000* Takes Us Behind the Scenes for the Netflix Revival." *Los Angeles Times*, April 12, 2017.

Index